Praise for *Mirror, Mirror Off the Wall*

"Brave and inspiring . . . Gruys admits to her all-too-human insecurities and describes her sometimes-difficult effort to live life without defining herself through beauty. Her story encourages others to do the same. This book should be required reading for those women who struggle with body-image issues—and even those who don't."

—*Publishers Weekly*, STARRED REVIEW

"Honest, heartfelt and quirky." —*The Boston Globe*

"Kjerstin Gruys writes with honesty, insight, and humor about her struggle to maintain sanity and self-confidence in a world where women are besieged with messages about the importance of beauty and image. Kjerstin's story will speak to anyone who is seeking to make peace with what she sees in the mirror and discover her own inner beauty."

—PEGGY ORENSTEIN, *New York Times*–BESTSELLING AUTHOR OF *Cinderella Ate My Daughter*

"Kjerstin turns her thoughtful gaze to the complex nature of feminism and beauty in this gripping memoir. I couldn't put this book down—as I flipped through page after page, I found myself nodding along with Kjerstin's astute observations. It's high time we stop picking ourselves apart and start focusing on what really matters: something deep inside, beyond what any mirror can reflect."

—CAITLIN BOYLE, AUTHOR OF *Operation Beautiful: Transforming the Way You See Yourself One Post-it Note at a Time*

"Kjerstin nimbly deconstructs the internal struggle between the desire to accept ourselves and the desire to be accepted by others. Her story is an important reminder that what we see in the mirror is not just our reflection but a reflection of the society in which we live."

—GOLDA PORETSKY, AUTHOR OF *Stop Dieting Now: 25 Reasons To Stop, 25 Ways To Heal*

"Gruys is an engaging, empathetic, and insightful storyteller, and her story needs to be heard. In a world full of conflicting messages about women's beauty and worth, it can be difficult to trust our own feelings about our bodies. Her year-long experiment illustrates how unchecked self-scrutiny can aggravate existing body-image issues, and how mirrors often play multiple roles in a woman's interior life. The media machine instructs women to control and monitor appearance at all costs, but Gruys shows us that there is freedom in letting go."

—SALLY McGRAW, AUTHOR OF *Already Pretty: Learning to Love Your Body By Learning to Dress it Well*

"*Mirror, Mirror off the Wall* is not just about Kjerstin Gruys's 365 day mirror-less odyssey. It's also about the psychological cataclysm that results when So-Cal bride meets feminist sociologist inside the mind and heart of the same person. Gruys grapples with the ubiquitous wedding 'shoulds' and puts her own body image advocacy to the ultimate test. She emerges with powerful lessons about trust, friendship, love, and being at peace with your own body."

—Cynthia Bulik, Ph.D., FAED, Director, University of North Carolina Center of Excellence for Eating Disorders

"*Mirror, Mirror off the Wall* is an engaging and entertaining read. Kjerstin Gruys strikes the perfect balance between much-needed social criticism and honest self-reflection. Gruys reminds us that in an image-obsessed society, something as small as looking in a mirror—or not—can be a political act."

—Natalie Boero, Ph.D., author of *Killer Fat: Media, Medicine, and Morals in the American "Obesity Epidemic"*

"Would you have the courage to give up looking in the mirror for a year—including your wedding day? Kjerstin Gruys did, and in doing so, learned to question her assumptions about appearance, trust, feminism, and the wedding-industrial complex, all of which she shares in this thought-provoking and honest account of her year without mirrors."

—Lynn Peril, author of *Pink Think: Becoming a Woman in Many Uneasy Lessons*

"The body issues, the issues about having body issues, the balancing act of genuine self-care: Kjerstin Gruys, quite simply, gets it. Glimpses of her interior life were articulated so honestly and with such precision that at times I felt like I was in her head—or, more accurately, that she was in mine, and that of every woman who has ever looked in the mirror and seen not how we look but how we feel. Without offering an easy solution to the anything-but-easy body image concerns that plague so many women, this book functions as a model of possibilities of what might happen if we looked more critically at our body narratives."

—Autumn Whitefield-Madrano, founder and editor of *The Beheld*

"In *Mirror, Mirror off the Wall*, Kjerstin Gruys lets us in on a fascinating social experiment. Combining smart, insightful research on body image and the politics of appearance with deep honesty about her own personal struggles, Gruys is a great guide through the sometimes funny, sometimes treacherous waters of women and appearance. By describing her year of looking away from mirrors she helps us turn our attention toward deeper, more meaningful, and more enduring sources of beauty."

—Lynne Gerber, author of *Seeking the Straight and Narrow: Weight Loss and Sexual Reorientation in Evangelical America*

"Through Gruys' thought-provoking storytelling, the cerebral reader and the lover of self-help books will find satisfaction in this unique memoir. For many years, I have personally witnessed women and girls being torn apart by our culture's desire for them to fit someone else's idea of 'perfect.' Kjerstin wrested herself from this peril and has lived to tell about her journey to the center of herself. Kjerstin lived in the gray areas of uncertainty as she uncovered important truths—not just for herself, but for women living in mainstream society. Every woman—of every age and background—can learn something profoundly meaningful about herself from Kjerstin's desire to separate herself from appearance obsession."

—JENNIFER BERGER, EXECUTIVE DIRECTOR OF ABOUT-FACE

"Kjerstin Gruys holds a critical mirror up to weight prejudice, revealing how it distorts our lives and our society. Her year-long experiment and powerful insights point the way for people of all sizes to reject such distortions in favor of already-available fabulousness."

—MARILYN WANN, AUTHOR OF *Fat!So?: Because You Don't Have to Apologize for Your Size*

"Kjerstin Gruys has written a frank, intimate and entertaining account of how she tried to overcome her body image insecurities by not looking at herself in a mirror for a year. Interspersing this personal account with insights from sociology and psychology research, Gruys shows how her own struggles are taking place within a broader social context, thereby holding up a mirror to contemporary American society. Highly recommended for anyone who has felt herself peering a bit too intently in the mirror."

—ABIGAIL C. SAGUY, AUTHOR OF *What's Wrong with Fat?*

Mirror, Mirror
Off the Wall

HOW I LEARNED TO LOVE MY BODY
BY NOT LOOKING AT IT
FOR A YEAR

Kjerstin Gruys

AVERY
a member of Penguin Group (USA)
New York

Published by the Penguin Group
Penguin Group (USA) LLC
375 Hudson Street
New York, New York 10014

USA · Canada · UK · Ireland · Australia
New Zealand · India · South Africa · China

penguin.com
A Penguin Random House Company

First trade paperback edition 2014
Copyright © 2013 by Kjerstin Gruys
Penguin supports copyright. Copyright fuels creativity, encourages diverse voices,
promotes free speech, and creates a vibrant culture. Thank you for buying an authorized
edition of this book and for complying with copyright laws by not reproducing, scanning,
or distributing any part of it in any form without permission. You are supporting
writers and allowing Penguin to continue to publish books for every reader.

Most Avery books are available at special quantity discounts for bulk purchase for sales promotions,
premiums, fund-raising, and educational needs. Special books or book excerpts also can be
created to fit specific needs. For details, write Special Markets@us.penguingroup.com.

The Library of Congress has catalogued the hardcover edition as follows:

Gruys, Kjerstin.
Mirror, mirror off the wall : how I learned to love my body by not
looking at it for a year / Kjerstin Gruys.
p.   cm.
ISBN 978-0-399-16017-2
1. Gruys, Kjerstin.   2. Feminine beauty (Aesthetics)   3. Body image in women.
4. Self-esteem in women.   I. Title.
HQ1219.G79   2013   2013003694
646.7′042—dc23

ISBN 978-1-58333-548-2 (paperback)

Printed in the United States of America
1   3   5   7   9   10   8   6   4   2

Book design by Susan Walsh

This book is dedicated to my parents, Julie Elmen and Ken Gruys, who enthusiastically allowed me to dress up as a bowl of salad for that Halloween costume contest at Kehrs Mill Elementary. From Day 1, you have unfailingly nurtured my creativity, celebrated my passions, and embraced my special brand of weird. Thank you for raising me to challenge injustice, and for loving me unconditionally.

A NOTE TO THE READER

A year from now you will wish you had started today.

KAREN LAMB

N 2011, THE AVERAGE AMERICAN BRIDE SPENT JUST OVER $1,200 on her wedding dress. While planning my October 1, 2011, wedding, I spent almost $2,400 on four of them. You read that correctly: *four.* Depending on how you look at it, this makes me either a fantastic bargain hunter or just plain nuts. It's fair to say that I was a bit of both. Despite my determination to stay true to my frugal midwestern roots and to not become a bratty bridezilla, I desperately wanted to look stunningly beautiful and fashionably fabulous in my wedding dress. To complicate matters, I was a body-image expert who wanted to lose weight before the big day (or at least find a dress—or four!—that would make me *look* thinner). When I began freaking out about my appearance, I was told by many people, "Oh, don't worry. That's *normal.* You're going to be a bride! Just have fun with it." But I did worry, and I wasn't having as much fun as I'd hoped. I realized that what our culture views as "normal" for brides-to-be wasn't what I wanted for myself.

Planning my wedding brought forth a fundamental mismatch between my values and my vanity. This book tells the story of how I came to recognize this mismatch, what I decided to do about it, and what I learned along the way.

What, exactly, did I do? I challenged myself to give up looking at myself in mirrors—and all reflective surfaces—for a year. Some might say that by shunning mirrors, I simply replaced one form of insanity with another. Fair enough, but my journey wasn't motivated by a desire to be perfectly sane (how boring!). Rather, I was desperate to contend with some painful contradictions in my character, and I decided that feeling authentic and taking care of myself were more important than being a "normal" bride. Sometimes you have to do something extreme and crazy in order to find balance and sanity in the end.

I hope that reading about my year without mirrors will encourage you to take steps in your own life to more closely align your everyday habits with your values and sense of authentic self. Maybe you're a bride-to-be who is facing similar frustrations with the wedding industry. Or maybe getting married is the last thing on your mind, but you still struggle to feel authentic in your choices. Or perhaps it's as simple as this: You hate your thighs (or stomach, or boobs, or hair, or . . . whatever), but a part of you also hates yourself for hating your body. I know how you feel. With a multibillion-dollar beauty and fashion industry telling us how to look, how to act, what products and clothes to buy—and promising us a happy life if we *keep* buying—we have a lot stacked against us when we try to carve out space for individuality, authenticity, and healthy body image (not to mention responsible spending!). All together, these goals may seem like an overwhelming challenge, but they are worth pursuing.

This book is not a self-help guide, just a story of how I helped *my*self. It is shaped by my unique goals, experiences, and my appetite for trying weird things. Your path will be different, but I hope you're able to learn something from mine. At the very least, I can promise a few chuckles at my expense along the way.

INTRODUCTION

*Bewilderment increases in the
presence of mirrors.*

TARJEI VESAAS

BOUGHT MY FIRST WEDDING DRESS THE VERY SAME WEEK THAT
I got engaged. In my giddiness at being officially betrothed, I at-
tended one of those epic Los Angeles sample sales with a friend
who was also planning her wedding. We were both broke graduate
students at UCLA, with low budgets but high-fashion aspirations.
The sale promised "designer gowns at bargain-basement prices!"
and we were amped and idealistic. I rehearsed my high school basketball boxing-out moves in my mind as we waited in line. Soon it
was our turn.

You know how these things work: If you find a dress you like,
you have to pounce on it like a Bengal tiger wielding credit card
claws, lest it be wrested from your grasp by another bride-to-be. The
shop was crowded, but I persevered and managed to grab an armful
of contenders. I could barely see over the pile of lace, silk, organza,
and taffeta stacked in my arms, but somehow I made it past several similarly overburdened brides-to-be on my way to the commu-

nal fitting rooms. An overly cheery sales associate examined my choices (for what, I don't know) and pointed me to a corner. Another saleswoman—this one *underly* cheery—paced through the crowd to assist the throngs of women trying on dresses. At first I assumed that this second woman's job was to make sure our dressing needs were being taken care of, but it quickly became clear that her primary goal was to protect the merchandise from damage. (Brides *are* a dangerous sort, I suppose.) Shrugging to myself, I stripped down to my undies and the requisite nude strapless bra and got down to business.

Now, at five-feet-five and 155 pounds, I'm pretty average in size (an 8 or 10 at most middle-America mall stores), but most of the dresses I picked were too small. I was prepared for some of this. I'd heard rumors that bridal sizes typically ran smaller than everyday clothes, but still, you'd think the "sample sizes" would be more accommodating! Considering that the average American woman wears a size 14, it seems more than a bit shortsighted for bridal boutiques to carry samples only in even-smaller-than-usual sizes 8 and 10. This was mildly frustrating, especially when I was interrupted mid-zip by the underly cheery sales associate announcing loudly that I wasn't ALLOWED to try on one of my selections because the dress zipper threatened to break from the strain of being zipped over my ass. *Ugh! Fail.*

A few other dresses managed to zip up without causing a commotion, but in each one I looked as uncomfortable as I felt. *These damned curves!* I cursed to myself. I am built more like a Coca-Cola bottle than the ever-coveted hourglass. My mother affectionately calls it "Body by Bartlett" (as in the pear).

But then one dress in particular caught my eye: a *gorgeous* blush-colored gown made of elegant slubbed silk, with hand-tatted lace detailing and a dramatic train of pleated taffeta layered with more lace. The ex–fashion merchandiser in me was starry-eyed and en-amored by the fancy details and high-end label. The current penny-pinching grad student in me was relieved by the 80 percent discount. It fit the bill, and my butt—and it was a size 8! I tried calling my mom for advice, but I couldn't get through. However, my friend, the saleswomen (both suddenly cheery again, now that I seemed on the verge of purchase!), and my aunt Sarah—who lives in South Dakota and had received pictures via text—all approved of the dress enthu-siastically. So I bought it. I loved it. It loved me. Until somehow we fell out of love.

Mirrors were to blame. Damned mirrors. I tried on that amaz-ing, gorgeous, fantastic dress at least once every few weeks for three months, just to look at myself wearing it again. I wanted to envision how glamorous and sophisticated I'd look while sashaying down the aisle. But each time I saw myself, I felt a bit less sure. Despite zip-ping smoothly over my derriere, the dress was, undeniably, a bit tight around my waist and hips. Coca-Cola bottles, as you know, start rounding out at midsection. Through the delicate slubbed silk, I could see the shadow of my belly button (or, more specifically, the doughnut of flesh surrounding it). Still, it was a negligible tightness—the type remedied by a month of skipped desserts and two pairs of Spanx. At first I confidently told myself that it would be easy to fit into the dress in time for my October wedding—a full eleven months away. I also knew that, at the very least, the gown could be let out a smidge by a skilled seamstress. But as the weeks wore on, I became less and less excited. Trying on my wedding dress was supposed to instill confidence and positive anticipation for the big day, but the sight of a bit of belly behind the fabric was disheartening. Sometimes I felt like I couldn't breathe when it was fully zipped. I began to re-sent the dress, and myself.

What's wrong with me? I wondered. *Why am I having so much anxiety about my looks? Why now, when I should be feeling my most beautiful?*

It bothered me tremendously. Not only because I wanted to feel happy with my appearance, but also because having a poor body image made me feel like a total hypocrite. Why a hypocrite, you ask? Well, in my final years of high school and beginning years of college, I suffered from anorexia. I was lucky to have fought my way into recovery by the end of college, but the experience changed my outlook on life profoundly. I've always had a thing for fashion, so after college—where I majored in sociology and minored in women's studies—I worked in the fashion industry for a few years, but it wasn't the right fit (pun intended!). Having battled an eating disorder and embraced feminism along the way, it felt utterly wrong to work in an industry known for glorifying emaciation.

So, as much as I loved the creativity and glamour of the fashion world (not to mention all the freebies and discounts on great clothes!), I gave up my career to return to school and earn a PhD in sociology. My chosen topic of study? Our beauty culture and how it shapes women's lives. Since then, I'd published academic articles about how the U.S. media reports on body size, I'd publicly lectured about the dangers of eating disorders, and I'd actively encouraged my students and friends to accept and celebrate their diverse bodies. I even volunteered at a nonprofit organization, About-Face, which works to improve teen girls' body images. In other words, I'd made it my life's work to help women feel confident, strong, and beautiful. Yet I was still struggling to accept my *own* body. I was a body-image expert with a body-image problem.

I wasn't starving myself anymore, but I still spent a lot of time and energy attending to my appearance. I rarely left the house without makeup, I indulged in mani-pedis every few weeks, and I enjoyed frequent bargain shopping to spruce up my wardrobe. I subscribed to several fashion and fitness magazines and, since becoming engaged, had added three bridal magazines to the list. I was mostly okay with these vain-ish interests; as a scholar, it comforted me to know that human beings in virtually every known culture alter their appearances to express themselves and to communicate social standing. My concern with appearance was a part of my humanity. Yet I also suspected that, like most things in life, when it came to beauty there existed a point of diminishing returns. I felt myself approaching it.

And I had many reasons to feel beautiful, or, at the very least, to feel attractive enough to accept myself and get on with enjoying my life. I was engaged to Michael, a brilliant and kind man with a sexy, dimpled smile and gentle gray eyes. Michael found me gorgeous and attractive, and told me so all the time. I had wonderfully close friendships with several strong, smart, and funny women—all whom I saw as stunningly beautiful, though none looked like supermodels. Most important, I was lucky enough to have been raised by parents who consistently emphasized the importance of my character over my appearance. My mother is one of those rare American women who has never dieted, and I have no memory of her berating her body in front of me. My younger siblings, Hanna and Peter, and I were taught that our bodies were wonderful because of all the things they could *do* (play sports! give hugs! make art!), rather than for how they looked. So, unlike a lot of women, I really had a fighting chance to love my body. But I didn't. And seeing myself in that too-tight wedding dress was dragging me down a path I recognized as dangerous.

And so it was that I found myself frantically scouring eBay for a replacement gown. It was more than seven months till my wedding, but all of the bridal magazines I'd been reading told me that I ought to have my dress ordered at least seven to nine months ahead of time. Having already spent almost $1,000 on dress number one, I was determined to find a real steal this time around. I gave myself an ambitiously low budget of $300 (about as much credit as was still available on my Visa card) and vowed to find something simple, elegant, and affordable. A cream-colored silk sheath from J.Crew, with cap sleeves and a cutout back, seemed like it might be the answer to my problems. It was elegant, minimalist, and—most important— available in non-bridal size 10. For $250, and with swallowed pride, I clicked the "Buy Now" button and crossed my fingers.

And then, just before I could sign out of eBay, the screen automatically flashed several "similar items" that might interest me. Sure enough, my eyes caught sight of an adorable short-skirted dress made of creamy embroidered shantung silk. The description charmingly called it the "Little White Dress." Visions of an elegant ceremony gown followed by a less formal reception dress shot into my imagination. For a *mere seventy-five dollars more*, I could pull a Kate Middleton and enjoy two grand entrances! *Click*.

Two weeks later, the sheath dress (aka Dress #2) arrived. Much to my chagrin (and additional portions of swallowed pride), it looked terrible on me. Not only was the dress about ten inches too long, but all of the proportions seemed generally geared toward a woman much, *much* taller than my five-five frame. The thinness of the fabric accentuated all the *wrong* curves (was that *back* fat?!?) and— adding insult to injury—what I'd taken to be cream was actually *beige*, a notoriously awful tone for pale-skinned blondes like myself. I'd made another awful mistake. With $1,300 in credit card debt and no stomach for further financial risk and embarrassment, I resigned myself to making things work with Dress #1. But a big question weighed on my mind: Should I spend a few hundred bucks to have the dress altered, or should I lose weight? The former would be expensive, but the latter could be dangerous. I decided I still had time to think this over. At least my little white reception dress (#3) was cute!

Flash forward a few more weeks to March of 2011. I found myself back in my childhood hometown of St. Louis, visiting my parents while attending the Midwestern Sociological Association's annual conference. I was booked to give four presentations in two days, but I hoped to sneak in some quality family time in the evenings. My mom, who hadn't been able to go wedding dress shopping with me the first (or second! or third!) time, had heard enough of my kvetching about the dress situation and had made appointments at area bridal salons, "just to look." I told her I was sick of looking at wedding dresses, but I was really just sick of looking at myself in them, not to mention embarrassed to have already blown my budget on poor choices.

Mere minutes after my final conference presentation, my mom called to let me know she was on her way to pick me up at the conference center. We were bound for bridal salons, and despite my post-presentation exhaustion, my mom's excitement was contagious. I felt myself becoming optimistic. *Aren't brides supposed to shop for dresses with their mothers? Maybe I jinxed myself on the first gowns by not following tradition!* Truth be told, I'd imagined this day for ages: My mom and I would bond over the subtleties of ivory vs. diamond white and sip champagne while being fussed over by charming sales associates. I'd use my well-honed aesthetic sensibilities to find the gown that perfectly expressed my unique personality and taste in fashion while morphing me into my best self; I'd feel like a beautiful fairy-tale princess when I finally found "the one." Besides, my mom has always been my favorite shopping partner. Like me, she's in it strictly for the bargains and is always on the lookout for flattering classics with a quirky twist.

Unfortunately, our joint venture actually started out *worse* than my first bridal salon experience, and felt all the more disappointing because of my high expectations. Instead of bonding, my mom and I bickered over directions the whole way to the store. Nothing builds anticipation like a few U-turns and wandering around strip-mall parking lots. Once we arrived at the first salon, instead of being fussed over by an attentive pack of fairy-godmotherly sales associates, we were treated with disdain by yet another snooty saleswoman (I was sensing a trend here) for daring to request last season's discounted samples instead of the pricier new designs. "Oh, they're in the back," she said, dismissing us with a flick of her hand to fend for ourselves in a poorly lit walk-in closet stuffed with dresses in various states of disrepair. It smelled of mothballs, and the carpet was stained. Suddenly bonded again, now that a shared enemy had made herself known, my mother and I persevered. Release the hounds; the hunt was on!

After an exhaustive search through the sample rack, we found my Wedding Dress #4. It was a strapless A-line gown, with lace trim at the bust, asymmetrical ruching across the waist, floral appliqués at the hip and on the back, and a long train with a delicate lace overlay. Pulling it out of the garment bag, I remember thinking that I didn't even need to bother trying it on: It was *so not* my style. I'd always hated ruching (it reminds me of mummy wrappings) and floral appliqués (too girlie). And yet, thanks to my mother's urging, I soon found myself standing in front of the shop's massive three-way mirror, seriously considering a dress with both. I worried that this gown, however flattering, was lacking in the haunting uniqueness I was looking for; I doubted if it could possibly be "the one." But my mom was certain it was.

"Oh, Kjerstin. This could be it. I think it is. It's beautiful! I'm getting goose bumps!" And she was. My mother actually got goose bumps. I was puzzled. Shouldn't *I* be feeling something goose-bumpy if I was wearing "the one"? At the very least, I thought, I ought to be crying and flapping my arms around, like those crazy women on *Say Yes to the Dress*, right?

But I had to admit, it fit beautifully—though Ms. Snarky Snooty-pants Saleslady couldn't resist mentioning with a huff that it seemed "a bit tight behind your armpits." Minuscule back fat be damned, my curves looked balanced instead of wonky. There was no dough-nut in sight, thanks to the powers of asymmetrical ruching. I could breathe.

The price tag read $700, a steal at 85 percent off the original price. I still wavered, protesting that I wasn't sure, but my mother insisted. "I'd like to buy this for you," she offered. I was touched. I sensed that buying me my wedding dress would feel like a gift to her as much as to me.

I still had my doubts, but I was also broke, frustrated, exhausted, and couldn't face another minute of second-guessing my taste or my body. Hearing my mother tell me that she was certain came as a relief. I needed a dress in which I felt comfortable, and in that shared moment with my mom, I also realized that I needed to give up my plans for bridal perfection (though I had no idea how). Perhaps I'd fall in love with the dress over time. Good enough would have to be good enough. I nodded my head, my mom wrote out a check, and then it was done; I owned a fourth—and hopefully *final*—wedding dress.

After months searching for and trying on wedding gowns, I was relieved to have found a dress I felt comfortable wearing. But I was also getting really, *really* sick of staring at myself in the mirror. While shopping for dresses, I'd become the worst version of myself: insecure, indecisive, and vain. My vanity had already cost my family and me over two thousand dollars in white dresses, an amount higher than my monthly salary at UCLA! Worse, I'd lost both time and emotional energy in the process. The dress shopping had pushed me to an uncomfortable edge, and—with the requisite dress fittings (plus bridal makeup and hair trials)—there was only more vanity to come. I'd definitely reached that point of diminishing returns, and something had to give. It was time to take a serious look in the mirror.

Or was it?

March

BEAUTY, LOVE, AND THE
ANGST OF SEX AFTER PASTA

*People think a soul mate is your perfect fit, and that's
what everyone wants. But a true soul mate is a
mirror, the person who shows you everything that is
holding you back, the person who brings you to your
own attention so you can change your life.*

ELIZABETH GILBERT

FOUR CONFERENCE PRESENTATIONS (AND ONE MORE WED-
ding dress acquisition) in two days left me exhausted but
proud of myself. I was ready to go home to California, and
soon found myself on my five-hour flight back to Los Angeles. I'd
made grand plans to "get some work done" en route and, as usual,
my intentions for work devolved into something more closely resembling a self-help therapy session between my inner thoughts and the
personal journal I keep on my laptop. At the beginning of the flight

I was all business, but by the time I landed, I'd hatched a crazy plan to shun mirrors for a year.

After settling into my cramped-yet-cozy window seat and waiting anxiously for the cue to stop hiding my electronic devices, I opened up my laptop and began to review the syllabus for my upcoming freshman-only seminar, titled "Gender, Appearance, and Inequality: From Evolutionary Psychology to Contemporary Feminism." I'd taught this course once before, but it had been over a year since then and I needed to reassess the planned readings and assignments.

Teaching this seminar had been one of the greatest joys I'd experienced since entering my graduate program. I was the sole seminar instructor to a small group of students and was allowed to choose any topic I wanted and customize the syllabus as I saw fit. I took it upon myself to design and teach a class I wish I'd been able to attend during my own college years. Over the ten weeks of the class, my students would be learning about the relationship between a person's looks and her opportunities. Each week, we would explore how appearance shapes our experiences in a different social arena, including childhood, education, our careers, our romantic relationships, and our health and health care. We would consider how our culture's beauty standards reinforced inequality across other social categories, like gender, race, class, sexuality, and age. As I perused the prior year's lesson plans, I skimmed over article titles and book chapters, noting any that needed to be replaced with more current research.

I could hardly wait for the first class, scheduled for the upcoming Monday afternoon. I enjoyed nothing more about my job than opening my students' eyes to the various ways in which having (or not having) "beauty" shaped their lives, and then giving them tools to combat these issues. And yet, it sometimes felt as though I had only depressing news to deliver (well, depressing to anyone who wasn't a supermodel). Whether one subscribed to the tenets of evolutionary psychology or to those of feminist sociology, the facts about beauty and one's life chances were the same: Appearance dramatically shapes our lives, and in predictable ways. At *every* single life stage, and in almost all social relationships and interpersonal interactions, good-looking people tend to be advantaged over less attractive people.

Indeed, psychologists have identified a widespread belief that people who are beautiful are also kinder and more intelligent than people who are plain. This so-called halo effect has enormous impact on our life experiences. More adorable babies are paid more attention by their parents than homely babies. Ugly children are presumed by their teachers to be less intelligent than good-looking children (although extremely beautiful children are often penalized for their looks, purportedly because their teachers resent them). Overweight girls are less likely to attend college, regardless of their academic preparedness. Above-average-looking women earn 12 percent more than average-looking women throughout their careers (the effect is even higher for men, at 17 percent). In fact, if you compare the best-looking workers with those who are the most homely, you see a difference of approximately $230,000 in lifetime earnings. Beautiful women tend to marry better-looking and higher-earning men. Attractive people get better terms on home loans (although they are more likely to default, since lenders overestimate their ability to pay). Even good-looking *criminals* tend to receive lighter sentences compared with homely criminals committing the same crimes. Statistics like these made me feel like apologizing to my students at the end of each class for causing them emotional trauma!

I could anticipate how these facts and figures would make my students feel because I knew how they made *me* feel. Even after spending an entire week of class discussing the subjects of social change and activism—not to mention the years of research and real-world experiences I had behind me—it was difficult for me to envision a world in which beauty didn't afford so many privileges. I knew that most of my students would be disgusted by some of what they read—including stories of parental neglect and peer bullying of overweight children, of "hogging" (a cruel bar game in which men intentionally "seduce" fat or unattractive women and then let their buddies and the woman in on the joke), and of court cases in which companies blatantly refused to hire (or made a practice of firing) workers who didn't fit the right "look"—but I couldn't control how my students would make use of this information. I hoped that they would feel angry, and that their anger would motivate them to change the world. But I feared that, instead, my students would feel fearful that such atrocities could happen to them, and that they would then use this fear as an excuse to change *themselves*. I wavered between these reactions on a daily basis myself.

Even with the embarrassing multiple wedding dresses saga fresh in my mind, as I read through my syllabus on the plane, I couldn't help but wonder if I ought to be spending *more* time and money on my appearance instead of less. Didn't this body of research basically prove that improving my looks would improve pretty much every aspect of my entire life? More money! More respect! Lighter criminal sentences for my hypothetical crimes! By these accounts, investing in and obsessing about my appearance wasn't vain or silly, but instead strategic and rational.

I caught myself before this thought went too far. It amazed me how easily my anorexic conscience could sneak its voice into my internal debates. I knew the data, but I'd been leaving out part of the story: In addition to all of the "beauty makes your life perfect" re-search, I also knew that, despite all of its perks, beauty has only a negligible impact on overall happiness. For example, in a recent study on the connection between beauty and happiness, participants were asked questions about their levels of happiness while, unknown to them, their looks were being rated on a one-to-five scale by re-searchers, either face-to-face or from photos. Those who were rated to be in the top 15 percent in terms of beauty were found to be 10 percent happier than those in the bottom 10 percent in terms of beauty.

Although a 10 percent increase in happiness may *seem* pretty meaningful, I couldn't help but note that this meant that the most stunningly beautiful people in the world would be only 10 percent happier than the most strikingly unattractive. In other words, the most anyone could (theoretically) gain by improving his or her looks would be a 10 percent increase in happiness, and that was only if that person went from strikingly ugly to strikingly beautiful, which seemed pretty impossible. By that same logic, moving from "aver-age" looks to being strikingly beautiful (which still sounded pretty difficult) would have an even smaller effect on improving happiness.

In a similar study, researchers found that, despite being highly prized by respondents, physical attractiveness again predicted only small variances in survey respondents' reports of pleasant feelings, unpleasant feelings, and life satisfaction. Clearly, even if people *be-lieve* that beautiful equals good, beautiful does not actually equal happy. As Leo Tolstoy wrote, "It is amazing how complete is the delusion that beauty is goodness."

Making sure my seminar students understood these findings would be of critical importance if I wanted them to make fully in-formed decisions about the time, energy, and money they spent on their looks. For the same reasons, reminding myself of these studies felt timely.

While I considered this body of research and how I would present it to my students, my brain quietly switched from teaching mode to self-overanalyzing mode.

It was obvious—*scientifically* obvious—that being what our culture considered beautiful was no recipe for happiness. I knew this on an intellectual level and from personal experience. And yet I felt as though being anything less than beautiful wasn't good enough, wasn't safe enough. I opened up a blank document in Microsoft Word and started journaling.

The FACTS:

Beauty = good for $$$, dating, not getting "hogged," & home mortgages

Beauty = not that great for being happy

Clothes + makeup + celebrity-endorsed organic juice fasts = expensive

Anorexia & Dieting = getting sick, being in pain, being miserable, feeling insane

The average American woman is 5'4" and 165 pounds.

The average runway model is 5'9" and 110 pounds.

I am 5'5" and 155 pounds.

The FEELINGS:

Being very thin = feeling safe and good about myself

Being 5'5" and 155 pounds = feeling ugly, ashamed, and unattractive

THIS IS SO MESSED UP!!!

I knew I wasn't ugly. In fact, if people who said I looked like my younger sister, Hanna, were telling the truth, I was probably pretty, or at least cute. But for some sick reason, despite all of my accomplishments and good qualities, the idea of being *merely* "cute" or *just* "pretty" felt like a failure.

It may seem strange that I could feel so insecure about my appearance while imagining myself to be above average in looks. A weird combination, I admit, but a common one: Research suggests that 80 percent of adult women are dissatisfied with their bodies, and that this problem starts early, with 42 percent of first- to third-grade girls wanting to lose weight and 81 percent of ten-year-old girls afraid of being fat. Yet we also know that the *majority* of women believe themselves to be above average in looks (a mathematical impossibility, which is why psychologists call this a positive illusion). In other words, *most of us are dissatisfied with our looks while thinking that we are above average in appearance.* Strange indeed, but it made perfect sense to me: Being above average (or "cute") doesn't mean squat when your culture tells you that anything less than airbrushed supermodel perfect is actually the same thing as being ugly. Add to this the widespread messages from our media suggesting that a woman's beauty (or lack thereof) is her most defining attribute, and suddenly it's easier to understand why a healthy body image is so rare among girls and women in our culture.

My own body insecurities have mostly had to do with how a romantic partner might view me. I'd always known that my family would love me no matter what I looked like, and I'd even begun to suspect that my academic colleagues took me a bit more seriously in my current "geek-chic" style and slightly chubby state, rather than if I were glamorously en vogue and very thin. I've always loved my friends for their intelligence, kindness, goofiness, and quirks, and had learned to appreciate these things in myself—when it came to *friendships*, that is. But I didn't believe that I could ever be lovable in the *romantic* sense if I wasn't skinny. Instead, I'd long imagined that being stylish and beautiful was a trade-off I could offer my boyfriends in exchange for my numerous faults, such as being bossy, impatient, emotional, neurotic yet messy, and a know-it-all. In particular, I worried that my feminism needed apology. I'd often imagined that dating an outspoken feminist like me was something any decent modern man *ought* to accept, but also something that few would really celebrate. I told myself that being a feminist might be more palatable if I could at least look *really hot* while passionately defending gender equality. I aspired to be a feminist trophy wife, as if such an oxymoronic state of being could possibly exist.

Of course, falling in love with Michael—and having him love me back—was hard evidence that I didn't have to look like a Victoria's Secret model to be loved. He even seemed to cherish my outspoken feminist side. Despite realizing this on an intellectual level, it was still hard to accept emotionally. I was always waiting for the other shoe to drop, for Michael to suddenly come to the realization that he'd made a mistake and could do better, either by finding a more beautiful woman with my personality or by finding a more agreeable woman with my looks. This was my greatest fear.

The next thing I typed into my journal was important:

What matters more to my happiness, my looks or how I feel about them?

And then:

Other than me and my imagination, does ANYONE ELSE actually have a problem with the way I look?

My family, my friends, my colleagues, and my soon-to-be husband didn't seem to have a problem with what I looked like. I was the only person in the entire world who did. (Okay, to be totally honest, I was a little worried that my future mother-in-law, Sherry, didn't think I was pretty enough or thin enough for her beloved firstborn child, but I tried to temporarily set aside this nagging suspicion.)

My insecurities clearly had little to do with my actual appearance, and everything to do with how I felt about it. I didn't have a body problem, but a body *image* problem. In addition to being a perfectionist about my looks, I'd somehow allowed them to determine too much of my overall value as a person; I'd conflated my body-esteem (how I felt about my looks) with my self-esteem (the feelings I had about myself as a whole).

Even worse: In addition to affecting my happiness, my poor body image was having a ripple effect. I'd recently read that a woman's body image accounts for almost 10 percent of her husband's overall marital satisfaction and 19 percent of her own marital satisfaction. My thoughts about my body weren't just confined to myself, but had seeped into my relationship with Michael, too. Michael and I weren't married yet, but we would be soon, and I didn't want my issues to continue to cause problems.

Numerous studies have shown that our partners almost always see us as more attractive than we view ourselves (another type of positive illusion), and this was certainly the case in my relationship. But rather than appreciating this, I frequently treated Michael as though he had bad taste for finding me attractive. To borrow from Groucho Marx, I acted as though he were the club I oughtn't join precisely because it had accepted me. To make matters worse, I almost always refused to make love if I "felt fat" (i.e., "Honey, sorry, but I can't get frisky right now; I ate that entire plate of pasta and I feel enormous"). It's no surprise that married couples in which the wife has a healthy body image report more frequent and more satisfying sex than couples in which the wife has a poor body image. It frankly surprised me that Michael had been so understanding and patient with these issues. Growing up with close relationships to his mother and younger sister had certainly taught him the futility of calling a woman beautiful when she didn't believe it herself. And yet he said I was beautiful anyway.

Michael, a biomedical engineer, and I have a wonderful relationship, filled with respect, appreciation for each other's geeky ambitions, lots of laughs, and mutual love for camping, animals, *Law & Order: SVU*, local hamburger joints, and California's amazing gastronomic culture. We like to joke that we met on craigslist, which was true, but not in a creepy "casual encounters" sort of way: I'd advertised the second bedroom of my condo for rent, and he'd responded to the listing. Michael was spending four months in Los Angeles for an internship at a local medical device company. When he came to my place to check out the second bedroom, I was smitten at first sight. We hit it off immediately, spending almost an hour chatting about what it was like to live in Los Angeles, having both grown up in the Midwest.

By the time Michael left, I'd developed a huge crush. As tempting as it had been to offer him the room, I decided against it. What if he turned out to be a bit of a lothario, bringing his conquests back home to my place?! Besides, I didn't want to feel pressured to look like a cute future feminist trophy wife at all hours of the day and night. But in my e-mail giving Michael the news of his rejection as a rental applicant, I casually asked if he wanted to join my friends and me for a beer at a local Irish pub. He responded enthusiastically, which of course meant I had mere hours to pull together a group of friends to go out with! We had a blast that night, and he asked me out on our first solo date by the end of the evening.

Two years later we became engaged in epic style, by winning my engagement ring in a local event called the L.A. Diamond Dash— an *Amazing Race*–style scavenger hunt in which the grand prize was a beautiful diamond engagement ring. An embarrassing video of the proposal is still floating around the Internet somewhere. Being engaged to Michael was a dream come true, not to mention evidence that being "cute" was lovable after all. I owed it to myself and to him to stop obsessing about my looks, but I didn't know how. Years of therapy had strengthened my resolve to take care of my body, but I still didn't know how to accept it.

I reflected further on my recent wedding-dress(es) saga and felt increasingly ill at ease. Hoping for a distraction, I put away my laptop and opened a new book, *The Birth of Venus* by Sarah Dunant. I looked forward to losing myself in the adventures of a feisty young female protagonist coming of age in Renaissance Italy.

Within two paragraphs of the prologue, a seedling of a plan was planted in my mind. Here is what I read:

> No one had seen her naked until her death. It was a rule of the order that the Sisters should not look on human flesh, neither their own nor anyone else's. A considerable amount of thought had gone into the drafting of this observance. Under the billowing folds of their habits each nun wore a long cotton shift, a garment they kept on always, even when they washed, so that it acted as a screen and partial drying cloth as well as a night shift. This shift they changed once a month (more in summer when the stagnant Tuscan air bathed them in sweat), and there were careful instructions as to correct procedure: how they should keep their eyes firmly

fixed on the crucifix above their bed as they disrobed. If any did let their gaze stray downward, the sin was a matter for the confessional and therefore not for history.

A *lifetime* spent without seeing oneself. The concept made me pause, my brain whirring. *What a different life those nuns lived, compared with my appearance-obsessed world of Los Angeles!* I thought. *Could I go even one day without looking at myself in a mirror? Maybe I should. Hell, why not a year?*

I didn't have a vision for exactly where the idea would lead, but my values and behaviors had clearly been at odds. Shunning mirrors would force me to *do something* about it. It might be the step back from vanity that I needed, a way to refocus my energy toward worthier things, like my relationships, my research, my students, and ultimately my health and happiness. But could I do it? How? And with what effects on my life, self-image, and personal and professional relationships? Was it possible that removing mirrors from my life might actually cause me to become *more* obsessed or insecure about my appearance? Would I completely lose the ability to apply makeup, style my hair, or select flattering and chic outfits? Would my appearance change, and—if so—would Michael still find me attractive? Despite these looming questions, I knew that I was on to something important.

N ATURALLY, I COULDN'T KEEP MY EXCITING PLAN A SECRET. I called my mom as soon as I stepped off the plane. I wanted her to tell me whether I'd stumbled upon brilliance or insanity. Her reaction was exactly what I needed: "Kjerstin, that sounds great! It's a perfect project for you." And then: "But you'll wait until *after* the wedding, right?"

I wasn't sure how to respond. On the one hand, it was all the "beautiful bride" pressure that had precipitated my moment of inspiration, and in the coming months, more than ever, I would really need help resisting the extra pressure I was feeling. On the other hand, my mom had always been the first person I called when I needed advice. She'd rarely led me down the wrong path, so if she had concerns I wanted to take them seriously.

The next person I called was my sister. Hanna is my closest friend and my most sensible confidante. A medical assistant with dreams of becoming a nurse-midwife, Hanna is smart, funny, and strikingly beautiful, yet refreshingly unconcerned with her looks. Her attitude toward fashion and makeup had always been the down-to-earth San Francisco yin to my high-maintenance Los Angeles yang (a particularly apt metaphor given that we each actually lived in these cities!). Unsurprisingly, she liked my plan to forgo mirrors, as long as she wasn't expected to do my wedding makeup. This was fine with me. I'd long known that her maid of honor duties would involve emotional rather than cosmetic support.

Michael picked me up at LAX, and after I gave him a quick hug and kiss, I immediately launched into the same hurried explanation I'd given my mom and sister. He seemed bemused. When I told him that my mother had suggested I wait until after the wedding, he raised his eyebrows and said, "Well, I'm sure your mom wants what's best for you, but I think that all of the wedding pressure is the exact reason you should start now!" He was *so* right. Perhaps it was lingering teenage rebellion, but this was the deciding moment. I knew I had to proceed, and right away. I needed his support, and his next comment didn't disappoint. "What's the game plan? I think we need to lay out a strategy!" *We.* He was in.

Michael was right about my need for strategizing. In fact, it seemed pertinent that I strategize *about* my strategy. Succeeding at this project would require more than just making a decision. Staring at myself in the mirror had become a daily, sometimes hourly, habit since puberty, one that I'd never thought to break. Mirrors were embedded within my routines. They hung on the walls of almost every room in which I lived, worked, played, and peed. To say that avoiding them for a year would test my willpower was an understatement.

I stared out of the passenger's-side window and watched reflections of my face bounce back to me in both the window and in the side mirror. *Straight blond hair, brown eyes, pale skin, round flushed cheeks.* Would I miss this sight? I surprised myself by thinking I looked lovely, happy even. Then my surprise saddened me. Did I view my face as lovely only in the prospect of not seeing it again for a long time? I watched myself frown at the thought and then reflexively noted a few new wrinkles, cringing at the fleshiness of my neck. *Ugh, I hate my chins,* I thought. *I'm so ugly and gross.* Yikes. This was not a healthy way to think. Was I lovely or ugly? I didn't know, but it was time to stop constantly asking myself the question and move on to more important things.

RESOLVED TO GO A YEAR WITHOUT MIRRORS THAT EVENING, AND by the following afternoon I'd accumulated an impressive collection of books and academic journal articles to help me achieve my goal. My first priority was to learn how to maximize my willpower and aptitude for personal change. I'd never kept a New Year's resolution in my life, and giving up mirrors seemed dramatically more ambitious and complicated than my usual plans to "stop picking at my cuticles" or "remember to write thank-you notes." Given the challenges ahead, I needed to learn as much as I could about how to be successful at changing myself. A quick search of Amazon's vast book inventory promised an enormous amount of self-help titles on the topics of personal change and willpower. I wanted this information in my arsenal, but needed my books on a budget; time for a trip to the library!

The titles I amassed from the self-help section of my local library branch ranged from pop psychology texts on the interesting topic of change itself (such as Chip and Dan Heath's *Switch: How to Change Things When Change Is Hard*, Cass Sunstein and Richard Thaler's *Nudge: Improving Decisions about Health, Wealth, and Happiness*, and M. J. Ryan's *This Year I Will . . . : How to Finally Change a Habit, Keep a Resolution, or Make a Dream Come True*) to inspiring narratives of other women's yearlong personal change adventures (including Elizabeth Gilbert's *Eat, Pray, Love: One Woman's Search For Everything Across Italy, India and Indonesia,* Judith Levine's *Not Buying It: My Year Without Shopping,* Vanessa Farquharson's *Sleeping Naked Is Green: How an Eco-Cynic Unplugged Her Fridge, Sold Her Car, and Found Love in 366 Days,* and Gretchen Rubin's *The Happiness Project: Or, Why I Spent a Year Trying to Sing in the Morning, Clean My Closets, Fight Right, Read Aristotle, and Generally Have More Fun*). After stumbling across more options through some online research, I tracked down the syllabus of a Stanford University course, "The Science of Willpower," and requested an advanced copy of Roy Baumeister and John Tierney's soon-to-be-published book, *Willpower: Rediscovering the Greatest Human Strength.*

Finding room for my new collection of readings was an adventure in itself; my desk at home was already covered with tangled piles of bills, my treasured collection of Anthropologie catalogs (hence the bills), and a smattering of interview transcripts for my dissertation, which examines how appearance shapes workplace discrimination. After some rearranging, I managed to squeeze the pop psychology texts onto one corner of my desk and decided to stack the narratives on my bedside table; I would research by day and then lull myself to sleep with uplifting and inspiring stories of other women's real-life adventures in change and transformation.

M Y READINGS ON WILLPOWER TAUGHT ME THAT I COULD DO much to improve my chances for success. Of primary importance was setting the right kind of resolution in the right kind of way—something I'd already begun, but needed to refine. For example, the very act of *making* an official resolution was important in itself. A psychologist at the University of Scranton studied two groups of people in 2002, both of which had identical goals and comparable motivation to change. At the six-month mark, the people who had made formal resolutions were ten times more successful at achieving their goals than those who wanted to change but hadn't made specific resolutions. Only 4 percent of the non-resolvers succeeded, compared with 46 percent of those who made formal resolutions. Further, it turns out that the act of resolving is further strengthened by telling others of your goals. After reading this, I turned to Michael and—in my most formal voice—said, "I resolve to not look at myself in the mirror for one year!"

"Yeah, I know," he responded, with a puzzled look, "but thanks for reminding me." With a shrug, he turned back to his e-mail, and I turned back to my journal articles. The statistics I'd read were compelling, but still a bit depressing. Even with a formal resolution to go without mirrors for a year, I had a less than 50 percent chance of successfully making it to the six-month mark. I clearly had more work to do to improve my chances.

So far I'd told only my mother, Michael, and my sister about my plans, but the literature on resolutions suggested that *broad* social support would further strengthen my resolve. (Well, actually, it suggested that telling a ton of people might make me too embarrassed to quit.) So I looked over my calendar and made note of every upcoming opportunity to tell my friends, students, and mentors. I hesitated on the last category: I wasn't a hundred percent certain that it was a good idea to share my plans with the members of my dissertation committee. It was important to me that these people took me seriously as a scholar, and sometimes that meant keeping my personal life . . . well, personal. I "resolved" to play that one by ear.

What I learned next, from my readings on the science of willpower, really surprised me. I figured that I already knew plenty about willpower, thanks to my experiences with anorexia. What I *thought* I knew about willpower was that I either didn't have much of it or had all the wrong kinds; willpower was an elusive stubbornness that couldn't be trusted or counted on.

In high school, what had started out as a bad habit of skipping lunch (because I didn't want to run into an ex-boyfriend who had recently broken my heart) turned into an intentional diet, once people started complimenting me for losing weight. As a student athlete with decent eating habits, I'd been at a healthy weight before this happened, but being admired for my new skinniness felt good, and at sixteen I craved approval.

My anxiety and heartache made it easy to continue skipping meals, and I started to pride myself on having what I thought was an admirable trait: willpower. I added additional rules and strategies to my secret diet: Each morning my dad would make breakfast for my siblings and me, and I would take mine to go but throw it away before I arrived at school; lunches were skipped, save for a side of Tater Tots eaten by myself in the library (eating small portions of junk food made me feel indulgent); two hours of basketball practice or track-and-field training each afternoon meant that I could eat a normal dinner with my family and use this as an excuse to brush off my parents' concerns about my weight loss. If I wasn't light-headed during practice the next day, I'd decide I'd eaten too much the day before.

But then I lost control; my willpower broke down. I began alternating restriction with episodes of binging. Suddenly I was a failed anorexic. Some weeks I dieted, while other weeks, racked with guilt, I indulged in "bad foods." I hated my inability to stick to my strict diet and mourned the willpower I'd once had. This cycle of binging and restriction would continue for years, until I finally committed to recovery in college, after several bouts of kidney stones and being diagnosed with borderline osteoporosis. Looking back, I know now that what felt like an unexplainable and unwanted loss of willpower was simply my body's refusal to be starved; an unwelcome survival instinct had kicked in.

To recover, I called on willpower once again, but this time it was to *stop* restricting, to *stop* binging, and to *stop* purging. These behaviors had become so ingrained that they felt irresistible even as they made me miserable and unhealthy. As before, I sometimes had willpower for recovery and other times it eluded me. As always, when I didn't have it, I felt like a failure.

Most people who, like me, struggle to keep their resolutions blame themselves for not having enough willpower; we assume that our failures in self-control are largely an issue of character. Contemporary research disagrees with this. Stanford psychologist Kelly Mc-

Gonigal, who created the "Science of Willpower" course I mentioned earlier, wrote the book *The Willpower Instinct: How Self-Control Works, Why It Matters, and What You Can Do to Get More of It* as a guide to understanding the science of self-control. In it, she argues that willpower should be regarded as a mind-body response rather than as a test of character; it is not so much a virtue, but rather "a biological function that can be improved through mindfulness, exercise, nutrition, and sleep."

I learned even more about willpower after talking with my cousin, psychologist Holly Miller, who conducts lab experiments examining how glucose levels effect the willpower of dogs (really, imagine the canine self-control required to "stay" for ten minutes with a doggie treat a few feet away! I couldn't do it). Holly helped explain that willpower is not an unlimited resource, but is in short supply physiologically. We fail when we literally run out of it, similar to how an amateur marathoner's muscles run out of glycogen at mile twenty (or mile eight, in my half marathoning case). Indeed, much like our muscles during exercise, our brains require steady supplies of glucose in order to work at their best during mental tasks, including the exercise of willpower. Even seemingly small mental tasks deplete our brains of available glucose, reducing our self-control, willpower, and capacity for responsible decision-making skills.

Take, for example, an experiment in which several dozen undergraduates were divided into two groups. One group was given a two-digit number to remember, and the second group was given a seven-digit number to remember. Then the students were told to walk down the hall, where they were presented with two different snack options: a slice of chocolate cake or a bowl of fruit salad. Here's where the results get interesting: The students with seven digits to remember were nearly twice as likely to choose the cake as the students who were given only two digits. It seems that those extra numbers took up valuable space in the brain—they were a cognitive load—making it more difficult to resist a decadent dessert. In other words, willpower is so constrained that all it takes is a few extra bits of information before the brain starts to give in to the temptation of a few bites of cake! This study hit close to home. Looking back on the years I'd spent struggling to avoid a few bites of cake (and most other foods, for that matter), I felt a surge of compassion toward my younger self. But would I be able to feel compassion for my current self during this year without mirrors?

Another study recommended that people focus on only one resolution at a time as a way to prioritize limited willpower. Since avoiding my reflection would certainly require ample willpower, my year without mirrors would therefore be a bad time to restrict myself to a tight budget, to give up any of my other bad habits, or to go on a crash diet, for that matter. This all sounded fine with me! Considering how tempted-to-go-on-a-crash-diet I'd been feeling, reminding myself to avoid cognitive overload was one more source of motivation I could give myself to stay healthy while planning my wedding.

My favorite study on willpower pointed to the importance of controlling one's environment. This University of Chicago study, which tracked people's reactions to different temptations throughout the day, showed that the people with the best self-control are, paradoxically, the ones who use their willpower the least often. Instead of fending off one urge after another, these people set up their lives to minimize temptations. They played offense instead of defense, using their willpower and self-knowledge in *advance* to set themselves up for success.

This rang bells of truth from my own experiences. During my recovery from anorexia, I'd had to direct my willpower toward *repressing* urges to be obsessive and unhealthy about food, which was a constant battle. Even though I was committed to recovery, when left to my own devices, I tended to either rigidly eat the exact same "safe foods" at every meal or fall into bingeing free-for-alls. To work around my food quirks, I eventually learned to keep my home free of foods that triggered binges and to satisfy my urges to track food by keeping an online food diary, which helped me make sure I was eating a healthy variety of nutritious foods (including treats!) in normal portions and at regular times. I also gave myself permission to obsess and read labels to my heart's content while shopping at the grocery store, even if shopping took extra time, as long as I left the store with a healthy variety of foods. This helped me feel more comfortable eating whatever I felt like when at home. These tactics helped me learn to eat more mindfully, which, to me, meant paying enough attention to my food to ensure that I was eating a balanced and nutritious diet, but not being so wary and restrictive that I became inflexible or missed out on eating for pleasure.

These strategies were enormously helpful in terms of keeping my body fully nourished, but I'd had mixed feelings about them. I'd felt guilty for not having the willpower to simply snap out of my disordered eating by eating completely intuitively, i.e., without the added structure of careful grocery shopping, limiting the types of foods in my home environment, and keeping a food and exercise journal. But with my newly refined understanding of willpower, I felt proud of myself for developing strategies that prioritized my willpower where it mattered most—at the point at which I kept myself healthfully fed and sane. Realizing that I already had the skills to cultivate willpower was motivating. It reminded me that I would be bringing almost thirty years of life experiences to my no-mirrors project.

In *The Happiness Project*, Gretchen Rubin outlined a list of overarching principles to guide her throughout her quest to become happier in one year. She called it her "Twelve Commandments." Encouraged by this idea, I gave some thought to what *I* had learned over the years, scouring through several of my old journals for revelations I'd arrived at along my path. I compiled a list of the ten most important things I'd discovered about myself, my body, my core values, and how to live in accordance with those values. In the spirits of Rubin and comedian David Letterman, I decided to call this my Top Ten Ways to Be Kjerstin list. Here it is:

1. Challenge your assumptions by doing exactly what scares you the most. (If you don't, you'll never know and you'll never grow.)
2. Good enough is good enough!
3. Your body is perfect, but your mind could use improvement.
4. Equating your body size with health is the fastest route to poor health. Focus on healthy behaviors, not the number on the scale.
5. Look to your role models for guidance at the crossroads. Act in accordance with the confidence you had as a three-year-old. If that doesn't work, channel Miss Piggy.
6. *Be* a role model.
7. Fake it 'til you make it.
8. Ask for help and accept it when offered.
9. Sanity comes first.
10. There is beauty in the breakdown. Let go.

My Top Ten Ways to Be Kjerstin list, I hoped, would serve as a guide for me over the next 363 days in my quest to avoid mirrors and become a *better* Kjerstin.

ENCOUNTERED THE FIRST OPPORTUNITY TO DRAW STRENGTH from my Top Ten list the very next evening. I'd been invited to a dinner party at the home of my mentor at UCLA, Dr. Abigail Saguy. Abby, as I called her, had been my primary advisor since the first day I started graduate school. In fact, she was the reason I applied to UCLA in the first place. Abby's research—which explores how larger body size has come to be understood as a public health crisis—was at the forefront of academic knowledge about the politics of body size, and I wanted to be there, too.

As a mentor, Abby was generous with both her time and willingness to share credit on collaborative projects; we'd worked closely together on several research papers and, throughout the prior five years, become friends. I was practically bursting with my news, but I questioned whether I should say anything. What if Abby told me I shouldn't do the project? Going without mirrors for a year—though serious to *me*—wasn't necessarily something that would be taken seriously by "the academy." Was this one of those "better to apologize than ask permission" situations?

Luckily for me, "the academy" hadn't been invited to Abby's dinner party. Instead, the group consisted of Abby's family (including her lovely French husband, who had a penchant for gourmet food, and two adorable kids) and a visiting scholar from Israel, who specialized in research on eating disorders. *Challenge your assumptions!* I reminded myself. *Abby isn't going to kick you out of grad school for doing this.* Then I thought, *What would my three-year-old self do?* The answer was clear: My three-year-old self—a confident and curious tomboy with short hair, a lisp, and elastic suspenders—wouldn't have given a fig about what other people thought of her ideas or wacky projects. In preschool I'd collected bugs and slugs as pets and entertained grand ambitions to someday become "either an archaeologist, a veterinarian, a pastor, or a doctor *and* a woman!" and I even started a small business selling pet rocks to my neighbors for five cents each. I probably made at least two bucks, thanks to my excellent customer service (I went back to every customer a week after my sales to "see how things were going"). Anyway, the point I had to remind myself of was that my three-year-old self had been a weird kid, but she'd been too focused on doing what she wanted to do to give much thought about what other people wanted her to do. I needed to regress in order to move forward. I took a deep breath and went for it:

"So, I had this crazy idea over the weekend and I think I'm going to go for it," I offered to the dinner table, while we nibbled on bite-size chocolate confectionaries for dessert. The kids were off playing, whispering giggle-inducing jokes to each other in fluent French.

"Oh? What's that?" Abby asked.

"Well, you know how I've been getting a little bit obsessive about wedding stuff, right?" I began.

"I *may* have noticed, just a little," Abby conceded with a smile. I'd been caught perusing wedding websites during one of our recent team meetings.

"Well, I hit a wedding-planning wall last week while I was wedding dress shopping with my mom," I explained.

"Wait, I thought you already *had* a dress!" Abby interrupted.

"Uh, yeah, that's part of why I hit a wall," I responded sheepishly. "Anyway, I've been feeling kind of obsessive about things—especially all the beauty stuff—so I've decided I want to stop looking in the mirror for a while. I want to see if it helps me focus less on my looks and more on other things." No one at the table said anything.

"Wow, that could be really . . . interesting!" exclaimed Abby's husband, breaking the silence.

"Would it be kind of like an autoethnographic experiment?" Abby asked. I nodded. (*Autoethnography* is a more science-y term that sociologists prefer to use rather than call something a memoir or autobiography.) Conducting an autoethnography basically requires that the autoethnographer consider her own subjective experiences in light of wider cultural, political, and social meanings. It's a pretty cool concept, but even so, "the academy" doesn't always take autoethnographies very seriously. I was okay with that; I wasn't doing this to please "the academy," just myself.

"What if avoiding mirrors makes you think *more* about your appearance instead of less?" Abby asked next.

"If that starts happening, I'll stop," I replied, pleased with myself for knowing the answer without hesitation. My self-protective survival instincts were still going strong. Sanity comes first!

We chatted as a group for a bit longer, throwing around some ideas for how I would manage to avoid mirrors and what might result from the attempt. The conversation ended with Abby's suggestion that I not let the project distract me from my dissertation research and writing. Hearing this made me feel a bit anxious, but she had my best interests in mind; as tempting as it felt to dive into this project with total abandon, I knew I oughtn't do anything that might risk my ability to finish my dissertation and someday find work in academia. Altogether, telling her had felt like the right thing to do, and I knew that her concerns were justified—this was going to be a lot of work!

THE FOLLOWING DAY MARKED THE FIRST DAY OF SPRING QUAR-
ter classes at UCLA. As I got ready in the morning, I was oddly
conscious of each step taken and every product used as I put on my
makeup and fixed my hair. As usual, my hair was a bit lumpy from
sleep (I'm a night showerer) and needed some coaching to stay in
place. *How the heck am I going to pull this off without a mirror?* Suddenly I was running late and couldn't worry anymore.

During my walking commute to UCLA, I noticed mirrors and
reflective surfaces *everywhere*! To my right, shiny store windows
lined every block; to my left were dozens of freshly washed (and thus
reflective) cars parked curbside, bumper-to-bumper.

Later that afternoon I stood in front of a small classroom and
introduced myself to the seventeen students who had signed up for
my course. After introducing myself and describing my expectations
for class, I shared my plans for a no-mirrors year. Half a dozen
hands shot into the air.

"How will you do your makeup?" asked one heavily made-up
young woman incredulously.

I explained my hope to teach myself mirror-free makeup skills,
and then waited to see what other questions my students would ask.
This was fun! Only half of the raised hands remained in the air.

"What about your hair?" asked the next student, who, I couldn't
help but notice, was wearing faux eyelashes and stripper heels to
class. I wondered whether her waist-length platinum blond hair was
homegrown or—ahem—synthetic.

Stop judging! I admonished myself silently. I'd learned that the
same internal voice that told me I wasn't good enough had a habit of

judging other women, too. They fed into each other, so it was best to quell such thoughts before they gathered strength.

I responded similarly to her question, but was then a bit disappointed to see that the other students' hands were no longer raised. Apparently protecting my beauty routines made up the totality of their concerns. With an internal shrug, I turned back to my lesson plans, determined to push these students a bit further than just worrying about hair and makeup by the end of the quarter. But would I be able to achieve this for myself?

April

MIRROR, MIRROR, OFF MY WALLS!

*If you wish to avoid seeing a fool you must
first break your looking glass.*

FRANÇOIS RABELAIS

ITH THE FIRST DAY OF CLASSES BEHIND ME, I FI-
nally felt ready to begin really strategizing for my year
without mirrors. Of utmost importance was deciding
on the official rules I would follow. My readings had taught me that
it was important to make resolutions as simple and specific as possible. By this logic, a person resolving to "get healthier" would be less
likely to have success than a person who resolved to "go to the gym
for thirty minutes on Mondays, Wednesdays, and Fridays." This had
made sense to me, but I wasn't sure how to incorporate the advice.
What part of shunning mirrors for a year would be simple? After
some thought, I decided that I could help myself by coming up with
a set of specific and (hopefully) simple rules.

I had much to decide on, from choosing the official dates that the project would commence and conclude to outlining the inclusions and exceptions for exactly *what* I would be avoiding. Mirrors of all kinds, shapes, and sizes were obviously out, but what about other reflective surfaces? Would it be cheating if I peeked at my reflection in the window displays at Anthropologie, or if I saw myself in the security video greeting shoppers standing in line at Nordstrom Rack? (Clearly I had fashion on the brain!) And what about photos, or "virtual" mirrors, like the built-in cameras and video recorders on my smartphone and laptop? Would I have to give up Facebook, Instagram, and Skype? Finally, what the heck was I supposed to do about the side and rearview mirrors in my car? I wanted my project to be ambitious, but not dangerous! I began drafting a list of possible rules and some potential exceptions. I had a pretty good idea of what I wanted, but I needed a second opinion I could trust.

I decided to call my younger sister for advice. Unlike Michael, who would be sharing a living space with me, Hanna wouldn't be worried about whether or not my project might cause *her* any inconvenience. I figured she'd be tougher on me, and I wanted that. My mind was built to search for exceptions to every rule. Knowing this about myself, I needed to plan ahead for potential loopholes, to protect myself from myself.

"How about when I'm driving? What should I do about my rearview mirror and my side mirrors?" I asked Hanna.

"You're kidding, right?" Hanna exclaimed, already exasperated. "You shouldn't be able to see yourself in those mirrors anyway—at least not without moving your head. They're supposed to be angled to show you the other cars on the road, not your face. Geez, no wonder you get into so many fender benders!"

Gulp. She had a point there. My cherished lipstick-red Saab hatchback was riddled with "love bumps," and the rear bumper was practically concave. I knew that a British study had recently found that 20 percent of female motorists admit to having applied makeup while driving, and that 3 percent had caused an accident while doing so. With a cringe, I recalled the streaks of waterproof Maybelline Great Lash mascara decorating my car's interior ceiling; abstract art, it was not. I hastily wrote *Car mirrors MUST be used, but for safe driving only!* to my growing list of rules. Even if my year without mirrors didn't successfully revamp my self-image, this particular rule had the potential to save my life.

"Okay—what about my wedding photos?" I asked. This was sure to be a weak spot.

"No exceptions means no exceptions," she shot back. Then, she more softly pointed out, "It's not as if you'll *never* get to see them, just not right away. It will be good for you."

I still wasn't convinced about the wedding photos. I made a mental note to myself to poll a few more friends for feedback on this particular point.

The only loophole Hanna agreed to was my suggestion that I be allowed to see my shadow. I knew that there was a chance I'd occasionally peer at my silhouette to check for egregious errors in self-presentation (i.e., Mohawk-size ponytail bumps or major muffin-top), but I sensed that this wouldn't become a crutch the way that looking at photos or video might. Besides, I had to draw the line somewhere, and considering all the shiny store windows lining the sidewalks of my walking commute to work, I wasn't sure where else I'd be able to look except down at the ground in front of me.

Then Hanna asked, "What are you going to do about makeup?" Unlike my sister, I rarely left the house without at least foundation, blush, and mascara (if not also concealer, face powder, eye shadow, eyeliner, and lip gloss), and she knew this.

Thanks to my students' queries, I'd already given plenty of thought to the makeup question. "I'm going to keep wearing it, but probably less," I replied with confidence. "I'll have to learn to put it on without looking." As much as I wanted to spend less time and energy on my looks, I wasn't interested in completely abandoning my personal sense of style and femininity. Wearing makeup most days helped me feel more pulled-together and professional. I knew dozens of women who rarely wore makeup, including my sister, and I didn't think any less of them for it (rather, I admired this in the same way that I admired *any* woman with a strong sense of individual style), but it wasn't for me.

Hanna and I both agreed that my official "year without mirrors" ought to begin retroactively, on March 25, 2011, the day that I had first thought of the idea. A retroactive start date may sound suspicious, since I hadn't yet begun avoiding mirrors, but this choice was very important; I wanted my project to emphasize thoughtful self-improvement instead of perfection, and beginning the year with my first tiny steps in the right direction, however small, reinforced this intention. In the same spirit, this meant that if I happened to falter at any point throughout the year—either by seeing myself by accident or in a moment of weakness—instead of quitting or beating myself up, I would do my best to mindfully learn from my mistake and keep moving forward. After all, avoiding mirrors was not itself my be-all-end-all goal, but a means to a greater end: I wanted an improved relationship with my body.

I also knew that there were risks to waiting. Just as yo-yo dieters tend to binge on junk food just before beginning their diets, I could see myself "binging" on vanity at the last minute. Sephora shopping sprees and Glamour Shots portrait sessions were *not* in my best interest, emotionally or financially.

After hanging up the phone with Hanna, I reviewed my notes and wrote out a finalized list of rules:

> My no-mirrors project started on March 25, 2011, and will end on March 24, 2012.
> Any and all reflective surfaces count.
> Virtual mirrors (i.e., photos, videos, Skype videos, etc.) also count.
> I will use my rearview and side mirrors when driving, but not for checking myself out.
> I'm allowed to see my shadow.

Reading over what I'd written forced me to consider the enormity of the changes I would be making in my life. For years I'd gravitated toward my reflection without thinking; every mirror, every store window—not to mention the occasional piece of well-shined cutlery—had been another chance to assess the goods. Succeeding at going a full year without mirrors wouldn't be as easy as simply avoiding them; I would have to retrain my very instincts. If I managed to change my behavior around mirrors, would this, in turn, lead to changes in my thinking?

This wasn't the usual order of things. Typically, behavioral changes are the goal, with changed thinking as the first step. Indeed, an entire field of contemporary evidence-based psychotherapy, cognitive behavioral therapy, is based on the premise that changing maladaptive thinking leads to changes in feelings and behavior. And this idea isn't even particularly modern. Lao-tzu, sixth century BC philosopher and founder of Taoism, wrote the following:

Watch your thoughts, they become your words.
Watch your words, they become your actions.
Watch your actions, they become your habits.
Watch your habits, they become your character.
Watch your character, it becomes your destiny.

Clearly, common thinking insisted that thoughts shaped behavior, but I was betting on the opposite. By focusing first on action, my project would have me skipping a few of Lao-tzu's oft-quoted steps. At the very least I would jumble their order. I hoped that my path would instead follow the wisdom of Harry S. Truman, who said, "Actions are the seed of fate. Deeds grow into destiny."

I knew that my habits couldn't change overnight, so I decided to dedicate the first month of my project to transition. Over the next three weeks I would examine the practical details involved in navigating a world without my reflection, from plotting out all of the mirrors (*and* reflective surfaces, *and* virtual mirrors) I encountered in a typical day, so that I could find reasonable solutions for handling every one of them, to teaching myself how to apply makeup, style my hair, put in my contact lenses, and choose outfits without seeing myself.

In terms of strategizing, I decided to start small. Before tackling the entire world of mirrors, I would focus on the ones in my home. I counted seven: two in my bedroom, one in my bathroom, three in the living room, and a wall of mirrors that lined one side of my building's foyer. It seemed important that Michael and I work together to figure out exactly how I would do this. We'd be living in the same place soon, and Michael wasn't planning to give up mirrors as well. Supportive as he was of my project and its goals, I sensed that he was worried about how it might impact *his* life, not to mention our relationship.

Like me, Michael is a worrier, a people-pleaser, and a perfectionist. He likes drawing diagrams and has a penchant for using unneeded and typically inexact similes to explain his thinking, even for basic concepts. (This drives me crazy!) Despite fancying himself to be a free-spirited, laid-back guy at heart, he is admittedly more risk-averse than me, and is extremely wary of hastily made decisions. He'd been paralyzed by indecisiveness when we'd begun talking about getting engaged. I'll never forget the time he'd plaintively whined, "I'm one hundred percent certain that I would be happy spending the rest of my life with you, but *deciding* to get married is so overwhelming. This would be *so* much easier if you just got pregnant. If you were pregnant, I'd marry you tomorrow!" Luckily, I wasn't impatient enough to test his hypothesis, and, sure enough, a few months later he signed us up for that fateful Diamond Dash contest.

Despite Michael's wariness of big decisions, I've never doubted his love for me, or his commitment to our relationship; I just hate waiting around while he figures out stuff that I already know. Anyway, the point of all of this is to explain why I wasn't surprised when Michael wanted to help sort out the details of my no-mirrors plan. Despite his initial enthusiasm, he seemed anxious to know exactly what would be involved. So we made plans for a special Friday-night strategizing date. (Yes, we make plans to make plans.)

After scoring a prime people-watching table at our favorite neighborhood bar, we ordered a first round of drinks and settled into our seats. To get started, Michael drew a diagram on the back of a drink menu listing all of the mirrors I'd encounter before leaving my condo. We decided to try tackling them in the same order that I would encounter them on my way out the door each morning. Unfortunately, we got stuck on the first one.

Almost an entire wall of my bedroom was made up of mirrors. I had one of those very large sliding-door closets in my bedroom, and both closet doors were mirrored. This meant that when I woke up in the morning, if I were to sit up in bed and look straight ahead, I'd be staring directly at myself in *a really huge freaking mirror.* I'm not sure what *you* look like when you wake up, but I can tell you that looking into this mirror was not the best way to start my day. Thankfully, I was already in the habit of looking away from this mirror first thing in the morning, but that usually lasted only as long as my glasses stayed off of my face.

Michael and I tried brainstorming ideas for how to make this particularly huge and poorly placed mirror a nonissue. His first suggestion was to "close the blackout shades in the bedroom and never, *ever* turn on the lights." He exuberantly wrote the words *pitch dark!* on the diagram and drew a line linking his words to where he had scribbled *closet mirror.*

I immediately assumed that he was joking and took offense. Was Michael mocking the whole project? I wasn't amused, and it showed in my face. I took a big gulp of beer and then said, "Ummm . . . can't we, like, brainstorm some *practical* solutions?"

Michael hadn't been kidding. *Oops.*

Obviously, Michael and I had brought to the table dramatically different ideas about what our brainstorming date would entail. I'd imagined that we'd work together to come up with ideas, which I would then give a yea or nay. In other words, he'd be welcome to pitch, but I'd be the umpire calling the strikes. Michael, on the other hand, had recently gone through some formal training on creative brainstorming at work, and my plans apparently broke the cardinal rule of brainstorming sessions, which was that ideas should *never* be critiqued in the beginning stages. According to Michael, early criti-

cisms disrupt the flow of ideas. My knee-jerk scoffing had offended
him and kind of hurt his feelings. I felt embarrassed to be the jerk,
but also a little defensive; it was *my* project, right? If I wanted to be
the umpire, I should be allowed!

I made the mistake of saying as much, which prompted Michael
to suggest that, if it was indeed *my* project, perhaps he ought to just
let me do it however I want and not be involved at all. The increasingly tipsy control freak in me found the idea slightly tempting, but
I knew that this was just *his* knee-jerk reaction to my knee-jerk reaction. Besides, up until that minute, I'd really been looking forward
to making plans with Michael for the project. I needed his support
and wanted his involvement. Besides, the last thing I needed was to
piss off the guy responsible for telling me if I was leaving the house
with arugula in my teeth! Embarrassed, I apologized.

"April Fools?" I added weakly at the end, wiggling my eyebrows
in hopes that I might produce a laugh. He rolled his eyes and accepted my apology, but I could tell he was still kind of disappointed.

We tried to start over, but couldn't quite find that brainstorming
groove we'd both been romanticizing. Maybe that teamwork I
thought we'd perfected during our engagement ring race still had a
few kinks to work out. Still, we chipped away at the plans for a few
minutes and figured out a few things.

First, I'd hang a curtain in front of our bathroom mirror, which
would allow Michael to uncover the mirror when he needed to see
himself. I silently wondered if he'd remember to recover the mirror
at the same rate that he remembered to put the toilet seat down (90
percent fail), but decided against mentioning it. I also wondered
whether I'd be able to create curtains that actually looked cool, and
not like a puppet show was about to commence above my sink.

Second, to avoid the full wall of mirrors in the entryway to our condo building, I would be taking the back stairs to get to my car from that day forward. I felt seriously bummed that I wouldn't be able to pick up my mail from the front hall anymore. This had long been a daily pleasure of mine, my version of a scratch-off lotto ticket; even if most of what came were bills, those "just because" handwritten letters from my grandmothers were priceless. I consoled myself by envisioning the murderous thighs (à la *GoldenEye*'s Xenia Onatopp) I'd earn after eleven months of climbing nine extra stairs each day. More important, this tactic completely solved a major mirror obstacle.

By this point, Michael and I were still at the bar, but our brainpower was fading (glucose shortage?), and we were both sick of talking about mirrors. Michael suggested that we try another round of brainstorming in a day or two, and joked that we ought to use dry-erase markers to draw a massive brainstorming diagram on—what else—the huge mirrored closet doors in my bedroom. I loved the idea and agreed to call it a night.

ON THE FOLLOWING EVENING, A SATURDAY, MICHAEL AND I joined a group of friends for a birthday celebration in L.A.'s Koreatown. It was a flavorful *gogigui* ("grill your own meat") extravaganza, and the guest of honor was Dave Frederick, a friend of mine from UCLA who I'd collaborated with on a research project about weight-based prejudice. I admired Dave for his wry and silly sense of humor along with his encyclopedic knowledge of research on body image and cultural perceptions of attractiveness. Also in attendance were Dave's fiancée, Erica; Andrew, a psychology grad student who I'd taught with in the Sex and Gender course for the past two years; and our friend Ana, who worked for UCLA's

Institute for Society and Genetics. We made a delightfully nerdy and almost-but-not-quite-rowdy bunch.

Over bowls of spicy kimchi, bulgogi beef, and galbi short ribs, we caught up on one another's lives and made sloshing beer toasts to Dave's soon-approaching graduation. I brought up my no-mirrors project and, in doing so, subjected myself to an onslaught of well-meaning teasing.

"So you'll have no way of knowing if you have food on your face?! I'm going to mess with you all the time. This will be fun!" Andrew joked, making "You've got a booger hanging out of your nose" hand signals in jest.

"How will you do your makeup?" asked Ana.

"What about reflective surfaces?" asked Erica.

"You should start a blog!" suggested Dave.

A blog? "I'm not so sure about blogging. I've never even *read* one," I responded.

"You built your own webpage for your research, right?" he continued.

I nodded warily. His enthusiasm was becoming slightly contagious.

"Well, it can't be much harder than that. Aha! You could call it Mirror, Mirror OFF the Wall!" Nods and murmurs of agreement circulated around the table.

I took a cooling gulp of my beer and said I'd think about it. As much as I loved the title Dave suggested, I wasn't sure I wanted to put myself out there on the Web. I didn't know anything about blogging (unless you counted watching the movie *Julie & Julia*) other than that it was something *other* people did, specifically other people who not only had mad computer skills, but also were capable of writing something almost every day that was interesting enough or funny enough that other people actually wanted to read it. It sounded like a lot of work and unnecessary pressure. I was great at scribbling in my journals, but the private nature of journaling allowed me to do it haphazardly (i.e., whenever I *felt* like it) and—most important— without concern for my grammar or spelling, much less entertaining an audience! *One thing at a time,* I told myself. Blogging could wait.

O VER THE NEXT TWO WEEKS I STARTED TO PUT MY PLANS into practice. Any mirrors I could cover up at home were covered, and the rest I learned to avoid. I practiced the two-mile walking commute from my condo to my office at UCLA, mapping out all of the major mirrors and reflective surfaces in my mind. I trained myself to look straight ahead during my walk to work; if I glimpsed my reflection in my view or peripheral vision, I turned away as quickly as I could. To get used to this, I began pretending that my reflection was a person I didn't want to talk to, avoiding eye contact with myself the same way one might avoid eye contact with an annoying or unpleasant acquaintance. In doing this, I realized that there was an important distinction between accidentally *seeing* my reflection (and then immediately looking away) and intentionally *looking* at it; the former would sometimes be unavoidable, but the latter was in my control.

I even went so far as to figure out exactly which public restrooms in my building had stall doors that didn't open facing a mirror. I also realized that my days of aspirational window-shopping were coming to an end; my heart sank as my wallet rejoiced.

I knew that once my transition month was over, I'd have to rely on hanger appeal and comfort to dress myself, so I tried on every garment of clothing in my closet and weeded out anything ill-fitting or out-of-date. I was relieved to confirm that my wash-and-wear haircut looked identical whether I combed it out in front of a mirror or in front of a curtain (or not at all, for that matter). The only practical task that remained was training myself to apply my makeup.

As an academic (in training), I was lucky to be working in an environment that was fairly ambivalent when it came to grooming expectations. UCLA's Department of Sociology is a relaxed-but-professional place that purports to value minds more than bodies. In fact, some folks in my department seem mildly suspicious of people who seem too put-together, as though the time spent styling hair or putting on makeup (or wearing deodorant or making sure your socks match) was time that could have been spent—ahem, *should* have been spent—theorizing about the workings of the world. I enjoyed an even more relaxed "Just be yourself, so long as it doesn't involve stripper-heels" dress code for my volunteer work at About-Face.

It was a far cry from my three-year stint working in the fashion industry. In *that* world I'd felt scrutinized for being "too cerebral." (Cue Miranda Priestly in *The Devil Wears Prada* complaining about hiring the "smart fat girl.") And I'll never forget the look of disdain on my VP's face when I returned from a style-scouting exercise with a jacket I'd found on clearance at T.J.Maxx. Going back to grad school had been a welcome change in terms of my body image and sense of style. It was infinitely more fun to be on the cooler side of geek than on the geekier side of cool!

Knowing this about myself, I wasn't interested in completely losing the "cool" in my "cooler side of geek" persona during my year without mirrors. I knew that my love for fashion would persist, even if I couldn't see myself wearing it. Nevertheless, I decided that this would be a good year to rely on dependable, classic ensembles rather than chasing trends.

Similarly, I wanted to keep wearing makeup because—even if I couldn't see it, and even if I wore much less—I knew that the routine of applying makeup itself would help me *feel* like myself. Before the project started, I was wearing makeup almost every day. I even wore it on weekends and on days when I worked from home. Somehow it just made me feel more fully put together. I also knew that not wearing any makeup was likely to make me feel hyper-self-conscious. Giving up mirrors *and* makeup at the same time would have been too much change at once.

I wrote out a list of everything I was accustomed to putting on my face each morning and how I applied everything, in order of application:

1. SPF 30 sunscreen (rubbed on with my fingers)
2. Liquid foundation (applied with a foundation brush)
3. Concealer (applied with a concealer brush)
4. Powder blush (applied with a blush brush)
5. Two neutral eye shadows (applied with an eye shadow brush)
6. Eyeliner (applied with an eyeliner brush)
7. Waterproof mascara (after curling my lashes)
8. Lip gloss (dabbed on with my finger)

I had to laugh at myself when I read over the list. I wore all this to look *naturally* pretty!? I clearly had plenty of room to downsize. I sifted through my wares, and the sheer enormity of my makeup collection revealed lots of duplicate products, as well as plenty of things I'd purchased on a whim, to be used only once or twice, or never. It didn't matter that I could apply all of the above in ten minutes or less; precise applications and multiple fancy brushes weren't going to work without mirrors. I was also in the habit of frequently changing up my "looks" depending on the day's plans, my outfit, or even my mood. It was fun to experiment with different colors of eye shadow or shades of lip gloss, but this practice, too, would be abandoned during my no-mirrors project. I needed to master *one* look that I could use every single day—and for every possible occasion—over the next eleven months. It needed to be both basic and classic.

I decided to get comfortable downgrading in coverage from opaque to sheer products that I could apply mostly with my finger-tips. Sheerness was essential: Opacity would make mistakes more noticeable, and mistakes were bound to happen. Neutral colors, rather than bright colors, were likewise important, as they would translate more fluently across a variety of occasions and outfits. Luckily, my vast makeup collection already contained several prod-ucts that fit the bill.

I replaced my powdered eye shadow with a neutral cream shadow that I could smudge on with my fingers. Hooray! I similarly replaced my usual lip gloss with a sheerer lip gloss. Less pigment meant that there would be a lower likelihood of my leaving the house looking like I'd been making out with a clown.

My eyeliner, on the other hand, couldn't be replaced, so it simply went away. It didn't matter how many thousands of times I'd applied it since sixth grade; with fears vacillating between the unlikely (loss of an eye) and the *very* likely (arriving at work looking like a five-year-old's art project), I didn't trust myself to apply eyeliner without a mirror.

This was not the case when it came to the idea of giving up mas-cara. As many natural blondes with invisible eyelashes may under-stand, mascara felt necessary. I'd long been convinced that my eyes actually disappeared without mascara. So, with a little practice (i.e., going cross-eyed while watching the wand slowly approach my face), I managed to master mascara sans mirror! It turned out that my trusty four-dollar waterproof Maybelline Great Lash mascara was mirror-*optional*.

Finally, in my boldest move yet, I replaced my sunscreen, foundation, and concealer with one product: a tinted moisturizer with SPF. The great thing about tinted moisturizer is that, thanks to its sheerness, I could just squirt a blob into my hands and then smear it all over my face like I was applying regular face lotion. The not-so-great thing about tinted moisturizer is that it wasn't going to do much for me in terms of hiding pimples or under-eye circles. I tried to reassure myself about this by remembering that people probably didn't notice my flaws (or care about them) as much as I did. If my critical inner voice believed that a pimple or two might be the difference between being loved by my friends and being respected by my colleagues . . . well, this would be an important assumption to test! As Michel de Montaigne—Renaissance author and father of modern skepticism—once said, "Nothing is so firmly believed as what we least know."

I didn't own a tinted moisturizer, and a quick trip to Sephora introduced me to another challenge: Sephora had forty-five different options available, and sheer as they were, I had to try on about twenty of them before I found an acceptable combo of sheer coverage + SPF + my perfect shade of pallor. When I informed the sales associate helping me that I would be applying the "luxury product" I'd chosen with my hands instead of the recommended fifty-eight-dollar brush, she looked at me as though I were planning to smear feces on my cheeks and call it rouge. Had this happened a few months earlier, I probably would have bought the brush. Instead, I reminded myself that my new body image motto was "Good enough is good enough!"

Speaking of good enough, I decided to keep my regular powder blush, since it was already sheer enough to be mirror-optional. My new mirror-optional list of products and application methods cut my original makeup list in half.

I began practicing my mirror-free application skills over the next few days and was pleased by my progress. I applied my makeup one step at a time, without looking at myself in the mirror. In between steps, I'd take a peek and make note of any blunders. After a few days I began skipping my peeks between each step until I'd completed the entire process sans mirror. Dare I say that I looked almost as put-together as before, but more "natural"? Good enough? Indeed!

SEVERAL DAYS LATER I FOUND MYSELF WATCHING TV ALONE after dinner on a Tuesday evening. Michael was in Palo Alto for the workweek, and I'd decided to spend the final days of my transition month really perfecting my mirror-free habits. I'd spent the entire day successfully avoiding mirrors and was pretty proud of myself, but completely exhausted. The amount of mental energy that I'd had to put into avoiding my reflection—combined with my regular workload of teaching, catching up on research projects, and a meeting that day with my therapist, Gia—had left me drained. Gia had given me her enthusiastic blessing to try my year without mirrors, so long as I promised to quit if the project triggered any disordered behaviors or thoughts. Gia reminded me that "one of the most powerful things you can do to challenge negative thoughts and behaviors is to test them out. You'll learn whether or not the assumptions that you're organizing your life around are based in reality or just in your mind. I'm optimistic!"

I stole a still-allowed glance at myself in one of my living room mirrors. It was the first time I'd seen my reflection all day, and I felt pleased that my makeup looked decent and that I didn't have any food on my shirt. I gave myself a minute to actively peer, noticing that this previously frequent and mundane act was beginning to feel precious. What was it that economists said? Increased scarcity predicts increased value? Or perhaps in simpler terms, the (anticipated) absence was making my heart grow fonder? Something along these lines was beginning to unfold, and it felt like a positive omen. My eyes looked tired and my hair was limp and scraggly thanks to my sweaty walk home, but I felt a surge of appreciation for the body that had carried me throughout my long day. I turned away from the mirror and returned my attention to the task at hand: relaxation.

I poured myself a full glass of six-dollars-a-bottle merlot from Trader Joe's, broke into a package of dark chocolate–covered marshmallows, and settled into my favorite chair with my two fluffy orange tabby cats, Dolce and Diesel. Surely wine, chocolate, and a few episodes of *Law & Order: SVU* would set things right. The day's stressors began fading away. Suddenly I was jolted out of my relaxation by the blaring of a TV advertisement, projecting at a volume far exceeding that of my TV show.

EAT WHATEVER YOU WANT, AND STILL LOSE WEIGHT!!

THAT'S RIGHT!

EAT WHATEVER YOU WANT, AND STILL LOSE WEIGHT!!

Whaaaat?! Another lying crash-diet commercial. Great. My thoughts shifted to the About-Face media literacy workshop I'd given my UCLA students the day before, in which I'd encouraged them to consider three questions when considering advertisements: (1) What is being sold? For instance, a potentially dangerous and unregulated diet drug. (2) How is it being sold? By, say, comparing a smiling thin woman with washboard abs with a frowning chubbier version of her former self. And (3) How does the advertiser want you to feel? Like a grotesquely fat and unlovable loser, maybe.

I shook my head, huffing and puffing, scaring Dolce right out of my lap. Diesel woke up from his nap, yawned in my direction, and went back to sleep.

"Fuck you, Hydroxycut!" I slurrily shouted at my television, pointing my fingers at the screen for emphasis. "And you, too, you, you . . . airbrushed Hydroxy*slut*! You're crap! You're poison! FUCK. YOU."

I was home alone wearing a ratty bathrobe, surrounded by two nervous felines, a half-drunk bottle of wine, and multiple empty chocolate wrappers. I probably wasn't my most composed self, and yet I'd never felt more empowered. The advertisement I'd just seen was evil, and I wanted to tell the world.

I am going to start a fucking blog! Right. Now. I decided, determinedly.

I stumbled into my bedroom to grab my laptop. Back in my living room, I poured another glass of wine and tapped "how to start a blog" into my online search engine. Five minutes and a few decisions later I'd built my blog, calling it Mirror, Mirror . . . OFF the Wall, just as Dave had suggested.

I wrote my first post that night, narrating the story of my wedding dress insanity and how it had led to my decision to give up mirrors. I threw in a photo of myself in Dress #1 and another in Dress #4. *These are the last images I'm going to see of myself for a year!* I realized with a gulp (of merlot). Eyeballing the now empty wine bottle with a wince, my index finger hovered over my keyboard. I clicked "post," and suddenly I was a blogger.

Vaguely recalling what I'd learned about keeping resolutions (and feeling particularly brave, thanks to the wine!), I copied the link to my first blog post and forwarded it to all of my Facebook friends. I promised to post two to three times per week throughout the project and crossed my fingers for support rather than ridicule.

Luckily, my virtual friends were as supportive as my in-person friends had been a few nights prior. I received a few dozen "likes" and several enthusiastic comments, ranging from, "Just subscribed! Very interesting project" to" "I'm following. What is Spanx?" and my favorite: "This will be good practice for if you ever become a vampire!" Indeed it would.

Thanks to Facebook, my project—*and* my blog—were now, truly, official.

O F COURSE, NOT EVERYONE I SPOKE WITH WAS A HUGE FAN of the idea. I'd scheduled meetings with two more of my dissertation advisors for the following day, and the reactions I received were mixed.

At my first meeting one of my advisors raised his eyebrows sky-high after I explained my project and decision to blog about it. He called the idea "interesting," but then added, "It all seems a bit ironic to me. I mean, your goal is to be less vain and self-involved, but blogging about yourself is an inherently vain enterprise, wouldn't you agree?" (Faculty mentors are known for ending abrasive statements with questions like "Wouldn't you agree?" As in "Your research questions are unimportant and your methods are inappropriate, don't you agree?" or "I assume that this is only your *first* draft, am I correct?") I was used to dodging these types of questions when discussing my research, but wasn't quite sure how to respond this time.

"I realize that there's some irony to the idea, but I also think that there's an important difference between obsessing about my appearance and being introspective about my experiences. I guess they're both *technically* self-involved, but I can't imagine any self-improvement project that wouldn't involve at least a little bit of self-reflection." I cringed as the word "reflection" came out of my mouth. Pun *not* intended!

"I imagine that you know autoethnography isn't very well received by the discipline," he continued.

"This isn't a formal research project," I offered, weakly.

"Well, at least you aren't doing this at the same time that you're on the job market, right?" he concluded, laughing.

"Right!" I chirped, laughing along. I was pleased to have something we actually agreed about.

But when I left his office I realized that I didn't actually know what we'd just laughed about in agreement. I turned around and knocked on his door. He answered, and I asked, "When you said it was good that I wasn't doing this project while I'm on the job market, did you say that because you don't think people would take me seriously because of the project, or because you don't want me to go on job interviews without looking at myself in the mirror first?"

"I was thinking it would be bad to have lipstick on your teeth while giving a job talk," he answered.

"Oh. Okay, thanks for clarifying," I said, sulking away.

My next meeting went considerably better. Wary of receiving the same critiques, I prefaced my explanation by clarifying that I was embarking on a *personal* project. I felt okay saying this, since I'd occasionally babysat for this advisor and his wife; having wiped his two-year-old daughter's bottom more than a few times, it seemed only fair that I could share a bit about my life outside of academia without reproach.

"That sounds really interesting!" he said warmly. "It reminds me of one of the bedtime stories we read to our daughter. Have you heard of George and Martha?"

"The first President of the United States and the first First Lady?" I suggested.

"No, George and Martha are characters in a children's book series. They're hippopotami," he explained.

My brain snapped to an unexpected word association: "Split pea soup?" I blurted, immediately feeling like a complete ass.

"Yes!" he exclaimed excitedly. "George hated Martha's split pea soup, so he hid it in his loafers to avoid hurting her feelings."

Aha! I suddenly remembered these picture books from my own youth.

The story—titled "The Mirror"—goes something like this:

Martha was having a bit of a vanity crisis. She couldn't stop looking at herself in the mirror! (Remind you of anybody we know?) Her good friend George was getting really annoyed by all of this, so he devised a plan to teach his friend a lesson. When Martha wasn't looking, George taped a horrid drawing of her onto the mirror.

Martha was horrified, as most of us would be upon seeing ourselves with green skin, wonky gold teeth, and eyes stacked on top of each other. She cried out, "What has happened to me?" Sly George was ready with an answer: "That's what happens when you look at yourself in the mirror." The tale ends with Martha's enormously cool/brave/awesome decision to never look in the mirror again.

It was clear that Ms. Martha and I had more than a few things in common. Martha truly enjoyed looking into the mirror (at least until George fooled her with his unflattering drawing), and at times I'd also admired myself in mirrors and felt pride and pleasure in my appearance. I'd felt beautiful or glamorous and, indeed, vain; very Martha-esque. Martha's best friend was George, and mine was Michael.

I'd also experienced the flip side of the mirror coin, in my crippling (indeed, disordered) body image throughout much of my high school and college years. Nobody ever drew an unflattering picture of me on my mirror (instead, Michael had recently helped me cover my mirrors), yet I managed to look upon myself with horror nonetheless.

But Martha stopped looking into the mirror to *protect* her vanity. Indeed, she abandoned mirrors only when their use supposedly threatened her looks! I'd chosen a similar path with the hope that avoiding mirrors would *reduce* my vanity. I was actually proud of myself for embracing the fact that my appearance might suffer a bit during my project. After all, what better way to prove to myself that my happiness and looks were not quite so tightly intertwined?

Reading an old children's book about a pair of hippopotami was a surprising source of insight and clarification of my goals. I was grateful to the advisor who lent it to me; perhaps not everyone in "the academy" would be concerned about my plans, after all.

THE NEXT DAY, I RAN INTO MY MORE SKEPTICAL ADVISOR IN the hallway while waiting for my lunch to heat up in the department microwave. I hadn't looked in a mirror all day and was feeling pretty good about my targeted expenditure of willpower.

"Dang! So I guess that no-mirrors project is off to a rough start, eh?" he exclaimed.

"Huh?" I responded, confused.

"Oh, I'm just kidding!" he said with a laugh. "No, really, you look . . . normal."

"Ummm . . . thanks," I answered, not sure what else to say.

"Well, I'll see you around!" he said, and then he was gone.

It took all of the (will)power in my being to not run immediately to the ladies' room for a peek in the mirror. I consoled myself by imagining that he wouldn't have made fun of me if I had *actually* looked "rough." Right? (That would have been mean; don't *you* agree?)

THAT EVENING, WITH ONLY ONE WEEK REMAINING BEFORE I quit mirrors cold turkey, seemed like a good time for reflection (pun intended this time). I felt bolstered by all of the support I'd received from my friends and family, but I was wary of the critiques. Hearing one of my mentors describe my project as ironic had hit a nerve, and I didn't want to flippantly dismiss his concerns.

Was it, in fact, incredibly, *ironically* vain to spend a year focusing on—not to mention publicly writing about—my experiences avoiding vanity? Was I blogging to share my experiences with others for *their* benefit, or for my own? Perhaps I was just a silly and self-absorbed narcissist who'd decided to swap her reflection for an audience? If so, which was worse?

I didn't yet know how to answer these questions, but I knew that they were important to ask. I vowed to be completely honest with myself as I came to the answers, and asked Michael to "tell it to me straight" if he started having concerns.

"Sweetie, you know I will, but you're overthinking this, as usual," he pointed out. "Just dive in and trust yourself to figure it out along the way. It will be okay, I promise. You're a good person."

I'm a good person. Maybe Michael was biased by positive illusions, but so what? It was soothing to hear this from somebody who had actually seen me at my worst and loved me anyway.

Later that evening I created a poll on my blog, asking my readers to vote on how I ought to handle photographs during my year without mirrors. I wanted to be able to look at old photos, but I wasn't sure how long I ought to wait before seeing new pictures of myself taken *during* the project. Should there be an exception for my wedding photos? I knew my sister's opinion, and knew that Michael didn't care, so I decided to leave it up to the masses (i.e., all of my thirty or so blog readers).

The overwhelming majority (63 percent) felt that I shouldn't be allowed to see photos of myself that were taken during my no-mirrors project until the full year was over. I'd expected this and knew it was for the best. I felt bummed and relieved at the same time. I worried that my world might feel less animated without being able to easily relive joyful memories a few days after an event, but adding photos to my list of "no exceptions" made things straightforward, simple, and, ultimately, nicer. It pleased me to imagine that for the next eleven months my life would be free of the self-bullying that frequently accompanied photo-viewing.

Still, I was delighted to see that there would be one exception to the no-exceptions policy: my wedding photos. Of the 63 percent of voters who wanted me to wait the whole year before seeing photos of myself, a slim majority (33 percent of *all* voters) felt that my wedding photos should be excluded from the ban. I was overjoyed. This was something I could look forward to, and it helped take away some of the anxiety I'd been feeling about the possibility that I might miss out on something priceless by not seeing myself on my wedding day.

And with that, my planning phase was complete. The rules were settled, the mirror-avoiding strategies in place, and I'd practiced my everyday grooming. It was time to get serious!

THREE

May

MY REFLECTION, MY FRENEMY

Men look at themselves in mirrors.
Women look for themselves.

ELISSA MELAMED

B Y THE TIME MAY ROLLED AROUND, I'D GIVEN MYSELF A month to figure out how to handle the practical aspects of avoiding mirrors, but I still didn't feel completely prepared. Sure, I'd plotted out all of the mirrors I'd encounter in a typical day of my life in Los Angeles, and I'd even spent several days successfully avoiding mirrors until bedtime, but the first week of May presented a challenge for which I'd been unable to prepare: San Francisco.

May marked a huge milestone in my relationship with Michael: After more than a year of splitting time between Los Angeles (my home) and Palo Alto (his home), we were finally, *finally* moving in together. I'd never lived with a boyfriend before (I'm an old-fashioned gal at heart!), so this was a pretty big deal for me, but I felt more than ready. To say that I was excited would be an under-statement.

As wonderful as it felt to pack my bags and hightail it to San Francisco to be with the love of my life, not everything about the move was ideal. Namely, moving to a new home meant I would have to navigate a whole new set of mirrors, not only in our new apart-ment, but also at a new office and in a new city. Even though I'd targeted May 1 as my first day of going wholly without mirrors, I ended up regressed back to my in-training mode for a few days while I adjusted. The good news was that our new apartment in San Francisco had only half as many mirrors as my place in Los Angeles, with one in the bedroom and three in the bathroom. The bad news was that, while moving in during that first weekend in May, I managed to take a nice long gander at myself in every single one of them!

By Sunday night Michael and I had managed to cover all of the mirrors, and I'd spent most of the following day practicing my reflection-free commute to About-Face, where I was going to be vol-unteering a couple of days a week (the rest of my time would be spent at home working on my dissertation), but I was still frustrated by what felt like a lack of progress. It had been almost forty days since I'd committed to giving up mirrors, but I had yet to spend a full twenty-four hours without at least a little peek. Even taking two extra days to "practice" felt like I was letting myself down, not to mention letting down the friends and family who were following my progress (or lack thereof) through my blog posts.

Over a celebratory thank-god-we're-done-unpacking meal of takeout Thai, I complained about all of this to Michael, who kindly suggested that I shouldn't feel discouraged. After all, he reminded me, it had taken me only a few days to prepare myself for the mirrors of San Francisco, which was a lot faster than the weeks I'd needed to accomplish the same in Los Angeles.

I begrudgingly accepted Michael's point. It was true that I'd begun to automatically look away from even the smallest glimpse of my reflection. I'd also grown increasingly comfortable and efficient with my scaled-back, mirror-free makeup routine. "I guess these are skills I can use no matter what city I'm in," I admitted between bites of spicy eggplant chicken, "but I also think that L.A. was harder because it just had more mirrors in general!" I didn't know if this was actually true (or, for that matter, why I was arguing with some-one who was just trying to make me feel better), but it wouldn't have surprised me. Los Angeles, home to Hollywood and all that comes with it, is about as appearance-obsessed as a city can get. It was a great place for studying body image, but—for the same reasons—a pretty lousy place for my own body image. Admitting this out loud made me wonder: If L.A.'s pro-vanity culture had caused me to be more appearance-obsessed about myself, then perhaps living in San Francisco's purportedly more laid-back milieu would prove to be a positive influence in the opposite direction. I was certainly excited to find out.

WELL-RESEARCHED BOOKS OFTEN INSPIRE ME TO HUNT down the original sources cited within them; these sources would further inspire me to hunt down *their* original sources, and so on. Mark Pendergrast's *Mirror, Mirror: A History of the Human Love Affair with Reflection*, one of the books I'd picked up in L.A., was one such book. Thanks to Pendergrast's detailed prose and copi-ous referencing, I'd developed a list of additional mirror-themed books and articles I was dying to hunt down. So, even though I hadn't yet finished all of the readings I'd already collected, I decided to take a trip across town to the San Francisco Public Library.

Of course, my list of books wasn't the only reason for my trip; I needed to apply for my library card. This, to me, is the equivalent of registering to vote or otherwise declaring official residency. Since childhood, I've always turned to books when feeling overwhelmed or out of sorts. I missed Los Angeles, but knew I'd feel immediately at home the moment I found myself surrounded by endless full bookshelves, the subtle smell of aging paper, the sounds of excited children and of kindly shushing librarians. After applying for my library card (approved! huzzah!) I claimed a study room and put myself to work.

Using Pendergrast's vast bibliography as a guide, I'd outdone myself by the end of the day. I couldn't possibly bring home everything I'd pulled off the shelves, but it was a pleasure to select my favorites and pore over my notes from the rest. I'd learned that many of the greatest philosophical, mathematical, and scientific minds have been inspired by both the mysteries of reflection and the potential scientific utilities of mirrors. I'd read (okay, *skimmed*) several mirror-themed writings from Plato, Aristotle, Pythagoras, Archimedes, Epicurus, Euclid, Newton, Descartes, and Einstein. I'd learned that the very ability to recognize oneself in a mirror is quintessentially human (okay, actually quintessentially human, ape, dolphin, and sometimes elephant!), and that this discovery had inspired modern psychologists to ponder the very nature of human consciousness and self-awareness. Yet some of the most interesting insights on the topics of vanity and beauty promised to come from the works of some of my favorite poets and novelists, including Jane Austen, Oscar Wilde, Louisa May Alcott, Emily Dickinson, Rumi, John Keats, Maya Angelou, Leo Tolstoy, and William Shakespeare. I took these home, along with a psychology textbook and a few classic feminist texts.

I especially wanted to find research that bolstered my motivation to become less obsessed with my appearance. I didn't have to search very long to find the goods.

The first esoteric gem I stumbled upon was this: Vanity makes us dumber.

Psychologists have found that focusing on our appearance consumes valuable cognitive resources, which ultimately impairs our ability to perform complex mental tasks. In other words, our brains can do only so much at one time, and thinking self-consciously about our looks (called self-objectification) steals brainpower away from other tasks. Like willpower, obsessive thinking is a major brain drain.

I suppose this shouldn't have surprised me.

A few years earlier I had locked myself out of my office at UCLA, thanksverymuch to vanity. The timing couldn't have been worse: It was a Sunday evening, when nobody—not even custodial staff—could be found to help. I'd been working for hours, intently editing what I hoped would be the final draft of my master's thesis. The deadline loomed, and I was in a panic to finish on time. Hopped-up on thirty-two ounces of Coke Zero, my bathroom breaks were frequent and distracting, though not as distracting as the huge zit on my chin. On the bathroom break in question, I remember washing my hands at the sink and then leaning forward into the mirror, chin first, to scrutinize the growing bump. I sucked my lips into my mouth, stretching the skin on my chin into pallor as I grimaced with frustration. *Nope, not ready to be fussed with,* I thought, itching to pick.

I'd performed these facial acrobatics numerous times that evening, each time huffing at my reflection in disgust, "Ugh, why haven't I outgrown these damn breakouts?" Always, I'd returned to my office determined to stay focused on the more important task of figuring out how to make my research sound smarter than I felt. But that last time, as I walked down the hall back to my office, I stopped halfway in a panic: *Where were my keys?* My hand—which should have gripped a veritable wind chime of keys for my home, office, and car—held only a damp, crumpled paper towel. I rushed back to the bathroom, heart sinking. My keys weren't resting on the counter. They weren't hanging in the stall, either. *Shit. Shit. SHIT!*

With growing alarm, I considered my phone and laptop, both taunting me from behind my office door. I was screwed. I'd have to leave my car on campus and walk home. I lived a little over two miles away, and it was getting dark. Sadly, this scared me less than missing out on the hours of writing I'd planned to complete that night.

My beloved car would be towed before morning. My thesis would remain unwritten. My promising academic career would be ruined! All because of a stupid zit.

Almost an hour passed before I found a way back into my office. First I tried climbing over a fence to reach my window from the outside, but found it locked. I tried to break into the student computer lab so I could e-mail an SOS for help, but I'd forgotten my passcode (naturally, it was recorded on a scrap of paper left in my office). Finally, while attempting to jimmy the lock with a bobby pin, something occurred to me: Why had I left the bathroom with a crumpled paper towel in my hand? Why hadn't I just thrown it away? *Wait. Maybe I threw something* else *away instead!* Sure enough,

I found my keys at the bottom of the restroom trash bin. I'd absent-mindedly thrown them out and walked off to open my office door with a paper towel. Oops.

This story came crashing into my memory while reading about the relationship between mirrors and body image. Here's what I learned: My ditzy behavior that fateful Sunday night was the perfect illustration of recent research linking increased self-objectification to decreased cognitive performance. Thankfully, vanity doesn't dull our minds permanently, but it does leave us less able to perform at our best while we're at our most appearance-obsessed.

This has been demonstrated experimentally by exposing people to self-objectifying situations and then having them complete math tests, memory tasks, response time tasks, or something called the "color-naming Stroop task" (most likely named after an otherwise unmemorable Dr. Stroop). In my favorite study, seventy-two men and women were required to try on either a bathing suit or a V-neck sweater in a dressing room that contained a full-length mirror. They were then asked to take a math test while still wearing the bathing suit or sweater. I presume—though the article did not confirm—that the sweater condition also involved wearing bottoms of some sort. Anyway, women wearing the bathing suit had significantly lower math scores than those wearing the sweater, presumably because they were too busy thinking about their thighs to contemplate trigonometry. Interestingly, the men participating in the same experiment actually scored *better* while wearing swim trunks. Go figure. Maybe the researchers should have used Speedos.

But I believed their conclusions; they echoed my own experiences, as well as those of other women. Eve Ensler, Tony Award–winning playwright of *The Vagina Monologues*, activist for global women's rights, and a personal hero of mine, wrote this in her book *The Good Body*: "Maybe because I see how my stomach has come to occupy my attention, I see how other women's stomachs or butts or thighs or skin have come to occupy their attention, so that we have very little left for the war on Iraq—or much else, for that matter." She goes on: "What I can't believe is that someone like me, a radical feminist for nearly thirty years, could spend this much time thinking about my stomach. It has become my tormentor, my distractor; it's my most serious committed relationship. It has protruded through my clothes, my confidence, and my ability to work." I could relate to this.

One article published in *Sex Roles* even argues that the intense focus on Sarah Palin's physical appearance during the 2008 presidential election (remember that $150,000 makeover?) might explain her frequent gaffes while in the public eye, ultimately shaping election results. They write, "Several lines of laboratory research suggest that this focus [on Palin's appearance] may have been detrimental to the Republican ticket because . . . it may have increased Palin's focus on her appearance, which, consistent with research on self-objectification, likely impaired the competency of her actual performance." I'd always assumed that paying attention to my personal appearance would boost my confidence and therefore improve my performance. Apparently not.

Having absorbed this information connecting vanity to brainpower, I felt a bit smug. I'd stumbled on a jackpot: To the extent that avoiding mirrors would decrease the amount of time I spent thinking about my looks, I'd soon be adding Mensa meetings to my social calendar!

By the time I left the library, it was well after dark. I'd become so immersed in my tasks that I'd lost track of time, and had to hurry home in a cab, arms and book bag filled with new reading materials. I gave Michael a swift kiss on the cheek, devoured some leftover frozen pizza, and then promptly put myself to bed, reading until I fell asleep with the light on.

The next morning I awoke earlier than usual with the realization that I'd just spent my first full twenty-four hours without looking in the mirror, and I hadn't even realized it. I'd been so blissfully distracted by all of the interesting things that I was learning that I hadn't given much care to what I looked like. I took note of this as an important lesson: If I truly wanted thoughts about my looks to take up less space in my brain, I needed to find more interesting and worthy passions with which to fill it.

M Y FIRST FEW WEEKS WITHOUT MIRRORS WERE PRETTY great, though I can't claim that they passed entirely without vanity. In fact, quite the opposite was true at times, as I awoke almost every morning with makeup on my mind. I was tickled by the idea that I'd mastered a more minimalist routine, and on days when I was back in Los Angeles, I walked the halls at UCLA silently daring my colleagues and students to compliment me on my cosmetic skills. To my delight, this actually happened several times, when friends who knew I'd started the project noticed that I "didn't look so different from before!" *Geez, why didn't I cut back on makeup ages ago?* I wondered. Five products were much faster than eight, they added up to lower expense, and apparently I still looked adequately put-together.

Noticing the extent to which my newly minimalist makeup sped up my morning routine led me to a new line of scholarly inquiry. It turns out that cognitive performance was only one side of the story. Vanity also steals from us something much more basic: our time.

A recent article in the *Journal of Socio-Economics* analyzed the American Time Use Survey, finding that American women spend an average of 49.68 minutes each day (with men spending an average of 33.48 minutes) on basic grooming alone. By my calculations, this number—which doesn't include nonbasic (complex?) grooming, such as time spent getting haircuts or shopping for clothes and makeup—translates to 302 hours per year, or the equivalent of *seven and a half workweeks*. Zeroing in more closely to the issue of mirror-gazing, cosmetic giant QVC conducted a survey among a thousand of its female customers to see how much time they allot daily for their beauty routine and how many beauty products they use. After reviewing the survey results, QVC released a press release announcing their finding that women spend a cumulative of *five full days* in front of the mirror each year. Other reports suggest that the average woman looks at herself in the mirror between thirty-four and seventy-one separate times per day (with men looking twenty-seven to sixty-six times per day).

This sounded like an awful lot of mirror-gazing, and I was curious to know whether my blog readers would relate to these numbers. So I created a poll on my blog asking, "How frequently do you look in the mirror?" Here are the options I gave my readers to choose from:

a. Never! Your no-mirrors project is nothing compared with me!
b. Rarely. Like, if I'm getting a haircut or trying on clothes.

   c. Several times each day, like when I'm getting ready or when I'm washing up in the restroom.

   d. Constantly! I check myself out whenever I can . . . in mirrors, windows, silverware, other people's sunglasses . . .

When the poll closed, 91 percent of my 134 respondents claimed to look at themselves in the mirror either frequently or constantly, with almost 30 percent selecting constantly.

In *The Beauty Bias: The Injustice of Appearance in Life and Law* (which I assign to my seminar students), Stanford professor of law Deborah Rhode further points out that "the more time women spend on elaborate grooming, the more time many men spend waiting for the results. A survey of British husbands estimated that they would spend an average of twenty weeks over their lifetime waiting for their wives to 'get ready for an evening out.'" Considering the fact that women's elaborate grooming is often aimed at pleasing their partners, I couldn't help but wonder whether men would consider the time to be wasted or well-spent.

I read this figure aloud to Michael, who bemoaned his fate. We were relaxing in bed on a weeknight.

"Well, you're never average, Sweet Pea," he suggested, in what started out sounding like a compliment but quickly devolved: "So unless we drastically cut back on our evenings out, I'm destined to be an upper-limit outlier. I'll probably hit forty weeks of waiting by the time we retire!"

"Oh, yeah?" I countered. "I suppose that might be the case, except we're already a *lower*-limit outlier in our frequency of date nights. We're skewed."

"What's that? You want to *screw*?" he punted back with a twinkle in his eyes. I just rolled mine.

"Speaking of statistical probabilities, how many times in your life has a line like that actually worked?" I teased.

"Well . . . never on *average* girls!" he admitted. Indeed.

WHO COULD HAVE PREDICTED THAT BUYING A BIKE WOULD have turned out to be one of the most challenging mirror temptations I faced during my first few months without mirrors?

One of the hardest transitions from L.A. to San Francisco was adjusting to rarely driving my car. Even though I brought my trusty love-worn "Saabaru" with me, I was barely able to use it because the parking situation in the city was so horrific. It cost thirty dollars a day to park in any of our neighborhood's pay lots, and if I wanted to park near the About-Face offices on days that I did volunteer work, it was up to ten dollars an hour in most garages. Because of this, if I managed to snag a free spot on one of the streets near our apartment, it took a lot to persuade me to drive away from it. This was a contrast to L.A., where I enjoyed the flexibility of driving whenever and wherever I wanted, knowing that I could always find free or cheap parking at my destination and that a reserved garage space would be waiting for me at home when I returned.

During my first weeks in San Francisco, I walked everywhere, so long as the trip was under two miles. If the route seemed dicey, or if I was running late, I'd take a cab. This worked fairly well, but I soon realized that walking half a mile to the nearest grocery store and then huffing and sweating myself back again with arms full of groceries wasn't so fun. Indeed, on particularly hot days I just stayed home all day to avoid getting sweaty or overspending on cabs.

Obviously, I could have taken the bus, but I am notoriously motion sickness–sensitive, and the numerous hills and turns involved in a typical San Francisco bus trip seemed like an invitation to throw up in public. And so, facing the impossible choice between house-bound isolation, blowing my budget on cabs, or puking several times a week, I decided it was time to buy a bike.

And so it was that I found myself perusing the sale options at my local bike shop. Walking into the store, I was surprised to spy a *huge* full-length mirror at the front of the sales floor. I imagined that, perhaps, serious bikers wanted to check themselves out on their bikes before purchasing. This was something I could resist—a piece of cake!

I flagged down a dreadlocked and enthusiastic salesperson and explained the purpose of my visit. I warned him of both my con-strained budget and utter lack of coordination. He promptly walked me down a long row of bikes (organized with the most expensive bikes near the front of the store and the cheapo options in the back where budget customers were less likely to bring down the ambi-ance). Once we arrived at the very end of the adult bike section, he pointed out a few suggestions and then rolled the best contender to the front of the store so I could fill out a test ride form.

And then, eyeballing me with squinting contemplation, he said it:

"Yep, well, you're definitely over five-feet-two and you've got pretty long legs, so you ought to be a size small in the coed bikes."

I couldn't help myself. "Long legs?" I asked, eyebrows raised. I'd heard "*strong* legs" and even the occasional "*great* legs" in my day, but *never* "long legs." I hoped he might say it again.

Without pausing, he clarified, much to my chagrin: "Well, yeah, I meant, like, in comparison to your torso. You have a really short torso. I need to make sure you'll be able to reach the handlebars."

Oh. Short torso. Right. Of course.

And with that, I learned what felt like an infinitely important detail about my body while standing about seven feet away from a humongous mirror I wasn't allowed to look at. Needless to say, I wanted to check myself out. Was it true? Did I indeed have a short torso with comparatively long(ish) legs? How could I not have known this about myself! Argh!

Look-away-look-away-look-away-look-away-look-away!!

Somehow, I managed to get myself outside for a test ride without stealing a glance.

On my breezy trip around the block, I was struck by two thoughts. First: *Wow! This bike feels awesome!* As promised, I was able to reach the handlebars without feeling off-kilter. The brakes worked. The wind whistled. The sun shone. I was loving it!

Second, a nagging thought: *Wait—didn't somebody else tell me that I have short arms? When was that? Who was that?*

Just as I arrived back at the bike shop, I remembered: At my first fashion job after college, one of the fashion designers had measured me to see if I could substitute as a size medium fit model so I could try on prototype garments to check for construction and style details. It turned out that even though my "boobs were in the right place," (thank goodness for that!) my arms were, unfortunately, "one half inch too short."

Seriously. One half inch too short. In that instant, my promising life of (fit) modeling was over!

Remembering this as I walked back into the bike shop, I knew that it must be true: I had a short torso and short arms to match. I'd been assessed by two unbiased experts, which made it official. I didn't know whether to laugh at the ridiculousness of this knowledge or

cry in frustration. I still really wanted to look at my officially dispro-
portionate body in the mirror, but instead I just bought the darn
bike and got the heck out of there, tires squealing.

The good news is that I fell completely in love with my new bike
within days. The experience even helped me come to terms with
the weird news about my torso. As annoying as it felt to be given
unexpected news about my body by a person I didn't know, I took
comfort in the fact that the salesman communicated the news nonchalantly. It wasn't like he'd said, "You may want to sit down . . .
(long sigh) . . . I don't know how else to say this, but . . . you have a
short torso. Here, take a tissue." Nope. It was just matter-of-fact. No
biggie. It was a fact, not a judgment, just a piece of information that
needed to be taken into consideration when choosing the right bike
to fit my body. Buying a customizable product that fit my body instead of trying to fit my unique body into something overly stan-
dardized: What a refreshing idea!

LATER THAT WEEK, I FOUND MYSELF SITTING AT MY DESK,
attempting to grade my students' reading responses. I couldn't
focus. I'd read for a few minutes, scribble a note or two, and then
reflexively look over my right shoulder at what used to be a mirrored
closet door. Instead, I stared at the blank white bedsheet I'd used
to cover the mirror. I became aware, suddenly, that I must have developed a habit of looking in the mirror frequently while working
from home. *What the heck?* I thought as I caught myself looking
again. A few times I even got up, as though to go *find* the missing
mirror, and then sat back down, blinking to myself in disbelief.
These self-peering instincts had been subconscious, but my non-
peering reactions were conscious and impossible for me to ignore.

The reports of women looking at themselves in the mirror thirty-four to seventy-one times per day had sounded outrageous when I'd first read them, but suddenly seemed less so. I *ached* to see myself. It made me anxious. And, surprisingly, lonely.

I realized then that I missed seeing myself for reasons quite separate from vanity. I'd counted on my reflection for *companionship* during long stints of time spent alone, especially on days I worked from home.

I've always considered myself a closeted introvert. In spite of my seemingly extroverted enjoyment of speaking my mind during class, or of standing in front of 150 college students to lecture in my own classroom, I am completely drained by the end of most social situations. On days that I teach, I arrive back home barely able to mumble a plaintive hello to Michael, and usually end up ordering him to leave me alone or at least stop talking while I recover from my day in solitude. While at parties during college, I often wished nothing more than to be curled up alone in my dorm, reading a book or watching a movie. I always looked forward to days in which I was able to work from home or alone in my office at UCLA, which were typically filled with writing, editing, and grading. They were not, however, filled with much social interaction. Or so I'd thought.

Was it possible that my reflection had served as a sort-of friend during my time spent alone? And, for that matter, exactly what kind of a friend had she been? More important, given all the horribly cruel and bullying things I'd thought and said to myself over the years, what kind of a friend had *I* been to *her*? I knew the answer: a "frenemy" of the worst sort, expecting silent support and companionship on demand while saying mean things about her behind her back—and sometimes to her face! But in this strange moment of realization, I had to ask: Who was I without her?

Without my reflection around to wave hello to me during my work-from-home days, I began experiencing strange moments when I questioned my very existence. If I couldn't see myself, did I exist? But how did I *know*? You know that saying about the tree that falls in a forest with no one to hear its sound? Well, I was starting to suspect that the tree would probably feel less shitty about the situation if it could at least watch itself in a mirror during the fall.

My cats, Diesel and Dolce, helped me work through these first weeks of solitude. Unlike stereotypically aloof felines, my boys were plain needy for attention. There's nothing more effective at halting a philosophical meltdown than the plaintive yowling of hungry animals. Apparently not only did I exist, but I existed for the sole purpose of feeding my cats.

The fact that I began questioning my own existence in the absence of mirrors started to make more sense when I learned that psychologists actually use mirrors to test other animals for self-awareness. Although *most* animals react to their images as if confronted by another animal, chimpanzees and orangutans (but not gorillas) show evidence of self-recognition when placed in front of a mirror. Similarly, two-year-old humans begin to develop what's called mirror-guided self-recognition at around the same time that they begin to show other evidences of self-awareness, such as using personal pronouns or smiling after mastering a challenging task. For both chimps and young children, the mirror-guided self-recognition test involves secretly putting a dot of red paint (for chimps) or a huge sticker (for kids) on the forehead of the primate in question. If the chimp/child notices this change to her appearance in the mirror and reacts by, say, touching the paint spot or reaching for the sticker—on her head and not on the mirror—she has passed the test. (Learning this, I couldn't help wondering whether the kids who passed this test got to keep their stickers. That would have made *me* smile after mastering the task!)

In this first month without mirrors, despite having some times when I felt more worried about my looks than ever before, I also experienced several blissful spells of not thinking much about my looks at all. These episodes—if I can call them that—are a bit hard for me to describe, mainly because I didn't realize I was experiencing them until they were over. (How does one describe the feeling of unawareness?) I didn't know what to call them, but I knew that during them I felt peaceful and fully engaged in whatever activity I was doing. It felt like progress and made me deliriously proud of myself whenever it happened. The moments in which I realized with pleasure that I'd gone hours or days without wondering what I looked like were infrequent, but promising.

No description for how this felt resonated quite so clearly as a passage I stumbled upon while rereading Jane Austen's *Persuasion*, which had been recommended to me by a friend who said it was filled with references to vanity.

In the passage, Admiral Croft, a sensible and kind man, has rented the opulent estate of Sir Walter Elliot, the exceedingly vain and spendthrift father of the book's reserved and practical protagonist, Anne. Anne visits Admiral Croft and his wife, and it pains her to see someone else occupying her home. Admiral Croft, sensitive to her feelings, mentions that they had changed very little about the home, explaining, "I have done very little besides sending away some of the large looking-glasses from my dressing-room, which was your father's. A very good man, and very much the gentleman I am sure—but I should think, Miss Elliot" (looking with serious reflection) "I should think he must be rather a dressy man for his time of life. —Such a number of looking-glasses! oh Lord! there was no getting away from oneself."

I was tickled by Admiral Croft's decision to rid his bedroom of mirrors (save for his "little shaving glass"), but it was his stated desire for "getting away from oneself" that really gave me pause. The idea of "getting away from oneself" resonated deeply, perfectly encapsulating what I'd found so rewarding about my episodes of calm engagement in my work and leisure activities. It was both poetic and ironic: In these moments of getting away from myself, I'd begun feeling like myself again.

I'd love to say that I learned how to feel this way all of the time, but that wasn't the case. Rather, in between episodes of getting away from myself, I continued feeling a bit lost without the self I'd previously been able to see in the mirror.

At times I even began experiencing some mild paranoia about my weight and the state of my skin. What had started out as a secret pride in my mirror-free makeup application skills quickly dissolved into illusions of rapid weight gain and acne. On a logical level I knew that my appearance couldn't have changed dramatically in such a short time. Yet I felt lost without the constant reassurance of viewing my reflection.

Having suffered from an eating disorder in the past, the weight-gain paranoia was a bit alarming. I knew I was being unrealistic, but a small part of me (the anorexic part) whispered, "Maybe you should go on a diet, just in case!" I resisted. But then one night I dreamt that I'd gained hundreds of pounds without realizing it. For all the body acceptance I'd accomplished and preached to others during my waking moments, some of these fears were still deeply ingrained. In my dream, I'd been walking up to my office building at UCLA with a friend when I caught a glimpse of myself in the glass doorway. I was as large and voluminous as Violet Beauregarde's blueberry-ballooned body had been in Willy Wonka's infamous chocolate-factory tale. I turned to my friend and, in a panic, plaintively begged for an explanation. "Why didn't anyone tell me?!" I wailed in terror and confusion. My friend only shrugged in response.

I woke up in a cold sweat and scheduled an appointment with Gia, my therapist, for the next time I'd be back in L.A.

"Is this dangerous?" I asked her.

"What do you think?" she countered.

"I think trying on wedding dresses was dangerous! Being a *bride* is dangerous!" I exclaimed. "But giving up mirrors is feeling kind of scary, too. What if the nightmare comes true? If I gained a ton of weight, it would freak me out so much that I might do something extreme."

"More extreme than giving up mirrors?" she asked, eyebrow arched. (Excellent point. I love a therapist who's not afraid to joke around a bit.)

"Ummmm . . . okay, well up until this week I've thought this was a good idea!" I explained.

She agreed, and then asked me if I'd actually gained any weight.

"Two pounds, but that could just be a normal fluctuation. Or because I used the scale at the gym."

"Definitely. That's normal. Are you weighing yourself regularly? That would probably keep your imagination from running too wild."

"My scale at home died an early death a few months ago. I didn't replace it because I thought I didn't need it anymore. Am I acting anorexic if I buy a new one, like, *immediately*?" I asked.

"No, that's normal, too. And you're a bride-to-be. Brides without any history of eating disorders go through this stuff, so don't be too hard on yourself. Go get yourself a new scale and see if that helps. Call me any time if you feel panicked, but I think you're doing fine. I think this project is going to be amazing."

I bought a new scale that very evening, and as promised, it helped calm my fears tremendously. My body wasn't ballooning out of control, just my imagination. I returned to my Top Ten Ways to Be Kjerstin list and underlined the third item: Your body is perfect, but your mind could use improvement.

DECIDED THAT CONSTANTLY ASKING PEOPLE "DO I LOOK OKAY?" ought to be informally against the rules (unless, of course, I was facing a particularly important occasion in which poppy-seed-teeth would actually be life-changing). However, one afternoon I found myself staring at Michael across our kitchen table, wondering with frustration why he couldn't read my mind to tell me not just *how* I looked (good, bad, so-so, etc.), but exactly *what* I looked like.

What kind of a soul mate are you? I silently implored. *How can you not know that I need to know this?*

He stared back at me and deadpanned, "What?"

"Nothing," I responded, playing it cool. He didn't take the bait.

Was my hair bumpy? Fluffy? Sleek? Was my makeup invisible-yet-ethereal? And how about that belly-button doughnut? I was at a loss. *Yeah, I used to not be so vain,* I thought, *but now I know better.*

To this day I'm convinced that Michael knew exactly what I wanted him to tell me, but also knew better than to feed into my obsessions. Or maybe he just liked to see me squirm.

The following day, my curiosity escalated to the point at which a blurry image of myself (reflected in my apartment building's brushed steel elevator door) became pathetically intriguing. Yes, random reflections were against my rules, but I couldn't resist. I stared at this blurry reflection for at least two straight minutes while waiting for the elevator. I felt a bit guilty, but I imagine that the blurred image I saw of myself was about as satisfying as Nicorette feels to most trying-to-quit smokers. Here's what I learned: My hair was still blond, my six-year-old Banana Republic blazer still fit, and I still existed. Good news on all counts, right?

Later that day I managed to lock myself out of the apartment.

Clearly, despite the time I'd spent getting away from myself, I was not yet benefiting from expanding cognitive resources.

I implored myself to be patient. After all, this was still an adjustment period (I hoped!). But I worried that I might be destined to spend more time wondering what I looked like than I had spent checking myself out in the mirror before the project started!

I couldn't know the answer yet, but in the meantime I celebrated smaller victories: getting out of the house in half the time I'd taken before; saving money; finding myself lost in work or play for large chunks of time without feeling the urge to look at—or for—myself in the mirror; getting in touch with my *un*self-conscious self. In these ways, life without mirrors was slowly becoming freeing.

In his book *On Self and Social Organization*, one of sociology's most famous theorists, Charles Horton Cooley, develops the aptly phrased (for my purposes) theory of the looking-glass self. Cooley's theory proposes that our sense of self is forged through our imagination of the way we appear in the eyes of others. In other words, we depend on interactions with others to provide feedback, telling us both who we are and how we should feel about ourselves.

Using mirrors as both metaphor and tools to explain how we see ourselves through other people, Cooley wrote the following in his book *Human Nature and the Social Order*:

> A social self of this sort might be called the reflected or looking glass self:
>
> "Each to each a looking-glass
>
> Reflects the other that doth pass."
>
> As we see our face, figure, and dress in the glass, and are interested in them because they are ours, and pleased or otherwise with them according as they do or do not answer to what we should like them to be; so in imagination we perceive in another's mind some thought of our appearance, manners, aims, deeds, character, friends, and so on . . .

Thus, even when we look into a mirror, our understanding of what we see is fundamentally social because it is mediated by reactions to us that we have seen in people we spend time with. As Cooley aptly puts it elsewhere in his book, "The thing that moves us to pride or shame is not the mere mechanical reflection of ourselves, but . . . the imagined effect of this reflection upon another's mind."

This theory speaks volumes to how mirrors themselves contribute to our self-images. On the one hand, in the purist form of Cooley's theory, mirrors are wholly unnecessary for understanding ourselves, so long as we have other people around. If the people we spend time with see us (and treat us) with love, affection, and approval, we will love, have affection for, and approve of ourselves. If the people we spend time with see us (and treat us) with disdain, disrespect, and condescension . . . well, you get the picture.

On the other hand, mirrors do allow us to actually see (at least in reverse reflection) what others are viewing when they look upon us. Thus, they add another step of self-awareness—and tool for self-adjustment—in this process of self-understanding.

Nicole Sault, editor of the book *Many Mirrors: Body Image and Social Relations*, extends the metaphor of what she calls the human mirror to ponder, "What if we had no mirrors, photographs, or videos to show us how we look? How would we see ourselves?" (Great question, Nicole! Somebody should try to find out!) She continues, saying, "Despite the fact that we have material objects to show us reflections of our selves, we are also social mirrors to each other, and we rely on the reactions of others to learn how we look and who we are."

We rely on the reactions of others to learn how we look and who we are.

Reading this made me pause. The theory made complete sense, and yet it didn't *feel* true. How much had I ever trusted the reactions of others for my sense of self? How many kind words spoken by loved ones had I dismissed in favor of my own, much harsher, critiques? The answer, I knew, was that I tended to stubbornly hang on to my own ideas about who I was, who I ought to be, and how I ought to improve myself. My reflection had been my frenemy, but now that she was gone, perhaps it was time for me to start paying more attention to what my friends and family had been telling me all along.

FOUR

June

HOW I (RE)DISCOVERED TRUST AND LEARNED TO STOP SECOND-GUESSING COMPLIMENTS

*Both within the family and without, our sisters hold
up our mirrors: our images of who we are and
of who we can dare to be.*

ELIZABETH FISHEL

F I'D BEEN ASKED ON THE DAY I STARTED MY NO-MIRRORS PROJ-
ect whether or not I generally trusted my friends, my family, my
fiancé, or even the average person one might run into on the street,
I would have answered with a resounding "Yes!" I thought of myself
as being, perhaps, even *more* trustful than the average Jane.

Growing up, my mother—a developmental psychologist who
specialized in achievement orientation in early adolescence—used to
always tell my siblings and me, "Positive expectations, positive results!" to describe her parenting philosophy. This personal mantra
was my mother's way of saying if you trust people to be good and do
their best, they'll be more likely to do so.

I've always looked up to my mom, so I've carried her wisdom with me, priding myself in looking for the best in people and expecting the best as well. I take pains to treat my students like smart, capable and morally sound adults, and am rarely disappointed in them; I ask perfect strangers to watch my belongings while I run to the restroom in coffee shops, and have never lost a latte, much less a laptop; I consistently vote in favor of social policies that provide resources and safety nets for the poor, and have never felt worried or angry about the possibility that underprivileged people might be taking advantage of the system (another cherished mantra from my mom: "Always remember, people do the best they can with what they have!"). In other words, I'm a trusting kind of gal. I really, actually, genuinely, seriously trust people.

And yet, the greatest challenge I faced during my year without mirrors was learning how to let go of control, to allow myself to trust.

It all started with something fairly simple: a shopping trip.

O N THE FIRST DAY OF JUNE, I CAUGHT MYSELF STARING AT the curtain covering my bathroom mirror. Unlike other days, when I usually tried to envision myself looking back at me from behind the curtain, this time I was actually staring at the curtain itself. It wasn't really even a curtain, just a navy blue bedsheet that Michael had (lovingly) MacGyvered into a quasi-curtain by draping it from the light fixture above our bathroom sink. Because we were subletting, I'd felt too nervous to put up proper curtains, which would have required a curtain rod and several forbidden holes in the wall. Our solution was very practical, but it was also very ugly. This wouldn't do. Michael's mom, Sherry, was visiting in less than a week, and I didn't want our apartment to look shabby.

Such began my very first mirror-free shopping adventure.

I headed out for what I *thought* would be a quick trip to San Francisco's downtown Ross store—you know, Ross of the "Dress for Less" variety. (The *"Dress* for Less" lingo should have been my first clue that the trip was unlikely to end with curtains alone.)

After walking into Ross, I attempted a beeline to the home goods section of the store, which was in the back corner of its third floor. Of course, along the way, I had to peruse—er, I mean traverse—three separate floors of clothes. (Even bees have to stop and smell the roses sometimes, right?) Even with my eyes directed downward to avoid all of the mirrors on the shop walls, a poster advertising "New Arrivals!" caught my attention. With eagle-eyed precision, I spied one of my personal retail adventure homing beacons: hangtags from one of my favorite clothing brands dangling off a scintillating display of discounted tops.

Upon sight of the hangtags, I made a snap decision and headed over to the "New Arrivals!" rack to start digging. With clothing sizes so unstandardized, I had to work my way through everything ranging from XS to XL, all the while scoping styles, speculating on size, feeling fabrics, surveying silhouettes, and computing costs. It had been more than two months since I'd stepped foot in a clothing store, and I'd really missed it. Besides, I wanted to make sure I had some cute clothes to wear for when Michael's mom was in town. Sherry always looked so chic, and I didn't want her to think of me as her dowdy future daughter-in-law! I emerged on the other side of the clothing rack with about a dozen potentials in hand and realized that, other than my not looking into any mirrors, things hadn't been going much differently from how my usual shopping went—so far, anyway. But what would I do next?

I held my potential purchases in my tiring arms, pondering whether or not I should venture forth to the land of mirrors (i.e., the fitting rooms). Or perhaps I ought to just buy everything (tempting) and try things on at home where I could get feedback from Michael or my sister? I'd never actually done that before, and the idea of trusting anyone else to decide what looked good on me was surprisingly nerve-racking. I wondered who I trusted more, my fiancé, my sister, or a random sales associate. Before I could worry too much about this question and what it said about me, basic math answered the quandary: I couldn't afford to charge $400 on my debit card. I would have to filter out at least half of my options, if not more. I wasn't sure exactly how I would do this, but off to the fitting rooms I went!

Along the way, I came up with what I hoped would be a simple, three-part dressing room strategy. First, I would try to cover the mirror in my fitting room, but if this wasn't possible, I would simply face away from it. (The trick, of course, would be to avoid seeing myself while deciding whether or not I could cover the mirror with the beach towel I'd just swiped from the home goods section.) Second, I would immediately disqualify anything that felt even remotely uncomfortable on my body. Finally, if too many garments remained after step two, I would ask for second opinions from the dressing room staff or from other shoppers. Mild panic ensued on this last point, but it seemed like it might be my only option.

I proceeded. After getting a number card from an apathetic teenaged sales associate, I ducked into the nearest fitting room and hung everything at the back of the room to avoid having to face the mirror until I was ready. My eyes traveled along the edges of the mirror, and when I saw that it was hung flush with the wall, it became clear that hanging a towel on it would be difficult. So I turned back around, peeled off my T-shirt, and started trying things on.

Three tops were too tight, and I managed to eliminate two more using my well-honed instincts for appropriate style-versus-price ratio. Twenty-five dollars for a basic T-shirt? Not unless it was cashmere! Only one top—a white tank displaying the delectable phrase YOU ARE BEA-UTI-FUL—was a definite yes, but I had six other shirts remaining in the undecided category. I poked my head out of the dressing room curtain to assess my options for a second opinion. No other shoppers were in sight. I felt relieved and disappointed at the same time.

Wearing one of the maybes—a bright yellow T-shirt cut on an interesting A-line that I hoped was skimming over my Coca-Cola belly and hips—I shuffled out of my dressing room in bare feet to see if I could drag an opinion out of Ms. Dispassionate at the front. I was skeptical, unsure whether this would even be worth my time. *What if she tells me I look great, but has really bad taste? How old is she, anyway? Can I trust fashion advice from a teenager? Is she wearing a cute outfit?* I tried to remember.

When I turned the corner, I saw that the young woman's fashion sense was probably a tad flashier than my own (neon yellow bra straps peeked out from beneath her blue blouse—could this be the Ross employee dress code?). However, her clothes fit well and flattered her body. I knew that I had little to lose by asking, but I was nervous. I couldn't remember *ever* asking a stranger for advice on my clothes. *Well, I don't trust just anyone's opinion!* I thought to myself as justification. But was that a good thing or a bad thing?

What's the worst thing that could happen? I asked myself. I then cringed inwardly when a few answers appeared: *Well, she could persuade me to buy something that actually looks awful on me. How embarrassing would that be!? Or, even worse, what if she says something mean that would cause my self-esteem and body image to spiral out of control, causing me to panic and look at myself in the mirror in attempts to regain my sanity, only to discover that whatever mean thing she said was true? ...*

My inner dialogue was getting a little out of hand. What was wrong with me? I reminded myself that I'd once worked in clothing stores and had always tried to give customers advice that fit their own tastes and sensibilities, even if they differed from mine. *Just do it!*

After catching the young woman's attention, distracting her from a listless stare into space, I asked, "Umm, does this top look okay?"

She blinked, looked at me for a split second, and said, "Sure." She turned back to her listless stare, and I grumpily turned back to my fitting room.

Sure? That's it? I thought. Sighing, I assessed the potential financial damage and decided to just buy the remaining seven shirts and bring them home. I'd figure out my next steps from there.

I felt mostly pleased by my choices, but not being able to see myself wearing them was terribly unsatisfying. The anticipation that had built up during my hunt through the sales racks remained unfulfilled, like a glaring "TO BE CONTINUED ..." announcement at the end of a suspenseful TV show. Realizing that I wouldn't be able to see myself in the mirror for another nine months was tantamount to receiving a second message announcing that the TV show in question was actually being canceled.

I thought to myself, *Shit. Is this how I'm going to feel on my wedding day?* The prospect was depressing. I needed to get myself the heck out of Ross. I'd deal with my wedding anxieties another time. To make matters worse, I'd spent almost $250, with only $15 going toward the new curtains for my mirror at home. I couldn't keep everything, so I would need to find some way to decide which shirts would stay and which to return.

Asking Michael for help felt particularly unwise—not only is the love of my life severely color-blind, but he is also somewhat fashion-challenged. (One of the first things I did upon becoming Michael's "official" girlfriend was to break the news to him that he'd been wearing the wrong size pants: a size too big in the waist and a size too short in the inseam. I'd been floored to learn that the current poor fit was actually the slightly improved result of a *prior* "floodwater pants" intervention on the part of his friends!) I'd asked Michael for clothing advice in the past, and his feedback was predictable: He'd tell me that everything looked equally fantastic, and then none-too-subtly suggest that I eliminate contenders based on price alone, keeping only the least expensive item or two. This approach worked fairly well from a purely economical standpoint, or if I wanted to hear that I looked cute even if I was wearing a potato sack, but it seemed like a poor strategy for stylish and expressive mirror-free dressing.

I went through a mental checklist of all of my female friends, recalling times when we'd shopped together. Sally, the fashion designer I'd worked with at my first job out of college, was a shoo-in for clothing advice, but she didn't live in the area so couldn't be of much help. Laila, another close friend from my days of corporate fashion, posed the exact same problem. I briefly considered e-mailing photos of my outfits for their consideration, but doubted my ability to do so without seeing myself. Thinking of all my other girlfriends, I realized that I'd rarely asked for help choosing clothes, and never without having first formed an opinion on my own. A stereotypical Virgo, I liked being in control. I was fiercely independent, and had been since childhood. It's not that I didn't like having friends or wasn't a good friend in my relationships. But I liked relying on myself. It felt safest that way.

I'd even developed a habit of shopping for clothes alone. I enjoyed the private project of quietly sifting through rows of hanging clothes and shoe shelves, of feeling the texture of different fabrics between my fingers, of finding fun and funky bargains, of trying on my finds and imagining myself wearing them at various social functions. Something about this solitary process was calming to me, almost meditative as it took my thoughts away from my other stresses and instead toward the visual and tactile experience of rooting through racks of clothes or stacks of shoes. Doing this with companions was disruptive to my meditative state, perhaps due to all of the expected catching up and inevitable back-and-forth asking of "What do you think of this?" types of questions. Of course, I enjoyed showing off my selections once I brought them home, but the act of shopping itself had slowly become a mostly solitary sport.

This surprised me. I had many fond memories of bargain shopping with Hanna, my mom, and my mom's sister, Sarah (the Aunt Sarah from South Dakota who'd approved of my first wedding dress via text). But the four of us hadn't been together in the same city for months, and my memories of these shopping trips conjured images of humorous chatter, flurried chaos, and frequent overspending. Inevitably, the visiting party would have to buy a new suitcase with which to bring everything home! I loved those times, but it was clear that shopping with my female relatives was a completely different sort of project from what I enjoyed when by myself.

This would have to change if I planned to survive my year

without mirrors while still recognizing myself at heart (if not by reflection!). Having just experienced the thrill of the hunt, I couldn't
fathom a year without mirrors *and* without shopping!

THIS QUESTION OF MY TRUSTING-NESS NAGGED AT ME. I
cringed to think of myself as just one more example of a woman
who didn't trust other women, but it seemed like it might be true. I
knew I wasn't alone in this, but it gave me little comfort. Our culture
is full of stories and myths warning women to not trust one another,
telling us that we are in competition with one another, both for men
and for prestige, and that we can count only on ourselves. We see
this in the fairy tales told to us in our youths, in which we learn
from Snow White, Sleeping Beauty, Cinderella, and the Little Mer-
maid that only the most beautiful girl will ever marry the prince,
and that older or plainer women (usually aging queens, sorcer-
esses, and witches) are threatened by younger and prettier women's
youth and beauty. As author Peggy Orenstein argues in her book
*Cinderella Ate My Daughter: Dispatches from the Front Lines of the
New Girlie-Girl Culture*, the Disney Princesses do little to encourage
girls to seek support from female friends: "There is only one princess
in the Disney tales, one girl who gets to be exalted. Princesses may
confide in a sympathetic mouse or teacup, but . . . they do not have
girlfriends. God forbid Snow White should give Sleeping Beauty a
little support."

I was well aware of these cultural tropes, but I'd thought myself
above them. I valued collectivity and cooperation over competition.
I'd believed myself to be immune to such unnecessary nastiness, by
refusing to make catty remarks about other women (at least out

loud!) and by actively embracing and celebrating the variety of talents and gifts that my female friends, colleagues, and relatives brought to the world. I was a feminist. I was enlightened. I wasn't a bully. All good, right? But apparently, when forced to do so, I didn't trust other women to live up to their end of the bargain.

Psychological research suggests that I am not alone in my tendency toward mistrust. On average, people have been shown to be quite cynical about the trustworthiness of others. But is this cynicism justified? Studies suggest not. Rather, most of us have what researchers describe as naive cynicism, that is, cynicism that is misguided.

In one experiment where psychologists had people play financial games in lab settings, the subjects honored the trust placed *in them* between 80 and 90 percent of the time, but estimated that others would honor *their* trust only about 50 percent of the time. Other research has shown that, when asked to think about strangers, people tend to believe that other people are more selfishly motivated than they really are, and less helpful than they really are. In a series of studies out of Columbia University, researchers tested people's estimation of how likely others were to help them out. The researchers had participants ask others to fill in questionnaires, to borrow cell phones, and to escort them to the gym. Across these conditions, participants underestimated how likely others were to help them by as much as 100 percent. Similarly, in another study, researchers asked participants to predict what would happen if they gave money to a stranger who then had the option to either split the cash with them or keep it. The givers thought the receivers would share the money around 45 percent of the time, but the actual number was nearly 80 percent of the time. This cynicism toward strangers has been shown to develop as early as seven years of age, and these patterns are not limited to our views of strangers; we are also overly cynical about our loved ones and teammates, assuming that they will behave more selfishly than they actually do.

Thus, there exists a mysterious trust gap between how people behave themselves and how they think others behave. One explanation for the trust gap is found in our egocentric biases: We find it difficult to understand what others are thinking and feeling because we are stuck inside of our own heads. Another explanation rests in the idea that our cynicism results from our experiences or, rather, from our *lack* of experiences. As explained in a Psych Central article on the trust gap, "The first time you trust a stranger and are betrayed, it makes sense to avoid trusting other strangers in the future. The problem is that when we don't ever trust strangers, we never find out how trustworthy people in general really are. As a result, our estimation of them is governed by fear. . . . It is lack of experience that leads to people's cynicism, specifically not enough positive experiences of trusting strangers."

By this logic, refusing to trust people and not giving people the chance to earn my trust had likely created a self-fulfilling prophecy. The only way to break the pattern would be to force myself to put trust in other people, even if it scared me. As promised by Psych Central, "If you try trusting others you'll find they frequently repay that trust, leading you to be more trusting." Or, as I'd written in my Top Ten Ways to Be Kjerstin list, I needed to challenge my assumptions.

I knew I'd never survive the next nine months without mirrors if I didn't take a leap of faith; it was time to practice trust.

As a baby step, I called Hanna and mentioned that I wanted to hang out soon. I was still horribly nervous about letting her decide which shirts to keep and which to return. Hanna and I have pretty different styles, and we weren't always good at picking out clothes for each other (I was always pushing her to ditch the yoga pants and sneakers to be more trendy, and she was always pushing me to be less brand-obsessed). Still, I knew in my heart that Hanna loved me and wanted only the best for me. Our tastes might be different, but she wasn't cruel or catty. If I couldn't learn to trust my own sister for advice, well, that probably said more about me than her.

WHEN MICHAEL GOT HOME LATER THAT EVENING, I HAD much to talk to him about. Shopping for clothes that morning had done more than just alert me to my trust issues; it had also reminded me of how much I loved and enjoyed clothes, fashion, and beauty stuff in general.

"Look, I don't want to be obsessive and insecure about my looks, or spend too much time and money and energy on my appearance, but I miss the creativity that comes along with fashion and beauty!" I exclaimed. "Can I take a step back from vanity without losing creativity and pleasure?"

"Do you think you could give up mirrors *and* fashion for the year?" Michael asked. I'd actually successfully sworn off shopping for a year a few years back, when our long-distance relationship had strained my budget to the max.

I thought for a minute, and said, "Yes, I think I could. But I don't want to. I'm trying to learn more about myself this year, and I learned something important today. I love the creativity and sensual experiences of fashion and I've missed experimenting with different looks. This project isn't supposed to be about denying myself pleasure, but about rejecting insecurities and obsessions." My cultural sociologist side took a turn at the lectern, saying, "Even if the fashion and cosmetic industries do make money by preying on women's insecurities, clothes and makeup aren't inherently evil themselves. Dress and body modification are found in every culture on the planet; all humans use these things for self-expression!"

"Whoa there, tiger!" Michael interrupted. "Where's the lecture hall? Look, I'm not asking you to defend your passions. I just want to make sure you don't spend all of our money or end up feeling miserable because your priorities are all out of whack. What, exactly, are you hoping to do?"

I was ready with an answer: I wanted to follow TheKnot.com's "Bridal Beauty: Countdown to Gorgeous" list for brides, but without looking in the mirror.

FYI, TheKnot.com is the biggest wedding-planning website in existence, and they published a countdown list as a "guide to looking fabulous by your big day." It details thirty-seven beautifying tasks that a bride should complete in the six months leading up to her wedding day.

At face value, the BBCTG list didn't seem easily compatible with the spirit of my no-mirrors project. Indeed, the very last of the thirty-seven tasks—to be completed moments before walking down the aisle—commanded the unthinkable: "Take a few moments to reflect on the meaning of the day before giving yourself one last once-over in the mirror." But my excitement wasn't just because the list involved a lot of girlie beauty stuff; it also had all of the makings of a great investigative project. How ridiculous could a bridal to-do list get? How expensive? How time-consuming? How presumptuous? How elitist? How gendered? How heteronormative?

The list was extensive and ambitious, almost to the point of hilarity. The numbered tasks ranged from simple (#20: "Drink lots of water") to much more involved (#7: "If you don't plan on using your regular hairdresser, make consultation appointments with potential candidates. Bring along pictures of hairstyles you like, even a picture of your veil and headpiece. If you want to wear your hair in an updo, discuss with the hairdresser how long it will take to grow out your hair so it's the right length for your desired look"). To be honest, almost half of the stuff on the list seemed silly to me, but that was part of the allure; as much as I looked forward to indulging in a manicure (#33) or reclining in "a long, relaxing bath" (#34), I also couldn't wait to snarkily report back to my bloggers on the delights of exfoliation (as TheKnot.com explained in #19, "Soft and silky elbows, hands, and feet are marriage musts!" Oh, please).

The BBCTG list had immediately reminded me of my favorite passage in Rebecca Mead's book *One Perfect Day: The Selling of the American Wedding*:

> What the bridal magazines promote . . . is the idea that a bride deserves to be the center of attention for the entire period of her engagement. . . . She deserves to be the center of her own attention, at least. . . . It is her privilege, her right—indeed, her obligation— to become preoccupied with herself, her appearance, her tastes, and her ability to showcase them to their best advantage. Being a bride, according to the bridal media's prescription, amounts to a quest for self-perfection, or perfection of the outward self at least.

These things seemed true of all the bridal magazines I'd been reading. How likely was it that anyone could actually follow all of their advice? But would tackling this vanity-based-project-within-a-vanity-rejecting-project make me a hypocrite?

I was a feminist bride-to-be equipped with the insider knowledge that TheKnot.com's list—and all others like it—encouraged vanity and self-absorption (and, of course, the spending of mucho money). These were all things I wanted desperately to decrease in my life. Yet I was still a bride-to-be. I was still a romantic. I was still the little girl who looked at my parents' wedding photos and wondered, hopefully, if I would look as beautiful on my wedding day as my mother did on hers. How could I merge these seemingly conflicting desires? How could I stay true to my values without becoming an ascetic martyr for my no-mirrors cause?

I said all of these things to Michael, who listened patiently. When I'd finally finished talking, he asked me one question: "Would this be fun for you?"

"Yes," I answered. I saw this list of bizarre beauty routines as the perfect way to more fully test my commitment to the project while also delving into the sociologically fascinating world of bride-dom. Even more important, I saw this challenge as a way to learn more about myself and who I wanted to be. I already suspected that I would find my most authentic self somewhere *between* all-out indulgent vanity and stringent self-denial. But I didn't know exactly where, between these two extremes, I would end up. What balance of behaviors would make me feel happiest, and the most like myself, while still honoring my values? I needed to keep swinging the pendulum back and forth for a little while, taking note of when things felt right and when things felt wrong.

"Then do it," he said. "Have some fun. Pay attention if something doesn't feel right to you, but don't overthink it."

He was right, and I was relieved by his support. I needed to follow my gut, with thoughtful determination, un-reckless abandon, creativity, and humor. Despite my decision to shun mirrors—and I was still fully committed to this decision, task #37 be damned!—I had no desire for an ascetic life.

I also hoped that this challenge-within-a-challenge would give me a better understanding of how to achieve balance and authenticity. Did having these things mean finding that one consistent "way to be"? Or would it involve a lifetime of shifting back and forth between different—but equally authentic—versions of myself (and if so, how many versions might there be?)? It was time to find out.

T HE FOLLOWING DAY, AFTER A MORNING OF GRADING, I TOOK a few minutes to skim over the full BBCTG list. It organized the beautifying tasks into a time line highlighting when they should be accomplished: "5–6 Months Before," "3–4 Months Before," "1–2 Months Before," "2 Weeks Before," "1 Week Before," "1 Day Before," and "On Your Wedding Day." According to TheKnot.com, I was already two months behind! To give myself a fighting chance to finish, I decided to try tackling *all* of the items on the "5–6 Months Before" list in one week, six tasks in all. These first six tasks targeted the following, in order: (1) stress relief, (2) wedding hair planning, (3) skin care, (4) nutrition, (5) exercise, and (6) weight loss. If I could manage that, I'd be caught up for the remaining items on the list.

As I read through this list, I felt confident that I'd manage to complete all within the week, but felt a pang of anxiety as I read over items 4 and 6, which focused on nutrition and weight loss, respectively. Nutrition and diet advice didn't always go over so well in post-anorexia Kjerstin-land. It was complicated, so I decided to deal with those things last, once I figured out how. The second task on the list would also be tricky; I had no idea what I wanted to do with my hair for the wedding, and I also didn't yet have a stylist in my new hometown of San Francisco with whom to "start experimenting."

This left items 1, 3, and 5 as the easiest places to begin. Accomplishing task 3 would be a cinch because I was already pretty fastidious when it came to skin care. This had been the case since around 1992, when my face hit puberty. Seemingly overnight, I'd gone from a peaches-and-cream complexion to something more closely resembling DiGiorno. Then it turned out that my mildly spotty adolescent years were only a warm-up for an inexplicable case of full-blown adult acne in my early twenties. Even though I now have "good" skin (thanks to two rounds of Accutane), to this day I always wash my face as the final step before exiting the shower—even if this means washing it twice—lest my hair conditioner pollute my pores.

Abandoning mirrors had thrown me off my game. Without being able to see my face in the mirror, the only way I could assess the state of my skin was through touch, and this presented a problem: I knew that touching my face too often could actually *cause* breakouts. If I wasn't careful, I'd create a self-fulfilling prophecy.

In the midst of all this worrying, I started to wonder: Why do we care so much about having "perfect" skin in the first place? These days we know that acne isn't caused by supposedly immoral behaviors, like eating a lot of chocolate or masturbating (or eating chocolate while masturbating, for that matter!). Having acne isn't a sign that you're a bad person, or even that you're dirty (indeed, no amount of cleansing will ever cure acne, and washing too frequently can just aggravate things). So why all the hype about zits?

Thanks to grad school, I was used to critically analyzing our culture, questioning beliefs, habits, and customs that we often take for granted as natural. We sociologists call this "making the familiar strange." And here's what I learned about zits: Our culture's modern obsession with blemish-free skin emerged as a result of increased access to . . . (drumroll, please!) . . . MIRRORS! Yes, *mirrors*. How perfect is that?

In her book *The Body Project: An Intimate History of American Girls*, Joan Jacobs Brumberg writes:

> When the mirror became a staple of the American middle-class home at the end of the nineteenth century, attention to adolescent acne escalated, as did sales of products for the face. Until then, pimples were primarily a tactile experience, at least for the girl who had them. But all that changed in the late 1880s with the widespread adoption in middle-class homes of a bathroom sink with running water and a mirror hung above it. . . . Mirrors made pimples accessible, but they also stimulated greater concern about the face.

There you have it: MIRRORS CAUSE ACNE! Okay, okay, maybe not directly. But they've certainly contributed to our culture's obsession with clear skin. Indeed, Brumberg goes on to mention that, by the 1890s, "anxiety about blemishes on the face" actually led to the popularity of hairstyles with bangs among adolescent girls. (And I'd always thought *I* was the sneaky genius who figured that one out!)

Knowing all this, I'd love to say that life without mirrors drastically decreased my concern with having clear skin, but instead, it was probably more of the opposite: Having dependably clear skin had made me more willing to banish mirrors from my life. That said, self-fulfilling pimple prophecies didn't sound so fun. Going to see a dermatologist didn't seem necessary, and monthly facials were way out of my budget, but I could certainly commit to maintaining my current routine. As I crossed off task #3 from my

BBCTG list, I also made a promise to myself that I would try my best to follow something I called Slow-Cooker Mode (i.e., "Fix it and forget it") by not touching my face during the day.

M Y NEXT ADVENTURE IN BRIDAL BEAUTIFYING WAS TO TACKLE item #5, which commanded, "If you don't already, start exercising. A few sessions with a trainer may help to jump-start your routine. Try practicing yoga; the postures build strength and are great tension relievers as well. You'll look great, feel better, and be less stressed out."

This seemed like an obvious next step, mainly because I'd had "start exercising again" on my own to-do list for quite a while. Back in high school I was an all-state track-and-field athlete, and I'd managed to push myself through a sporadic smattering of half marathons over the past five years—emphasis on *sporadic*—but it had been awhile since I'd had a consistent workout routine. Getting back in touch with my inner athlete would be like visiting an old friend, a friend who made me feel energetic, confident, and strong.

Paying for "a few sessions with a trainer" sounded absolutely lovely, but Michael and I weren't really in the financial position to hire a pro to "help to jump-start" my routine. That said, the suggestion to "try practicing yoga" sounded perfect. Not only did I hopefully have the vestiges of my last yoga practice hiding out in my muscles, but I knew that the stress-relieving effects of a few sun salutations might do me wonders in preparing me, mentally, for hosting the upcoming visit from Michael's mom.

Hanna had managed to score a great online coupon deal for a local yoga studio that I'd missed out on, but the studio still offered a negligibly affordable discount of three sessions for twenty dollars for new clients. Although $6.66 per workout was embarrassingly unsustainable for me in the long term, I figured it would be well worth the experience of getting back into yoga in the company of someone I wanted to spend more time with, anyway. Hanna and I made ourselves a yoga date.

Of course, I found myself out of breath and sweating before the class even began. I was running three minutes late, after having aggressively weaved through rush-hour traffic, cursing at pokey drivers like the totally un-Zen yogi that I was. Hanna, bless her, had arrived early and reserved a neighboring mat for me while she waiting with mild embarrassment (she has always been the responsible one). I plopped down ungracefully and cautiously looked around, prepared to avoid eye contact with myself in a room full of mirrors. Much to my delight, the room was completely mirror-free! It turned out that the owners of the studio felt that yoga ought to be more about the experience of feeling your body and less about looking at it. I'd practiced yoga on and off over the prior years, and this was a first! Not only was it convenient for my no-mirrors pledge, but it turned out to be really nice.

Based on what I saw while watching my sister, I probably looked completely ridiculous. We were instructed to "fold over" into Uttanasana (intense standing forward fold pose), and I realized, with dismay, that my stomach folds were preventing the act of folding. And yet I didn't feel the least bit self-conscious. If Hanna could flail around ungracefully and still be loved by her sister, so could I. At the end of the session, we'd both conquered headstands against the wall. Namaste, bitches! It was awesome.

Leaving the yoga studio, I caught a partial glimpse of my flushed face reflected in a mirror that had been tucked into a corner of the studio office. I don't remember details of what I looked like, other than very pink, but I remember that I *felt* happy.

Feeling sufficiently relaxed from our yoga class, I gulped back my anxiety and asked Hanna to come over to help me weed through my clothing selections from earlier that week.

"Wait, you want *me* to help *you* pick out clothes?" she asked. "This is a first."

"I'm desperate," I conceded, which made us both laugh.

Asking my sister for help picking out clothes—and actually trusting her opinions—ended up being fun. After it was all said and done, I kept three of the seven shirts and returned the other four. But had I learned from the experience? Would I allow myself to trust other women? *Ugh, why am I such a control freak?*

Well, this control freak was about to meet her match. Michael's mother, Sherry, was due to arrive the next day for a visit. Michael hadn't been able to get time off until the end of the week, so it would be up to me to entertain her over the next few days.

Mother-in-law/daughter-in-law relationships are known to be complex. James George Frazer, one of the founding fathers of modern anthropology, once declared that "the awe and dread with which the untutored savage contemplates his mother-in-law are amongst the most familiar facts of anthropology." My relationship with Sherry was no exception. Awe and dread. Yep, that sounded familiar.

The awe I had for Sherry was rooted in our similarities, which included both of us being bossy, outspoken, and—of course—quite attached to Michael. The dread I felt about spending time with Sherry rested in our differences. To put it plainly, Sherry and I stood on opposite sides of almost every issue that we both cared deeply about.

Our political difference alone would have been enough to raise any future daughter-in-law's blood pressure, but there was more. Like me, Sherry had dealt with some serious body image issues during her life. However, *unlike* me, instead of trying to change her mind, she'd opted to change her body (and several times at that) through dieting regimes and a handful of cosmetic procedures. Sherry was completely open about this and had gotten at least one face-lift, a few rounds of breast augmentation (first implants, and then reconstruction after she survived breast cancer), and was a regular Botoxer.

I didn't know exactly what to make of all this, but it worried me to wonder what Sherry thought about *my* body. Sherry had always gone out of her way to be kind to me, but every so often she put her foot in her mouth regarding my looks, usually by presuming that I was on a diet or wanted to lose weight. Even though we got along well, I was pretty sure she wished her son was marrying a thinner (and more politically conservative) woman. Sherry's visit would be the first time we'd be spending a lot of time together, just the two of us. I worried that our differing approaches to beauty and vanity might derail the progress I had made.

"You'll be fine, Sweet Pea," Michael insisted. "Just avoid talking about politics or dieting, and focus on things you have in common."

"She doesn't even believe in global warming!" I whined.

"Maybe so, but that doesn't make her a bad person, just . . . quirky," he insisted. "Besides, you've got your own quirks, too. Just go shopping together or something. If you can hang in there for three days, I'll be around to take over the major hosting responsibilities. It'll be fine, I promise."

The following morning I spent a few hours cleaning our apartment, with my eyes on the clock. Sherry was due to arrive downtown by early afternoon. Since Michael had taken our car to work, she'd bravely offered to take public transportation from the airport to Union Square. At eleven thirty, I received a text from her letting me know that she was on the train, so I slipped out of our apartment to begin my walk downtown. I told her I was on my way and hurried.

Union Square is a major tourist attraction, and it was crowded. It took a few minutes before I spotted Sherry standing with her suitcase mere yards away from some tap-dancing street performers.

"Sherry!" I shouted. "Over here!" I saw her look up and spot me. She waved at me with a smile and started heading in my direction. We met in the middle, and we shared a big hug.

"I'm so glad you're here! How are you?" I asked. As usual, she looked great. Bobbed blond hair carefully styled, subtle makeup, perfectly manicured nails, and a chic outfit. When I traveled, I usually wore stretch pants and Ugg boots, but Sherry always looked put together.

"Oh, I'm great! I can't believe the weather is so nice here. When I left Louisville it was eighty-five degrees already, at nine in the morning!" she replied in her slight southern accent.

We both turned to start walking back toward my and Michael's apartment, and a block later we almost bumped right into a large sign standing on the sidewalk. It read SALE in huge bold letters and stood right outside of my all-time favorite store: Anthropologie. I'd spotted it earlier and was secretly hoping that we'd stop inside. I knew that Sherry was also an Anthro fan and thought we might as well start off the week with something we had in common.

"Oh my gosh, I love Anthropologie!" she squealed, adding, "And a sale, too!" We charged in, dropping off Sherry's luggage at the front cash register without slowing down on our race to the racks! In a moment of bliss-induced generosity, my future mother-in-law said those beautiful words every young woman wants to hear: "If you find a top that you like, I'd love to buy it for you!"

If I could find a top I like? I'd already seen about four, and that was just one layered outfit done on a mannequin!

Skilled hunter/gatherers that we were, it didn't take long before both of us had accumulated heavy armloads of potential purchases. We traveled to separate-but-across-from-each-other fitting rooms (sharing would have been weird, no?) and proceeded to try things on. And that's when things started to get a lot more interesting than my experience at Ross.

It turned out that I had no problem trusting Sherry's opinion. Instead, I desperately wanted it. I believed her to have great taste in clothes, fashion, and flattering fit.

I was trying on my first top, an olive-colored sequin-embellished sleeveless blouse with an attached matching scarf. It was beautiful, but I couldn't tell if it fit well.

I called to Sherry from across the fitting room to request an opinion. She asked me to wait a second and then emerged from her own room. We were wearing the *exact same top* (I told you she's got excellent taste), and it looked great on her. We had a good laugh, and she told me the top was flattering on me as well.

We both hit the shopping jackpot that day. Sherry bought several tops and a pair of great denim capris. I left with five (five!) new tops, all on sale, and Sherry actually treated me to *two* of them. She said she couldn't bear to buy one of the shirts without its coordinating sweater. I'd had a ton of fun and felt touched by her generosity. We'd managed to get through the whole afternoon without talking about anything remotely challenging. I could only hope we'd be able to keep it up.

But a nagging voice inside my head bothered me. Getting along fabulously with Sherry had been a relief, but it surprised me that I trusted her taste in clothes so much more easily than I'd trusted my sister. What did it say about me that I trusted the opinion of someone who intimidated me more than the opinion of someone I felt completely comfortable with? Why was this? Did I think we shared the same taste in clothing? Or was something else going on? I knew that I was uncomfortable with Sherry's choices to diet and to have plastic surgeries, but for some reason, knowing how much she cared about her own appearance made me trust her stamp of approval over all others. An uncomfortable realization presented itself: I trusted Sherry precisely because I believed her to be a particularly discriminating critic. If Sherry approved of something, I knew it must surpass the standards of pretty much anyone else (including myself). But was this trust, or simply *mis*trust (of everyone else) in disguise?

THE NEXT DAY WE ENDED UP GOING SHOPPING AGAIN. IF IT ain't broke, don't fix it, right? This outing involved a trip to a fancy-schmancy department store in hopes that we might find some wedding jewelry I liked. Sherry—a retired high school art teacher who makes beautiful handmade jewelry as a hobby—had generously offered to design and make my wedding jewelry. I was pretty excited about this! After walking through the jewelry section and finding nothing to our liking, we began to make our way to the exit. Just then, Sherry saw the sales stand for a skin care line I'd never heard of.

"Oh my gosh! I know the plastic surgeon that invented this skin care line! He's from Louisville, Kentucky. The products are amazing. And *very* expensive—like liquid gold." Intrigued, we went over to take a look. Liquid gold, eh? My current skin care routine didn't involve many precious metals, save for the trace mercury levels in our water supply.

The sales representative manning the booth looked like a petite version of supermodel Agyness Deyn, all stunningly androgynous with white-blond short hair and pale-yet-glowing skin.

"Welcome," said Agyness Deyn 2.0, whose real name, according to her tag, was Beth. "Have you tried our products?"

"Oh yes!" said Sherry. "Actually, I personally know the doctor who invented the line! I'm from Kentucky and so is he. He's brilliant! I love your products."

"That's wonderful! And you?" Beth asked, turning to me.

"I'm just learning about it, actually. My skin is sensitive, so I don't usually try new products," I responded truthfully. Several mirrors rested on the display shelf. I edged back and started eyeballing the products to keep myself focused away from my reflection. The bottles of serums and cleansers and lotions and potions looked enticing, but at $250 for a teeny tub of eye cream, there was zero chance of purchase.

"Oh, don't you worry, everything was *designed* for sensitive skin. The products were designed to help your skin heal after peels and surgeries, right? Do you have any samples?" Sherry asked, turning back to Beth.

"Of course! We'd *love* for you to try our products," Beth exclaimed. She turned around and started fishing through a few drawers behind the counter. Sherry turned to me with a sly grin and winked.

Beth returned and handed me a dozen or so small packets of various potions. "First you use the skin oil, then the cleanser, then the toner, then the serum, and finally the moisturizer. There's one for daytime and another for night, and don't forget the eye cream. Pat it on, don't rub. I don't see too many wrinkles yet, but they'll sneak up on you if you aren't careful!"

I was surprised and delighted. I couldn't remember the last time I'd received so many free samples without first buying something. I thanked Beth profusely and we headed on our way.

As we walked away from the store, Sherry, who had been silent since asking for the samples, turned to me and said, "Well, she was certainly right that you don't have many wrinkles! Whatever you're using already must be working. Not so for me. At my age I have to really bring in the big guns."

I wasn't sure exactly which "big guns" she was referring to, although staple guns came to mind. Sherry had made no secret of her various cosmetic procedures. Indeed, on the first day we'd met she'd brought up the subject of breast implants while we sat next to each other at a minor-league baseball game. Originally, Sherry's implants had been "way bigger," but they'd been removed, and her breasts reconstructed, for her breast cancer treatment several years back. "Before the implants I barely had enough for a mammogram," she'd explained while we sat drinking beers at the baseball game. "That's when I decided to get them fixed, right then and there during my mammogram. I'd never been so embarrassed in my life." I must have looked worried (I hate it when women talk about "fixing" their bodies, as though their functional but aesthetically challenged parts were literally broken or defective), because her next words were of comfort: "Oh, don't worry, you're proportionate!" she offered. I summoned up a weak "Thank you" and quickly changed the subject.

I shook the memory from my mind and tried to focus on the present. Sherry was still talking. "So anyway, that lady was really generous to give you *so* many samples. I guess she only gives samples to people who haven't already tried their products." It suddenly clicked. *Damn it, she wants my samples!* Female competition shows up in the most surprising little ways. But there was only one thing to do, and I knew it.

I offered the samples to Sherry. "I think you'd enjoy these more than I would," I said. "They're the perfect size for traveling. Besides, with this whole no-mirrors thing I wouldn't even be able to see if they made any difference, anyway!"

"Oh, I couldn't do that! They're yours," Sherry countered, but I knew how this worked; I'd watched Michael dance this dance many times.

"No, I insist. Really," I replied firmly. As I said it, I realized that Sherry would, indeed, enjoy the samples more than I. Their allure gave way to the gratification of knowing that I was doing the right thing by giving them up. And, really, they were samples of face cream. How could they possibly be worth making my future mother-in-law feel slighted?

"Well, if you *insist*," she acquiesced, clearly delighted. "Thank you so much, that was very generous."

"No problem!" I responded, pleased with myself. *How strange,* I thought. Counter to my expectations, the two of us had been getting along really well. Maybe my anxieties about Sherry were more in my head than in reality.

T HE FOLLOWING DAY SEEMED LIKE AN IDEAL TIME TO CROSS off item #1 from TheKnot.com's BBCTG list, which instructed me to "Begin a stress-relief regimen. Reserve at least one night a week for some non-wedding fun or quiet time to regroup."

I laughed to myself as I read this. I wondered, *Does anyone*

actually spend every night of the week doing their wedding planning?
Come on! I doubted it. Maybe it was true for people with ambitious
plans and very short engagements, but for most of us this would be
overkill.

I suspected that TheKnot.com was applying a bit of sneaky reverse psychology; despite urging me to take "at least one night a
week" away from wedding planning, this to-do task subtly implied
that near-constant wedding planning was the norm, perhaps even
necessary or expected. Research shows that the longer a shopper
stays in a store, the more she is likely to spend. This is why milk and
eggs—the most common grocery list items—are always buried in
the *back* of grocery stores, so you have to pass by a ton of other things
you may be tempted to buy. Weddings must be like that, too; the
more time we spend thinking about them, the bigger and more expensive they become.

Reverse psychology or not, I was happy to comply with *most*
of TheKnot.com's instructions for this particular task. Having
played hostess to my future mother-in-law over the prior few days,
I was definitely in need of a "stress relief regimen," and I craved
"quiet time to regroup" with the intensity of an addict in her
first few days of rehab. Having some "non-wedding fun" sounded
great, too.

So, on Saturday morning, I used work as an excuse to head over
to a friend's house for the morning, laptop in tow. Michael and
Sherry could spend some mother-and-son time catching up with
each other, and I'd be able to catch up on some paper-grading, blogging, and friendly gossip.

My friend, Liz, was recovering from neck surgery, so I knew it
would be a low-key and relaxing visit. Even better, Liz's own mother,
Nancy, was in town for two weeks to help out, so I knew that Liz

and I would be able to empathize with each other regarding the mixed blessings and exasperations of hosting houseguests.

We chatted for a while about the frustrations of even the most pleasant visitors, and then Liz left me to work while she rested in bed. I graded a handful of my students' final papers, and then turned to my blog. It was Friday—time to update my readers on how things were going with my BBCTG challenge. I still wasn't ready to deal with the nutrition and weight-loss tasks, but task #2 had my attention. Here were my instructions: "Want to grow out your hair or try a new color or cut? Talk to your stylist and start experimenting now."

This one proved to be a challenge. First of all, I wasn't quite sure I wanted to do *anything* new with my hair. I liked my hair. Well, at least I remembered liking it before the no-mirrors project started. It's naturally a nice medium-to-light-blond color with natural highlights. It's pin-straight, fine, and there's a lot of it, which makes it pretty easy to style (or *not* style, which was more typical for me, especially without mirrors!). I didn't have much to complain about in the hair department. Why should I begin experimenting just because TheKnot.com said I should?

Of course, I did miss the *small* ways I'd typically experimented with my hair on a weekly basis. As a shower-at-night kind of gal, I'd typically woken up in the morning, peered into my bathroom mirror, assessed the state of affairs, and decided at that moment whether it would be a hair-up day, a hair-down day, a messy bed-head day, a sleek and smooth day, or some other variation in styling.

In other words, before my no-mirror days, my hair-styling habits were based on visual assessment. But now that I couldn't see myself, it was ponytails served up all day, every day. There was nothing wrong with this look. It was simple and fast and I liked it.

Still, I missed some of that "who knows what it'll look like today!" spontaneity.

This made task #2 a bit more intriguing. Was there a way for me to have fun experimenting with my hair—in a way that gave me some creative pleasure—without looking in mirrors and without doing anything stupid or expensive? Getting a new haircut seemed foolhardy, since I couldn't learn how to style it. New hair color was also axed, since I liked my natural color. And I certainly wasn't interested in making a drastic change just to have something to write about on my blog. I was stumped.

I mentioned my predicament to Liz, who had a great idea. "Why don't you check out one of those online makeover websites?" she suggested.

"Huh?" I asked, intrigued. I loved makeovers.

"I've never done it, but I know there are websites that let you upload a photo of yourself and then try on new hairstyles," she explained.

A quick Google search landed me on a fantastic website filled with totally fun makeover technologies. Not only could I experiment with different hairstyles and colors (the site had hundreds of celebrity photos to help with this), but it also used some really great Photoshop-ish technology to help experiment with different makeup styles and shades. Within minutes I'd uploaded a plain ponytailed photo of myself (from before my no-mirrors project) and was experimenting away!

Inspired by TheKnot.com's suggestion to "grow out your hair," I found a way to morph teen phenom Ashley Tisdale's Rapunzel-esque locks onto my face. The suggestion to "try a new color" was really fun, especially when I discovered that Tila Tequila's red-headed bob looked fantastic on me. To try a new cut, Anna Faris's platinum bob with short bangs fit the bill.

It was rad. I felt a huge endorphin surge from all of the creativity, and I surprised myself by loving the image of myself with Tila Tequila's coppery shade. I'd always thought of myself as having a redhead's stereotypically fiery personality, and now I knew I could actually pull off the look if I ever felt so inclined. I was in no rush to try it out in real life, but that's what made it so fun.

By the time I'd finished up my experimenting and written up a blog post about it, it was time to head back home. I met up with Michael and his mom just in time for us to go to a baseball game at the Giants' stadium. Our place was only a few blocks from the ballpark, so the whole neighborhood was out and about. It felt very festive; a perfect opportunity for some "non-wedding fun."

I should mention that Michael's father, Doug, and Sherry are insane baseball fans. How insane? Let's just say that when it came time for us to pick a wedding date, the Ackermanns declared that there were only *two* weekends between the months between April and October 2011 in which they would be available to travel. Luckily, after a bit of "you would miss my wedding for a minor-league baseball game?!?!" cajoling on Michael's part, they eventually came around. I digress. Anyway, Sherry was really excited for the game and had generously offered to purchase our tickets and all of our snacks and drinks.

Compared with the Ackermanns—well, compared with pretty much everyone else in America—I'm not much of a baseball fan. In my opinion, there are too many rules and the games last far too long. Sure, I'd loved watching *A League of Their Own* when I was a kid, but—let's be honest—that full-length film was about an hour *shorter* than an average nine innings, and a lot more dramatic (not to mention feminist-friendly)! In middle school my whole family went to a Cardinals game together, and I'd ended up being captured on the Jumbotron reading the novel I'd brought along. I didn't even realize it at the time (too engrossed in Nancy Drew), but my image had been broadcast to all the local stations, so I heard all about it the next day from the kids at school. It was not exactly my ticket to sitting at the cool kids' table at lunch.

The Giants game ended up being more fun than I'd expected. It was really cold out, so we all had to cuddle up to stay warm.

"Geez, I'm freezing!" I said, snuggling into Michael. He was seated between Sherry and me, prepared to be the moderator of any debates that sprung up.

"Must be that global warming, eh? Feels more like global *cooling*, if you ask me!" Sherry chided, raising her eyebrows for impact.

"Mom, for the last time, global warming is *not* a liberal conspiracy. I refuse to have this debate again," Michael interjected, saving me from any involvement.

Freezing or not, the beer was flowing, and by inning six I started feeling pretty buzzed and relaxed. I decided to cut myself off before I felt dizzy or said something liberal. Sherry seemed similarly intoxicated, but took a slightly different approach.

"It'll be last call in a minute!" she announced a bit slurrily. Her southern accent was thicker than usual. "Come on! We've gotta get in line before they stop serving!"

"Thanks, but I'm good," I responded. Michael said he'd have another beer, so Sherry went off on her own to get them.

"Should you go with her? She seems a little tipsy," I said to Michael.

"Oh, she'll be fine!" he answered back. "Besides, it's nice to have a minute alone." I was happy when he leaned in and put his arm around me.

Minutes later Sherry was back with not two, but *four* jumbo beers. "Two for one!" she explained, clearly proud of the bargain. I tried to refuse, but Sherry insisted. My elementary school D.A.R.E. program hadn't prepared me for this situation. I'd have to be scrappy. I took a few sips of the beer and then poured at least half of it out onto the ground when I thought nobody else was looking.

The three of us made our way out of the stadium after the Giants ultimately lost. Michael and I both took one of his mom's arms to keep her steady on her feet. The chemotherapy she'd gone through during her breast cancer treatment had weakened her bones, and we didn't want a small stumble to land her in the ER with a broken foot or worse.

Before we arrived home, Sherry started getting a little emotional. We'd just finished crossing a street in downtown San Francisco when Sherry stopped in her tracks, took Michael's hands in her own, and said tearily, "You are the most precious thing in my life. I love you so much. You are my precious boy, my precious boy!" She next turned to me and continued, "Kjerstin, I just love you so much, too. You love my precious boy. Michael is my soul mate, my *soul mate*! I know you'll take care of him for me."

Soul mate? I looked up past Sherry to see Michael's face, his eyes pleading with me to just go with the flow. *Sigh.* All I could muster up in response was, "I love you, too, Sherry. Now let's get you home, okay?"

Later that night, after we'd tucked his mom into bed on the futon, I caught Michael's eye while we were brushing our teeth.

"Soul mate, eh?" I whispered, eyebrows raised. I may have been feeling a bit competitive. *You're MY soul mate, not hers!* shouted my catty psyche.

"Oh, give it a rest, Kjerstin," he begged sternly. "She used to say the same thing about her parakeet until it died. She's had a few beers. It didn't mean anything. Besides, you know she was just trying to tell us she loved us."

"Fine," I snapped, "but I still think it was a weird thing to say." I knew I was being ungrateful for Sherry's generosity that day, but the selfish side of me—my closeted introvert, who also happened to be a raging feminist, a believer in global warming, and a surprisingly possessive fiancée—was aching for life to get back to normal.

Sherry headed back home the next morning. It was nice to have time to myself again, but I had to admit that—save for the soul-mate thing—her visit had gone much better than I'd expected. In fact, I'd really enjoyed most of it. Had I completely misjudged Sherry?

DON'T THINK ABOUT MY EYEBROWS VERY OFTEN. AS A NATURAL blonde, I'm actually pretty lucky in the eyebrow department because my eyebrows are just dark enough to show up on my face (so long as my complexion remains within the pallor-to-paler range). Yet they aren't dark enough for it to be particularly noticeable if I haven't kept them perfectly groomed. A bit of light tweezing every few weeks and I'm in good shape. It's not like my eyebrows are part of my signature look or anything like that. They just don't suck and don't require much work. As with finally having good skin, having decent eyebrows is something I've taken for granted and, therefore, rarely think about.

This was true until I spent a few months without looking in the mirror. At first I didn't think about my eyebrows at all, which was kind of nice. But after no tweezing every few weeks (or—ahem—*at all*), this changed abruptly. One day I caught myself mindlessly running a finger across my brow bone and realized that it felt like I was, instead, caressing Michael's stubbly jawline. Uh-oh! Had I been channeling Frida Kahlo without realizing it? Was it time to call Groucho Marx so he could swing by and pick up his eyebrows?

"What's up with my eyebrows?" I asked Michael in an accusatory tone. This is why I didn't trust him with these things. He had no eye for detail!

"Yeah, they're looking a little fuzzy, but I just figured you were growing them out or something," he responded sheepishly.

"Growing them out?! Are you crazy? What did you think, that I was going to French braid them for the wedding?!" I shot back.

"Sorry! They aren't that bad. Do you want me to help you pluck them?" he offered.

The idea truly frightened me, so I declined as graciously as possible: "You've *got* to be kidding me! No. Fudging. Way." (But I didn't say *fudging*.)

"Well, I think you look beautiful even if your eyebrows are kind of wonky!" Michael insisted. Typical.

"Yeah, that's the problem," I grumbled. For all I knew, I'd become known as "that lady with the crazy eyebrows" to the rest of the world. I knew, realistically, that it couldn't be *that* bad, but I still wanted to take care of things ASAP so I could get back to not thinking about my eyebrows.

Enter TheKnot.com's BBCTG challenge, which commanded, "Ever consider having your eyebrows professionally shaped? Why not? It's your wedding. Now's the time to try it." Indeed. It *was* my wedding (or, at least, it would be in a hundred days!).

After reading through a number of Yelp reviews, I decided to try a "brow bar" that had set up shop in the Union Square Macy's store. I figured I'd mitigate some risk by going to a place that specialized in eyebrows. "Good enough is good enough!" I repeated to myself, mantra-style, as I picked up the phone to make an appointment. "Practice trust!"

And so I traipsed down to Union Square and ducked into Macy's. I ventured into the brow bar, settled into a stool at the "bar," and anxiously awaited my fate. *What kind of bar doesn't serve cocktails?* I mused. A stiff drink would have helped take the edge off the pain that awaited me.

Within minutes, a cute aesthetician with auburn hair and perfectly groomed brows introduced herself and started pulling a kit of goodies out from under the bar. I watched as she lined up her torture implements one by one: tweezers, hot wax, teeny strips of fabric, makeup remover, some kind of soothing lotion, a few makeup compacts, and . . . a handheld mirror.

I quickly blurted out, "Oh, sorry! I can't look in the mirror. It's a blog thing, a project I'm doing. Sorry for the short notice!"

She paused for a second, and then said, "Wow! No mirrors? That's cool! You must really trust me, huh!"

Good question. Did I? Could I? I didn't; at least, not completely. But what else was I to do, other than letting my brows grow beyond recognition? (Okay, admittedly this wouldn't have been the end of the world, but professional brow shaping was on BBCTG list!) I couldn't very well groom my own eyebrows without looking, and a professional aesthetician with perfect brows seemed like a surer thing than a fiancé whose idea of "good enough" was quite different from my own. So I responded by saying, "Yeah. Well, I read that you

guys usually do a great job, so I figured I would be in good hands!"
Besides, I had a self-fulfilling prophecy to disrupt.

I closed my eyes and pursed my mouth as the aesthetician got to
work with her bounty of tools. It all happened very fast, and after a
few snaps of pain (which felt exactly like she was pulling a teeny-
weeny Band-Aid from my skin) she was done; my brows had been
cleansed, waxed, tweezed, soothed, and made up with concealer ("to
mask the redness") and brow pencil ("so they really POP!").

I wanted to take a look, but resisted the urge. Instead, I ran my
fingers across my face. I saw the aesthetician flinch, probably worried that I was smudging off the carefully applied concealer. Whatever. How else was I supposed to check? I could feel that (1) my
brows were mostly still there and (2) the skin above and below them
was smooth and soft, though a bit tender.

BBCTG task #14: done!

THE THIRD WEEK OF JUNE BROUGHT A SECOND SET OF VISI-
tors, this time from my side of the family. My sister and her
longtime boyfriend, Nick, were hosting a couples' wedding shower
for Michael and me that Saturday, and my parents and younger
brother had decided to fly into town for the party. Even though it felt
as though I'd barely gotten back to my normal routines after
Sherry's visit, it was nice to be able to spend time with my own family and friends. The fact that my parents had decided to stay in a
hotel helped take the pressure off as well!

I was excited to hammer out some wedding plans with help from
my mom. In addition to finalizing our guest list and ordering the
invitations, I wanted help with my wedding-day beautifying plans.

According to TheKnot.com's BBCTG list, it was high time that I started worrying about my wedding makeup. Item #8 suggested that "3–4 Months Before" my wedding, I ought to "Make consultation appointments with potential makeup artists. Be sure to take pictures, then analyze them. Do your features stand out? Do you look like you're wearing a mask?" Task #9 involved deciding on a makeup artist and then booking "him/her for your wedding date."

I was mightily pleased that TheKnot.com was enlightened enough to use both male and female pronouns when referring to makeup artists, but less pleased by the assumption that I (and *all* brides) had both the interest and the bucks to pay for professional makeup artistry on the big day, plus multiple trial appointments to weed out the options. I had been planning on some makeup help for myself, as a way to make a mirror-free wedding day less stressful, but I couldn't help noticing that, once again, the BBCTG list had communicated normalcy, rather than choice, on the topic of bridal over-consumerism.

I decided to have my makeup professionally done for the couples' shower as a way to "try out" a makeup artist. Since I couldn't "take pictures, then analyze them," I'd scheduled one appointment for myself and another for my mom. I wanted us to spend some time together, and I wanted her opinion on the end result. I was also secretly hoping that my mom would help pay for the makeup trial, since it cost $50 (and would cost another $150 on my actual wedding day!).

The experience itself was luxurious, and the makeup artist— whose own makeup looked natural and lovely, I thought—was incredibly sweet and personable. After almost an hour of dabbing various brushes into various pots and compacts and then onto my face, I felt optimistic about the results. It took me only five minutes to put on my own makeup without a mirror, so I figured I ought to look amazing after all the extra effort, time, and talent. The makeup artist stepped back to look at her work, smiled with a satisfied sigh, and squealed, "Oooh, you look soooo great!" Sometimes it was easy to practice trust.

My mom nodded, smiling. (Though, in hindsight, I admit that the nod wasn't particularly vigorous and the smile wasn't exactly glowing.)

I happily scampered off to have my hair styled on the other side of the salon, and my mom sat down to have her own makeup done. *I bet I look fab!* I remember thinking.

But I soon began picking up on clues that my makeup might not look quite as good as I'd hoped. The first clue was in seeing that my mom's makeup didn't look much different from her usual self-application. Well, except for the fact that her foundation was kind of settling into her pores (and out of her non-pores) in a weird way. *Wait, were those crow's-feet? And she looked a little pallid. Was she even wearing mascara?*

I tried to shake it off.

But then when it was time to pay, instead of treating for both of us, my mom hesitated, and then asked, "Sooo . . . how do we want to do this?" We each ended up paying for our own services, which was completely fine and reasonable, but it also served as a second clue. My parents expected my siblings and me to be financially self-sufficient, but every so often my mom liked to treat for special things. Whether a discounted wedding dress, a haircut at a non–Great Clips salon, or a new shirt or dress from T.J.Maxx, my mom liked to give us just-because gifts whenever she felt inspired. Sometimes this inspiration struck because of sentiment and tradition (e.g., Wedding Dress #4), but usually it was as simple as her seeing us try on an outfit, thinking we looked particularly put together, and wanting us to have it. Over time I'd noticed that this latter form of inspiration happened only if my mom loved the look of an outfit, even if I didn't. If I wouldn't—or couldn't—buy something my mom loved, she was likely to treat (well, as long as it was a great bargain), but this did *not* happen if the item in question wasn't to my mother's liking. In other words, if Hanna or I happened to fall in love with an outfit or haircut that my mom didn't like, we'd be on our own. No amount of hinting or twirling around a dressing room could move my mother to "treat" for something she found unflattering or distasteful. So the fact that my mom didn't feel inspired to treat for my makeup trial didn't quite certify that I looked like crap, but it certainly suggested it.

I got nervous on the way to the party and asked my mom if I should be worried. She told me that I looked "just fine," but admitted that she didn't think that the trial makeup application had been worth $50, much less the $150 it would cost on my actual wedding day. (And let's not forget that treating my bridesmaids to their own makeup applications, which seemed like a nice thing to offer, would add another several hundred dollars to the total.)

I was super bummed. What was I supposed to do? I couldn't afford to keep going to $50 makeup trials in hopes that I'd find someone who was worth the money. Besides, I'd really wanted my mom to help me figure this out. Luckily, she did.

"To be honest, I think your makeup looks just fine the way you've been doing it yourself," she offered. "All you'd need for it to be wedding-worthy is some help applying more eye makeup. I bet your bridesmaids could help!"

My self-applied makeup looked better than the professional application I just paid fifty dollars for? I was incredulous, but flattered.

A quick calculation confirmed that *not* hiring a makeup artist would mean saving more than $600. The math was certainly tipped in favor of self-application, but I wavered; would my bridesmaids find it tacky if we didn't offer them professional makeup applications? The past few weddings I'd been in had provided this, and I didn't want to disappoint my friends. Then I remembered something key: My bridesmaids are all competent and sane women who wouldn't give a fig about missing out on an unaffordable—not to mention *crappy*—makeover. If my mom thought my own makeup skills were adequate, that would be good enough for me. I knew she wanted me to look lovely on my wedding day, so she wouldn't have complimented my makeup application skills just to be nice or to save a buck. What was good enough for my mom would be good enough for me.

ATER THAT DAY, MICHAEL AND I HAD A GREAT TIME AT OUR laid-back couples' shower. Afterward I took a few minutes to consider how, if at all, giving up mirrors had affected my own attitudes about wedding planning. Thinking about how our culture encourages competition and mistrust between women made me consider the wedding industry in a new light. Aside from those mythical impromptu Vegas events, most weddings require at least some planning. Indeed, according to recent reports, there's a $161 *billion* wedding industry that seemed to survive—nay, thrive—on the constant one-up-womanship of brides (and mothers-of-the-brides) who are determined to not embarrass themselves with a subpar event. As much as we like to think of weddings as revolving solely around romantic commitment, they are also deeply embedded within a highly gendered consumer culture. Based on my readings—not to mention my own experiences—I felt convinced that the wedding industry thrived by reinforcing (and sometimes creating!) women's insecurities about their appearances.

American weddings and consumer culture are married to each other (pun intended). This is not news to anybody who has planned a wedding in the past few decades, but I had mixed feelings about my own role as a consumer-bride. The penny-pinching, bargain-hunting, "I got it on sale!" reveler in me was secretly thrilled by the epic challenges involved in wedding planning, but I was simultaneously peeved and appalled by the seemingly unavoidable and ridiculous expenses involved. And I couldn't help wondering how much my own grand wedding ambitions had been shaped by feelings of competition and comparison.

I knew from watching a few episodes of *Bridezillas* that the potential insanity of wedding planning could go so much further than my annoying body image woes, or a $700 dress of questionable bargain-worthiness. Watching women treat their friends, family, and fiancés with bratty disrespect was disheartening. Repeated again and again by these young women was the phrase "It's *MY* day!" I couldn't help being reminded of Peggy Orenstein's warning about the dangers of princess culture. The wedding industry was more than delighted to sell any bride on the idea that she ought to be a "princess" for "her" big day. The princess mentality might have been good for business, but it was bad for women (not to mention the poor souls who got screamed at along the way!).

Just a few months earlier I'd felt on the verge of slipping down my own slippery slope to Bridezilla Land. I obviously couldn't predict my future actions, but for the time being it seemed as though my no-mirrors project had put some serious treads in my slope-climbing stilettos. I noted three major changes.

First, since I couldn't look at myself in the mirror, I'd stopped trying on my wedding dress(es). (Well, to be completely honest, I did attempt to do this once without a mirror, but I felt stupid, and the dress was difficult to get in and out of on my own.) I calculated that, by not trying on my dress every week or so, I'd saved twenty to forty minutes of time per month, depending on how easily the damned thing zipped. I still felt a little bit worried about whether I'd ended up with the "perfect" dress—and I'm sure the wedding industry would have fully supported my purchase of infinite dresses in search of an unachievable "one"—but the feeling waned each day.

Second, I'd dramatically reduced my spending on beauty products. Before giving up mirrors, I used to peruse the makeup aisle at my local drugstore for fun, purchasing little goodies whenever I'd felt inspired. Now that I'd memorized my makeup routine using particular products, I didn't feel comfortable deviating. Although a small piece of me bemoaned the reduction in my cosmetic creativity, a quick peek at my makeup drawer confirmed that I hadn't been all that creative to begin with. (Nude lip gloss, anyone? I had twenty!) I probably saved ten dollars a week by staying out of CVS and Walgreens. If I counted all the random other stuff I typically felt inspired to buy on these drugstore trips, it probably added up to much more.

Finally, the very act of "announcing" so publicly that I'd needed to take a step back from the wedding craziness had been enough for me to take the task seriously in more realms than just my appearance. I'd caught myself not thinking about my wedding for entire days—egads! Yes, it was still fun to plan my wedding, but other things—like moving to a new city, teaching my students, volunteering with About-Face, spending time with family, and completing a long-overdue journal article—were competing for my attention. It felt great to know that all the foofy stuff would play second fiddle, at least temporarily.

I N THE FINAL WEEK OF JUNE, MICHAEL AND I TOOK OFF FOR A week of camping to celebrate the end of the school year. After the stresses of out-of-town guests, late-night paper-grading, and frantic BBCTG-sanctioned bridal beautifying, a week of solitude in nature sounded like heaven. Smartphones were silenced and laptops were left behind. Calls could be returned. E-mails could wait. Blogging could wait. Vacation couldn't.

We split our time between northern California and southern Oregon, with plans to spend our days alternating hiking among the world's tallest redwoods with wine tasting at some of the world's most amazing vineyards. Michael and I loved living on the West Coast pretty much every day of the year, but we always felt particularly enamored by our home when we went on our camping trips. This trip was as amazing as ever, with an added bonus: Spending so much time in the great outdoors ended up being great for my body image.

In some ways, camping made me feel more beautiful and proud of my body, and in other ways it simply reduced how much I cared or worried about my looks. Both of these things felt like progress. Having no mirrors around at all meant that I spent even *less* time thinking about my appearance. Although mirrors and other reflective surfaces are everywhere in the city, they are difficult if not impossible to find in the woods, even in campground potty shacks. None of the campground restrooms we used had mirrors. This may sound like no big change, since I'd been avoiding mirrors over the past three months, but it was gorgeously different because I didn't have to expend any energy to avoid them. Although banning mirrors from my everyday life had helped me keep my appearance in a healthier perspective, having to constantly and consciously work to avoid mirrors had the unintended side effect of keeping my forbidden reflection in the back of my mind throughout the day. Not so while camping, and it was sweet relief. Full disclosure: I did have to resist staring at myself in my car's side-view mirror whilst road tripping, but the epic scenery made my pale face pale in comparison.

Wearing even less makeup than usual made me feel like a confident nature babe. Surrounded by a rustic community of other campers, and often just Michael, I felt comfortable enough to experiment a bit with my makeup routine, which hadn't varied at all since Day 22 of the project. Specifically, packing limitations and nature-girl ambitions led me to cut back on products yet again, which further minimized makeup application time. I was down to only two minutes and four products (SPF 30 tinted face lotion, gel cheek stain, cream eye shadow, and a swipe of mascara), but I felt like a total hottie.

And also, tree-hugging inspired a bit of self-hugging. Camping in the woods meant spending a lot of time with trees. Big, beautiful record-breaking redwoods. Hanging out with my huge coniferous friends made me feel much smaller than usual (in a philosophical rather than skinnier sense), and yet somehow more majestic and connected. Trees have wrinkles, gnarls, warts, rough skin, and weird smells, and I loved them anyway. Trees get really old, and I cherished them all the more for it because their age bore witness to experience and strength. Trees get really big, huge, enormous, really, and I found them more majestic for it. No two trees are alike, yet all are magnificent and miraculous. Could I give my body the same respect and admiration? Eve Ensler posed a similar question when she was interviewed for the body-positive documentary *America the Beautiful*. In her interview, Eve spoke glowingly about meeting a woman from Nigeria who told her,

> Eve, look at that tree. Do you see that tree? Now look at that tree. [pointing to another tree] Do you like that tree? Do you hate that tree 'cause it doesn't look like that tree? We're all trees. You're a tree. I'm a tree. You've got to love your body, Eve. You've got to love your tree. Love your tree!

What a beautiful suggestion.

Finally, a few times I managed to talk Michael into chopping wood or setting up our tent while wearing his boxer briefs, a pair of sneakers, and not much else. Watching Michael perform these duties while wearing next to nothing made me feel like Cleopatra. Yes, I said it: sexually objectifying my fiancé made me feel like a sexy, all-powerful queen of the Nile.

When it came to housework we usually had a 50/50 split, but when camping, Michael probably did close to 70 percent of the "tent-work," including setting up our tent, building the fires, tending to said fires, fiddling with food cooking on said fires, and the careful leave-no-trace undoing of all of the above. My main responsibilities were blowing up our air mattress (using a battery-operated air pump), chopping veggies, and helping to unload and reload stuff from the car.

This division of labor might seem both unfair and completely unrelated to body image, but this wasn't the case. Feminists though we both are, Michael and I do enjoy excelling at things we are good at, even if our talents sometimes fall along the usual gendered lines. Thus, Michael takes some pleasure in successfully chopping wood, building fires, and growing a lot of facial hair in a hurry. Similarly, I take some feminine (and feminist) pleasure in watching him do so not only because these are (hetero)sexy-man "manly" activities that I find attractive (and which manage to subtly realign housework inequalities on a macro scale), but also because having somebody else take care of so many of these burdening details makes me feel cared for. Feeling cared for—while sitting back, eating a s'more, and watching a big furry man chopping wood in his Calvins—made me feel sexy, regardless of what I looked like. Trust me.

As the month of June came to an end, I felt grateful for the lessons I'd learned about trust and about myself. Thanks to my no-mirrors project, I'd begun to cut back on a lot of unnecessary and stressful wedding-planning hoopla, while also figuring which parts of bridal culture I actually *wanted* to engage in, both for fun and to satisfy my sociological interest. In other words, I was saving myself time, money, and stress, and also having a lot more fun. I'd even begun building a better relationship with my future mother-in-law. I hoped the remaining two-thirds of my year without mirrors would bring as much positive change.

FIVE

July

WHAT, EXACTLY, *DOES* A FEMINIST (BRIDE) LOOK LIKE?

*Remove those "I want you to like me" stickers from
your forehead and, instead, place them where they
truly will do the most good—on your mirror.*

SUSAN JEFFERS

AMERICAN FEMINISTS HAVE LONG BEEN SUSPICIOUS OF
beauty and fashion. As described by Linda M. Scott, author of *Fresh Lipstick: Redressing Fashion and Feminism,*
"Across the spectrum of academic and popular literature, feminist
writers have consistently argued that a woman's attempt to cultivate
her appearance makes her a dupe of fashion, the plaything of men,
and thus a collaborator in her own oppression." I am all too familiar
with these contentions. In college, I absorbed Naomi Wolf's *The
Beauty Myth: How Images of Beauty Are Used Against Women* with
the enthrallment of a newly converted religious devotee.

Above my homework-cluttered desk, I'd dutifully taped quotes

from my favorite feminist authors as inspiration for my burgeon-
ing empowerment. My favorite, written by Mary Wollstonecraft, author of *A Vindication of the Rights of Women*, became a daily mantra
for me while in treatment for my eating disorder: "Taught from
their infancy that beauty is woman's sceptre, the mind shapes itself
to the body, and, roaming around its gilt cage, only seeks to adorn its
prison."

I read from the feminist canon and felt enlightened and empowered, yet doubly burdened.

Beauty was oppression. Beauty was patriarchy. Beauty was pain
and loss and kidney stones and disintegrating bones. Beauty was
violence to the body and spirit. Beauty was wasteful and indulgent.
Beauty was antifeminist.

But I still wanted to be beautiful, or at the very least to be mod-
erately attractive and conventionally feminine (well, with an androgynous free-to-be-you-and-me tomboy twist thrown in here and
there). Did this make *me* antifeminist?

I was not the first woman to ask this question and I will not be
the last.

There have been seemingly endless internal debates on the topic
among feminist circles. According to Scott, the "founding feminists"
of the nineteenth century sniped at one another for being too fashionable or too ascetic, too sexy or too prim, too vain or too careless.
Feminist leaders of the 1920s grimaced at the grooming, dress, and
activities of the era's flappers, even as these young urban women
challenged gender roles at every turn. Fifty years later, second-wave
feminists insisted that liberated women oughtn't wear makeup or
shave their legs, and in 1991, Naomi Wolf's best-selling *The Beauty
Myth* influenced both academic and mainstream audiences, garner-
ing polarized debates about the role of beauty in women's lives.

Historically, the message from feminists has been accusatory: Beauty standards should be understood as tools of patriarchy, and one cannot challenge patriarchy while conforming to it.

Yet rejecting mainstream beauty standards isn't an easy choice, no matter how much one wants to change the world. There are personal costs to not conforming, and any woman who recognizes these costs is no dupe.

Messages such as those outlined above have long alienated women who believe in gender equality but aren't interested in being martyrs for the cause. Indeed, feminism's presumed antagonism toward mainstream beauty standards has been used by detractors to discredit the movement and to silence individual women within it. Key among these attacks was Rush Limbaugh's insisting in 1987 something to the effect of "Feminism was established so as to allow unattractive women easier access to the mainstream of society."

Accusing feminists of being "just a bunch of ugly chicks" sounds woefully immature, but has arguably been one of the most effective ways for contemporary detractors to discredit the women's movement. These attacks were so powerful and effective that the very same feminists who had once criticized their compatriots for conforming to mainstream beauty standards suddenly found themselves working to prove to the world that feminists *weren't* ugly, after all.

In the 1990s, T-shirts claiming THIS IS WHAT A FEMINIST LOOKS LIKE became all the rage. They were created to challenge stereotypes about what types of people supported gender equality. Although these still-popular T-shirts were originally intended to celebrate diversity among feminists across race, class, gender, and sexuality, images of actress Ashley Judd—a heterosexual white woman with class privilege—wearing the shirt have arguably become the most iconic (well, at least until 2008, when *Ms.* magazine put a Photoshopped image of Barack Obama wearing the T-shirt on its cover!). In other words, the only stereotype that Judd seemed to challenge by wearing her THIS IS WHAT A FEMINIST LOOKS LIKE T-shirt, and the stereotype that most captured the attention of the mass media and general public, was that of the "ugly feminist." Now, I'm not mad at Ashley Judd for being conventionally beautiful; she's a freaking fabulous feminist role model, who happens to champion several of my favorite women's causes. I bought myself the T-shirt after seeing her in it. Yet it fascinates me that, with all the famous folk seen wearing that T-shirt—Whoopi Goldberg, Patrick Stewart, Margaret Cho, and Camryn Manheim, among others—Judd's image was the one that came to represent the "new" face of feminism.

And so, by the time I began my year without mirrors, I'd spent close to a decade pondering this curious relationship between feminism and beauty and my own place within these debates.

It angered me that this antagonism seemed to reinforce the idea that a woman could be either pretty or intelligent, but not both. I agreed with the English writer and poet Elizabeth Bibesco, who insisted that "you don't have to signal a social conscience by looking like a frump. Lace knickers won't hasten the holocaust, you can ban the bomb in a feather boa just as well as without, and a mild interest in the length of hemlines doesn't necessarily disqualify you from reading *Das Kapital* and agreeing with every word." (Not that I've ever managed to read every word of *Das Kapital*!) Bibesco may have been speaking from experience; Virginia Woolf, one of her contemporaries (and an apparent frenemy), once snarkily described Bibesco as "pasty and podgy, with the eyes of a currant bun." Who would have expected Virginia Woolf and Rush Limbaugh to share similar strategies for demeaning their adversaries?

I agreed wholeheartedly that the beauty and diet industries

deserved my skepticism and disdain. It disgusted me to know that entire markets relied on—and actively reinforced—women's insecurities in order to turn a profit. I'd been a victim of these messages and would never forget it. And yet I remained confused by my own pleasure when partaking in beauty routines. Could I still be a "real" feminist if I shaved my legs and armpits? How about if I wore a push-up bra? Was I supremely naive to feel so empowered by a good hair day? And why did I feel so proud—as though I'd somehow "made it"—when I was interviewed for a book titled *Sexy Feminism: A Girl's Guide to Love, Success, and Style?*

I wondered if a love for fashion *and* feminism could exist in the same person, or whether these things were mutually exclusive. I'd also guiltily considered that I might actually be a more *effective* feminist teacher and activist if I didn't look like a stereotypical "ugly feminist," though I'd never gone so far as to wear my THIS IS WHAT A FEMINIST LOOKS LIKE T-shirts to class. Nevertheless, I felt certain that my students tended to take me, my politics, and the sociological research supporting gender equality more seriously when I looked like a "normal" woman. And one more thing: Why did feminists so easily give *patriarchy* all the credit for fashion's existence? Who were we to dismiss women's own creativity, autonomy, and pleasure when engaging in the world of style and self-expression?

I had plenty of questions, but no concrete answers. Little did I know, but my no-mirrors experiment was about to propel me smack-dab into the midst of these debates.

BY THE BEGINNING OF JULY I'D MANAGED TO MAKE A SIZABLE dent in TheKnot.com's "Bridal Beauty: Countdown to Gorgeous" list. Having started two months behind the recommended six-month schedule, I'd had my work cut out for me to catch up. I'd begun a yoga routine, enjoyed some relaxing time away from wedding planning, experimented with different virtual hairstyles, gotten "serious about skin care," and even jumped ahead of schedule by getting my eyebrows waxed by a pro. My blog readers seemed to be having fun with my mirrorless challenge within a challenge, and so was I. But I'd been intentionally avoiding a few things on the list. Specifically, I had yet to report back on either of the following two items:

> #4: Start paying attention to your nutrition. Bad food habits and too much caffeine mixed with wedding planning stress can transform a bride-to-be into Bridezilla.
> #6: If you'd like to lose weight before your wedding, consult your doctor to develop a nutrition and fitness plan. Set a weight-loss goal and meet it before your dress fittings begin. Once fittings are underway, you'll need to maintain your weight. (Or reconsider losing weight. Obviously your guy thinks you look great just the way you are.)

I didn't forget to do these two BBCTG tasks. In fact, I'd kind of been doing both of them since before my no-mirrors project even started. However, I'd been avoiding writing about them on my blog. At that point in time, my blog readers knew a lot about me, but they didn't know two important—and seemingly contradictory, and therefore very complicated—things: (1) that I was a recovered anorexic, and (2) that I had (sort of) been on a (sort of) diet over the prior several months.

I've never felt ashamed of having had an eating disorder. On the contrary, I'd usually been very open about it, especially to my students at UCLA and to the girls participating in my About-Face workshops.

Being recovered from anorexia helped define who I was and it helped shape my values and commitments to helping other women.

So why hadn't I already mentioned my eating disorder in my blog? I hadn't figured out how to. I never mentioned it in my first posts because I was new to blogging and didn't know how much personal information I wanted to share. I also didn't want my blog to be interpreted as an eating-disorder recovery memoir. But not bringing this up in the beginning made it harder to bring it up later. I didn't want to sound like I was making some kind of coming-out-of-the-closet-style announcement, since anorexia was in my past and being a recovered anorexic was only one part of my current identity. But I also didn't want to just sneak it into my writing, all casual-like, as though it didn't matter at all. I didn't want to trivialize my experiences, or those of other eating disorder sufferers. So I'd dealt with the situation by hinting around at it, by saying vague things like "I used to have disordered body image" or "I know from experience that dieting can be dangerous."

But when it came to explaining my thoughts on BBCTG items #4 and #6, I knew that it was time to talk about my experiences in plain language. As much as it made me cringe to do so, the post I wrote on July 1 was very coming-out-of-the-closet-esque. I wasn't scared to admit that I was a recovered anorexic, but I was terrified to admit that I was dieting.

Here is the gist of what I wrote:

Dear friends,

I want to address tasks #4 and #6 from the BBCTG list, but it's been difficult. I haven't told you the whole story about myself, which is what I owe you. Here it is.

I'm a recovered anorexic, I'm a feminist, and I'm on a diet.

Because of my experience with anorexia, I know how horrible things can get when one starts obsessing about "bad foods" and setting (and re-setting) weight-loss goals. My eating disorder made me miserable, and I have lasting health issues that could eventually shorten or lessen the quality of my life. This makes me angry and sad, though I try not to beat myself up about it because recovering from my eating disorder is part of what made me a feminist. While battling for my sanity and health, I became increasingly pissed off at the THIN=BEAUTIFUL*GOOD cultural environment we live in.

Our culture's valorization of thinness caused well-meaning friends to compliment me on my rapid weight loss, literally up until the weeks that I entered treatment. Even after entering treatment, some people didn't think I was skinny enough to be "really" anorexic.

In the end, I got better, got angrier, and ultimately rearranged my life so that I could stay healthy and continue fighting the good fight as my career.

We feminists typically view dieting—and, particularly, the diet industry—as an expression of patriarchy that is bad for women. As a scholar who studies the harmful effects of our culture's beauty standards, I agree with this. Diets (which FAIL 95 percent of the time) drain women's energy, happiness, and wallets—often while risking our health. "RIOTS, NOT DIETS!" has become a well-known rallying cheer for many feminists.

Dieting can also be understood as a type of "patriarchal bargain." As described by sociologist Lisa Wade on the blog Sociological Images, "A patriarchal bargain is a decision to accept gender rules that disadvantage women in exchange for whatever power one can wrest from the system. It is an individual strategy designed to manipulate the system to one's best advantage, but one that leaves the system itself intact."

*By strategically losing weight, we accept the THIN=
BEAUTIFUL*GOOD equation (which implies FAT=UGLY*BAD) and
propel ourselves into positions of greater social advantage. On an individual level, having "thin privilege" feels empowering. (Recall Oprah
Winfrey—arguably the MOST powerful woman in the world—has described "going to the gym when I really prefer wine and chips" as her
greatest accomplishment!) Yet these THINpowered feelings depend upon
a system of inequality in which power/privilege/respect are denied to
others on the basis of these standards.*

*Frustratingly, given the patriarchal bargain of weight loss, being rad-
ically anti-diet as a political stance doesn't always fit comfortably as
a personal stance. Because we live in a society that punishes women for
being fat, even the most dedicated feminists, like Eve Ensler and Naomi
Wolf, report struggles with body image. The threat of becoming a martyr
for this cause (i.e., by voluntarily giving up "thin-privilege," if we've got
it) can be terrifying. As Esther Rothblum so plaintively stated in the title of
her chapter of the (highly recommended) book* **Feminist Perspec-
tives on Eating Disorders,** *"I'll Die for the Revolution but Don't
Ask Me Not to Diet." I know the feeling.*

*Add to this the personal fact that I've gained an (subjectively) un-
comfortable amount of weight in the past year thanks to some unhealthy
emotional eating, and suddenly I'm facing a conundrum.*

What's a good feminist to do?

*You already know that I've challenged myself to avoid mirrors, but
what you don't know is that I'm also using the food tracking website from
a well-known weight-loss program to monitor my food and exercise. (The
"good feminist" inside of me is cringing as I write this, but so far the program has helped me avoid both restricting and binging. When it comes to
patriarchal bargaining, do the ends justify the means?) As an advocate of*

the Health at Every Size movement (which stresses the importance of
healthful behaviors but rejects the idea that there is a universal "healthy
weight"), I'm trying to judge my success based on my behaviors instead of
my weight. My goal has been to consciously reengage in healthful eating
habits and joyful activity, and then accept my body size and shape wher-
ever it settles. As much as I'm still tempted to "get skinny," I know I can
live with this, and (more importantly) I know my body can live through it.

Clicking "post" after writing all of this was cathartic. I felt
proud of myself for telling the whole story, but still nervous that my
readers—particularly my feminist readers—might think less of me.
I reminded myself that, even if following a diet program made me
a bad feminist, I was right to prioritize my mental health; "sanity
comes first," even before feminism.

SHORTLY AFTER SHARING MY ENTIRE BACKGROUND WITH MY
blog readers, I finally hit the one-hundred-days mark of my
project. Even though I wasn't quite a third of the way through the
full year I'd committed to (and thus didn't want to get too far ahead
of myself), it seemed like an auspicious time to give myself a progress
report on my growing independence from mirrors. Despite facing
doubts at times, with a hundred days of work behind me, I felt certain that I'd be able to make it through to the entire year. I was no
longer dependent on mirrors for my daily life, which felt phenomenal. That said, it had been incredibly difficult in a practical sense,
and sometimes I still had slipups. In other words, I wasn't yet 100
percent mirror-free. In truth, there had been only a handful of days
over the prior three months when I hadn't seen myself at all, and

most of those were days when I hadn't left the house. With mirrors
and reflective surfaces everywhere, even the most stringent preventa-
tive measures couldn't prevent accidental glimpses (damn those
ATM security cameras!). Those peripheral peeks were mostly benign, but every so often, "seeing myself" had led to "looking at myself," which was totally against the rules. This didn't happen more
than once every week or so, which wasn't too bad, but I wanted to do
better.

Even though I'd tried to find ways to compensate for the creativity that had previously gone toward my daily makeup and hairstyling routines and my outfit choices, I was still feeling a lot of
temptation when getting ready in front of my curtained bathroom
mirror. I'd look longingly at my (exceedingly excessive) collection of
abandoned beauty products and would feel incredibly tempted to
just push aside the curtain and play. The good news was that this
new temptation seemed motivated by body-positive creativity rather
than paranoid insecurity. This represented a form of progress indeed, but I still had work to do. To start, I decided to box up all of
my fancy makeup and hairstyling products and put them away until
the end of the project. A key lesson from my readings on willpower:
Why battle temptation when I could avoid it?

Had my body image improved since giving up mirrors? It had,
subtly. This was motivating. I never expected to reverse a fifteen-
plus-year issue in only a few months. That would be ridiculously
simple, and—as is true for most women—my body image remained
ridiculously complex. Yet I was seeing small changes, all in a positive
direction, and they gave me hope. I also believe that finally *doing*
something about my body image (rather than just thinking about it)
was one of the most empowering things I'd ever done. I was proud

of myself for what I was accomplishing, and that was starting to matter more to me than what I looked like.

Despite all of this pride and progress, I was still haunted by one nagging task on TheKnot.com's BBCTG list. According to TheKnot.com, the last thing I was supposed to do before walking down the aisle to marry Michael was to "take a few moments to reflect on the meaning of the day before giving yourself one last once-over in the mirror."

The "last once-over in the mirror" was definitely not permitted in my rules, but it's something I felt scared that I'd regret not doing. I knew that I'd probably be desperately curious to know what I looked like on my wedding day. This, alone, I could handle. After all, I've felt desperately curious about my looks on other days, managed to resist, and been okay. But a lot of people had told me that my wedding day would be different. So many trusted, sane, wise, and not-ridiculously-vain women in my life, including my own mother, had told me that I needed to spend a few moments alone to see myself in the mirror on the day that I got married. I'd been told that this moment wouldn't be about my looks, but about quietly recognizing myself for just one calm minute during a whirlwind day of momentous transition. This minute alone in front of a mirror would mark an important life moment for my own memory, and that didn't sound so horribly bad or wrong. Would I be able to create this important moment for myself on my own terms? I didn't know.

Or maybe this was just one more overly romantic bridal must-do myth, and by looking at myself on my wedding day I'd only be buying into the myth at the cost of my beloved project's integrity. I was at a complete loss about what to do. I was glad to have another three months to mull it over.

A FEW DAYS AFTER DAY 100, MICHAEL AND I FLEW TO ST. Louis to visit my parents for the great "parents meeting parents" weekend. Michael's parents, Sherry and Doug, were flying in from Louisville, Kentucky, along with Michael's sister, Mandy, and her boyfriend, Jon. I was sad that Hanna and Peter couldn't make it. I was excited for this weekend, almost certain that it would go well. Michael's mom had already met my family about a year earlier, when both were in San Francisco at the same time. Sherry and my mom are both known for their strong personalities and passionate politics, but they'd gotten along great (a huge relief!). Michael's dad and sister hadn't yet met my parents, but we weren't too worried about any clashing personalities on that front.

Both my dad and Michael's are successful, smart, sweet, and mostly laid-back guys. Although they're on opposite sides of the political spectrum, neither is known for aggressive debating. If anything, they're both conflict-averse peacekeepers. My dad and I have always been close, and I'd bonded with Doug over our shared love for books and thousand-piece jigsaw puzzles. Having both dads around for the weekend promised to tone down any potential drama.

Michael's sister, Mandy, has a lot of exuberance and energy, but thankfully is no drama queen. Born exactly two years after Michael, *to the day*, the two of them act more like twins than regular siblings. They share a bond that I sometimes find intimidating. Michael had always described Mandy as his best friend; she would be his "Best MANdy" at our wedding.

Michael's sister is tall and thin, with thick curly blond hair and bright blue eyes. She managed to drink like a fish, swear like a sailor, tell completely inappropriate jokes (frequent topics: dead babies and bodily functions), and enthusiastically narrate epically gross stories from her veterinary school case assignments, yet still turn the head of pretty much any heterosexual man on the planet. I loved hanging out with Mandy, but if Michael was around, I couldn't help noticing that he tended to stop acting like my fiancé and instead acted like Mandy's twin. The two of them went together like two peas in a pod, and I was, well, I don't know, some other food.

Feeling like the third wheel when the two of them were together always hurt my feelings a little bit, but there wasn't much I could do about it. How do you tell your fiancé that you're jealous of his sister? I'd mentioned this once to Michael, but he'd politely suggested that I was overreacting; he got to spend time with Mandy for only a few weeks every year and wanted to make the most of their visits. He had a point, so I tried my best to keep myself in check.

Still, despite all my progress in developing a generous spirit when it came to feeling competitive with other women, it was difficult for me to avoid comparing myself with Mandy. I felt jealous of their bond and of Michael's open admiration for her numerous talents and good qualities. Michael assured me that Mandy had her own insecurities, but she did a pretty good job of hiding them. She seemed so perfectly comfortable in her own skin and in her role as party instigator and creator of (according to Michael) the world's best Bloody Marys. She was his baby sister, and he had her on a pedestal. Frankly, I imagined that a non-filial version of Mandy was what Michael had probably hoped to find in a life partner, and this made me feel terribly inadequate; compared with Mandy, I was boring, uptight, and short. (Not that there's anything wrong with short. I've just never fully recovered from being exceptionally tall for my whole life until fourth grade, when I stopped growing. I played center for my elementary school basketball team; in middle school I was switched to forward; by high school I played guard, and in college I was benched.)

Of course, Mandy had always been incredibly nice to me and had welcomed me into their family with open arms, so I felt silly and guilty for feeling jealous of her bond with Michael.

Upon our arrival to my parents' home, Mandy whooshed in and gave me a huge hug. She bent down slightly, with squinted eyes, and wiped the side of my nose with her finger. "Much better, Martha! Your mascara was misplaced." I laughed and thanked her, and then got out of the way so Michael could get in his own hug. So far, so good. I braced myself for a busy weekend.

In preparation for the Ackermanns' visit, my parents had temporarily removed all of their Obama 2012 posters from the living room, stocked their liquor cabinet with Kentucky's finest, and bought tickets for all of us to attend a Cardinals game on Saturday. The date of the weekend, in fact, had been chosen to overlap with the Cardinals baseball schedule.

My mom insisted that we do a bit of prepartying at home before heading over to the stadium; her penchant for a deal was notorious, and I was delighted to see Sherry nodding in agreement. If nothing else, the two of them definitely had a love for bargain shopping in common. "The price of stadium beer is atrocious! Everyone should get started with what we already have here," she insisted. No one had any complaints about that, and by the time we headed out for the stadium, most of us were feeling a bit tipsy. Getting to the stadium involved a bit of a walk, plus a ride on the MetroLink, so we all poured ourselves to-go cups of beer to wet our whistles along the way. It was over ninety degrees out, with typical St. Louis humidity, so our ice-cold drinks were also helpful for temperature regulation.

After a few minutes of walking, we started separating into smaller groups of faster walkers and slower walkers. I ended up talking with Sherry for part of the way. We chatted just long enough for my blood pressure to rise.

"I read your blog post from last week," Sherry announced, patting my hand, "and I have to say, I am *so* proud of you for deciding to lose weight before the wedding. I lost almost twenty pounds a few years ago, and it was the hardest thing I ever did in my life. People thought it was easy because I lost it pretty quick, but it took a ton of work and discipline. It's hard, but I'm proud of you and I know you can do it. I'm rooting for you! You're going to look so beautiful in that wedding dress!"

I was speechless. This was one of the most enthusiastic and supportive things my future mother-in-law had ever said to me, yet she'd completely missed the point of what I'd written. Yes, I wanted to lose some weight, but I was really conflicted about it and needed to be exceedingly careful to avoid unhealthy dieting behaviors. I know it wasn't what she meant to communicate, but I was left with the distinct impression that Sherry thought I really needed to lose some weight, that I *should* be on a diet. That hurt. It was exactly the kind of comment (a Sherryism?) that kept me on my guard.

But I had to take a step back and think about what was really going on. I knew in my heart that Sherry had absolutely no idea that what she'd just said might have upset me. After all, I *had* blogged to the world that I wanted to lose a little bit of weight. Sherry knew what that felt like and was trying to empathize with me and let me know she was *proud* of me. She'd said so twice, in fact. How could I acknowledge her intent without bristling at the delivery? And how could I end the discussion before it went any further? I swallowed a big gulp of beer (and pride) before speaking.

"Oh, thank you, Sherry, that's such a nice thing to say. I'm trying to be healthier so I feel better," I said. It was the truth, after all.

"Yes, exercise is so important! I swim laps for an hour, every day that I can. It has really made a difference. And I only drink light beer," she joked with a wink, clicking her Solo cup to mine in a faux toast.

I called Michael over to walk with us, which made it easy to change the topic of conversation. I never in my life thought I'd say this, but I did: "So, how about those Cardinals?!"

We arrived at the stadium sweaty but in good spirits. My mom had made sure to order seats under a shaded canopy, though she hadn't been able to find seating for eight all next to one another. So we split up into groups of two, two, and four, with all of the parents sitting together and the two sets of twenty-something couples sitting on their own. The game went well, though we all had to take frequent breaks in the air-conditioned clubhouse to avoid heatstroke. Ample ice-cold beer helped, too.

Once the game ended, we all did our best to meet up together for our walk out of the stadium. Michael and I immediately noticed with relief that our parents seemed to have become fast friends.

"Your folks are going to visit us for a vacation in Florida!" boasted Sherry, my mom nodding vigorously beside her in agreement. I noticed that my mom had a slight wine mustache.

The stadium was packed full of people emptying into the streets below. None of us knew our way around, but we were determined to find a local bar within walking distance so we could keep up our good spirits with, well, more spirits. The crowds pressed against us, making it hard to stick together as we found our way. There were five or six iPhones between the eight of us, and nobody seemed able to get directions to pull up.

"We need a camp counselor to guide the way!" suggested Sherry. "I nominate Ken!"

Indeed, my dad, at six-three, was the most *visible* leader for the group and seemed the natural choice to safely lead us through the hectic crowd. I also knew for a fact that my father hated large crowds, so I wasn't surprised to see him take off at a decent pace. I doubted he actually knew where he was going, but just wanted to get away from where we were.

Just then, my iPhone dinged, letting me know it had directions to the bar we were looking for. They pointed in the opposite direction from where my dad was headed.

"Hey, everyone! I have directions! It's this way! Follow me!" I shouted exuberantly. I've always liked taking charge.

"This won't work," Sherry joked. "You're too short to be the leader!"

"I'm not *that* short!" I countered, also joking. I may have been the shortest person in our unusually tall group, but five-feet-five is *average* for American women. (And as I said before, there's really nothing wrong with being short!)

My mom came to my rescue. "Kjerstin isn't short, she's *just right!*" she asserted, giving me a one-armed hug. She said this with a smile, but I knew she was worried that my feelings had been hurt. It was nice to see my mama bear get all grizzly over the situation.

Sherry caught on to the possibility that she'd misspoken and corrected her earlier statement. "Oh no! I am *so sorry*. I didn't mean to say that you're short. I don't know why I said that. You're not short, really. I feel so awful." She truly looked ashamed. I appreciated that

Sherry didn't want my feelings to be hurt, but it really hadn't bothered me much. That said, I couldn't help wondering whether she was backpedaling so quickly because she *didn't* think I was short, or because she *did*. Either way, I just wanted the conversation to end. I was starting to feel embarrassed. This was turning out to be a night of uncomfortable Sherryisms.

Sherry turned to my mom and continued apologizing, saying, "I'm so sorry for saying that, Julie. Your daughter is lovely, and I don't know why I said that. She really isn't short." She paused a moment before continuing. "I'm just so lucky to have two tall children," she concluded with a proud sigh, as though that explained everything. I suppose it did.

My mom looked surprised, but quickly hit her stride. "Yes, we both have such wonderful children!" she asserted, shifting the subject away from the surprisingly contentious topic of my (relative) lack of height. I said a small prayer of thanks for my mother's adept social skills and hoped we were done talking about my body for the night.

Michael, who had overheard the entire exchange, made eye contact with me and gave my hand a squeeze. *Sorry!* he mouthed silently, not wanting the conversation to pick up again.

I mouthed back *Thanks*, and then announced loudly to the whole group, "We're here!" Thank god.

I was grateful that the rest of the weekend progressed without incident.

ON JULY 14, THE BLOG POST I'D WRITTEN ABOUT MY ANGST about dieting and feminism was picked up by two popular websites, Sociological Images and Jezebel. For a few hours I floated on air, feeling as though I'd officially "made it" as a blogger. The

Sociological Images post collected 438 Facebook "likes," and the Jezebel piece—actually just a two-sentence snip from my original essay—had been read by more than 25,000 readers. How exciting!

But then I read the comments, all 490 of them. I'd expected some discussion, and that's exactly what I got. My personal curiosity as to whether or not wanting to lose weight was antifeminist had stirred up some pretty strong reactions. I'd apparently blogged myself right into the midst of the "choice feminism" debates.

The term "choice feminism" was coined in 2005 by lawyer and scholar Linda R. Hirshman to refer to the popular feminist philosophy that, in her words, declared that "a woman could work, stay home, have ten children or one, marry or stay single. It all counted as 'feminist' as long as she *chose* it." Proponents of choice feminism support the idea that we shouldn't judge what any woman chooses to do with her life, because feminism exists precisely to give women choices. By this logic, self-proclaimed feminists who express disappointment in other women for not making the "right choices" are being elitist and doctrinaire. Since 2005, concerns about choice feminism have broadened from debates about housewives versus working gals to include numerous topics, including concerns about appearance. This is where I came in.

Some comments on my post reaffirmed my fears that being a "good feminist" required 24/7 vigilance and careful consideration of every decision, every word, and every thought. A lot of these commenters were frustrated by—okay, "fucking tired of"—choice feminism, and seemed to think that I was promoting it by asking the World Wide Web of feminists for permission to diet. Other comments, obvious examples of choice feminism, vigorously defended my right to diet. Many were somewhere in the middle, often empathizing with the angst I was experiencing and telling their own stories. The ones I found the most interesting, however, were comments that suggested that my choice to diet itself didn't matter, but that my *motivations* for dieting were the sticking points. This group thought it was okay—even commendable—for me to lose weight *if it was for my health*. But these same people seemed to think that the exact same behavior, dieting, would be unacceptable (at least from a feminist standpoint) if I was doing it to look better or to live up to anyone else's standards but my own.

This surprised me. Apparently, the greatest crime I'd committed when asking for "permission to diet" was not the diet part, but the asking permission part. This must be the flip side of choice feminism; just as passing judgment on other women's choices had been deemed antifeminist, so too was the act of *requesting* judgment. Wanting to please anybody but myself was apparently antifeminist. But I *did* want to please other people, preferably everyone!

My angst about being a good feminist seemed like just one more example of a chronic need for approval. I wanted to please everyone, from the most radical of feminists to my conservative and traditional future mother-in-law. By virtue of this, I also wanted to *be* everyone: I wanted to be a good feminist to my colleagues and readers, but I also wanted to be a good daughter to my parents, a good student to my mentors, a good fiancée to Michael, a good teacher to my students, a good future daughter-in-law to my future mother-in-law, and a good friend to my friends.

This wasn't a new thing. In high school I'd been a chronic overachiever of the worst sort. I was the student council president, an all-state track-and-field athlete, and the salutatorian of my graduating class. But these accomplishments didn't satisfy me. I felt disappointed in myself for not being the valedictorian, and a part of me was truly crushed when I wasn't voted onto the homecoming court.

(My mother had been the homecoming queen, so I believed I'd failed to live up to her legacy.) I cringed at these memories. How annoyingly self-involved I'd been. How in the world had my poor girlfriends put up with that crazed intensity and competitiveness? My desire to be the best at everything had left no room for me to appreciate and celebrate other people's gifts and talents. I felt ashamed by the memory.

But how much had I really evolved since that time? How many times had I promised myself I could have it all (which, of course, really meant *be* it all)?

As I read over the varied comments on my essay, it hit me: Even if all I'd wanted in life was to be a good feminist, it was clear that I wouldn't even be able to please all the *feminists*! Wanting to please everybody, and trying to be everything, was impossible. Recognizing myself as a chronic, lifelong people-pleaser felt so *lame* and disempowered. But I had to face it as a truth. I needed to let go of these crazy ambitions, or I'd never be satisfied with myself.

The more I thought about it, the more strongly I felt that my desire to please everyone by being everything might actually have *feminism* to blame, at least in part. Since childhood I'd been told that women could be anything we wanted and that I could have it all. I'd taken this message to heart, and then some, but it wasn't true or realistic. It wasn't even fun. There were too many contradictions embedded within my ambitions. I could be many things, but I'd have to choose which ones were most important to me, and I'd have to stop asking permission to be myself.

I decided it might do me good to make a list of all the people— real or imagined—I hoped to please, and then list them in order of importance, keeping my own name at the very top. Below the list I copied a phrase I'd recently seen at a coworker's desk: "I can only please one person per day. Today is not your day. Tomorrow isn't looking good, either."

But would a decision to "stop asking permission" be at odds with last month's commitment to practice trust? I decided that this wasn't the case; succeeding at both being myself *and* trusting others would involve choosing the right people to trust, and the right (wrong?) people to ignore. But how would I know the difference? Clearly this would involve more than simply trusting my gut (which sought universal approval); I would have to consciously contemplate my values and priorities and then ignore people whose opinions pushed me in the wrong direction. I would have to refine my "please everybody" instincts to become "please only those who make me a better person."

I realized then that I didn't want to ride the wave of choice feminism any longer. I didn't want to surround myself with people encouraging me to "do whatever I felt like" and telling me that any choice I made would be an empowered one. Instead, I wanted to surround myself with people who challenged me to do *better*, to live in accordance with my values. I wanted my choices to matter. I was reminded that the driving spirit of feminism had never been rooted in simply offering women more choices (although we do have a habit of chronicling successes along these lines). Rather, the core goal of feminism was to challenge structural inequalities, even if this meant sometimes harping on women who reinforced structural inequalities through their supposedly empowered "choices." I knew that sometimes *I* was one of those women, and that I could never expect myself to be a perfect feminist. Still, I could do better. My choices mattered.

We all have habits and urges that draw us away from our principles, but this doesn't mean we should seek out enablers. Indeed, our ability to suppress instincts in favor of ethics is perhaps the most defining characteristic that separates human beings from other animals. I needed to stop trying to please everyone, and instead seek appropriate role models whom I could trust for guidance and feedback if I began to falter.

Contemplating this balance between trusting people and following my own path led me to a phrase I thought worth sharing. As I journaled my thoughts, I kept circling back to the saying "People who matter don't mind, and people who mind don't matter." It seemed to be the answer to my puzzle, but something was missing. It didn't feel right to me that anyone, no matter how different from me or disapproving, could ever just not matter. I recalled my decision to avoid conflict with Sherry, when I opted to acknowledge her thoughtful intentions (even if I didn't like what she'd said). That had felt right, too. A mantra began to take shape. In my journal I wrote: *Act in accordance with your values. People who matter don't mind, and people who mind don't matter (but it's still important to treat people as though they matter!).*

This concept worked well. First, it prioritized values over anything else, and second, it provided guidance for accepting the support of people with my best interests at heart, along with permission to walk away from those who didn't. Finally, my decision to treat all people as though they mattered felt like a path toward empathy and connectedness. Awesome.

N THE AFTERMATH OF MY "AHA" MOMENT, I FOUND MYSELF feeling more at peace with myself than I had been before. I felt curious and pleased by the prospect of *discovering* myself, rather than shaping myself around what I thought other people wanted me to be.

It was during this week that I realized that I'd been having more and more episodes of not thinking much about my looks, while simultaneously feeling unusually focused on my work, errands, and even my relaxation activities. I was "getting away from myself" more than ever, and yet I felt like I was spending more time just *being* myself than ever.

I discovered several references that offered explanation for what I was going through. I suspect that during these episodes I was experiencing a form of what psychologists often refer to as *flow*. Otherwise known as living in the moment, being fully present, being in the zone, or being in the groove, flow offers a state of simultaneous pleasure and productivity in the absence of self-consciousness—a perfectionist's dream. (Along these lines, I suspect that writer's block is the polar opposite of flow, though I haven't seen any scientific statements making such claims explicitly.) I knew that I'd slipped into episodes of flow before forgoing mirrors, but never with as much frequency or ease as I did after removing mirrors from my surroundings.

This made perfect sense in light of the fact that mirrors are often used by psychologists to *induce* heightened feelings of self-awareness. (Other ways that psychologists induce heightened self-awareness include forcing research subjects to stand in front of a crowd or to listen to their own recorded voices.) We've seen some of this already in the research I mentioned earlier, on the relationship between self-objectification and mental capacity. However, psychologists suggest that increased self-awareness can be a *good* thing (at least when it isn't preventing underclothed people from performing well on their math tests). For example, in one famous study, Halloween trick-or-treaters were greeted at a researcher's door and left alone to help themselves to a bowl filled with candy. A note asked them to take only one piece. For half of the children there was a full-length mirror placed right behind the bowl of candy, while for the other half there was no mirror. Thirty-four percent of those without the mirror took more than one piece of candy, compared with only 12 percent of those with the mirror. The theory behind this study is the idea that people who are self-aware are more likely to make sure that their behaviors are in line with their values.

Self-awareness doesn't just improve the behavior of children; laboratory research with adult research subjects shows that people who are looking at themselves in the mirror are less likely to use stereotypes, are more helpful, and are more likely to behave morally if given the opportunity to cheat in a game. Another study found that eating in front of a mirror slashed the amount of food that people ate by nearly one third, which saddened but didn't surprise me; our culture is fraught with guilt tied to eating. These studies all illustrate something I'd experienced: The presence of mirrors increases self-awareness. That said, since flow requires a *lack* of self-awareness, it stands to reason that the presence of mirrors may *inhibit* flow, or at least make it more difficult to achieve. I imagined that removing mirrors from my environment helped me—and might help others— reach flow more easily.

The concept of flow helped give scientific explanation for my episodes of mirror-free bliss. It was pretty cool to forget about my looks for a while. However, sometimes this caught up with me.

Buying a new tube of mascara every three months on the dot wasn't something I'd ever done. Sure, I'd read numerous times that mascara is the cosmetic product that is (supposedly) in most need of frequent replacement, but my frugal side has always scoffed at those guidelines. In my mind, rigid makeup expiration dates seemed to benefit cosmetic companies much more than me; with the exception of sunscreen, I have always strategically pushed the limits of my products' supposed use-by dates.

Thus, I've always tried to use each tube of five-dollar mascara until it obviously wasn't working as well as it should. I refused to discard it one minute before this happened. Not doing this would feel deeply wasteful; I'd be racked with guilt.

That said, not being able to see the state of my mascara without looking at myself in a mirror may have legitimately pushed things past their limit. One day, after I was applying my mascara while sitting at my desk (Why at my desk, you ask? Why not? If you're not putting on your makeup in front of the bathroom mirror, you can put it on pretty much anywhere else!), clumpy flecks of mascara fell off the wand and onto my work space. Bits of mascara littered my keyboard, and a few specks had settled onto my left wrist. I smeared the fleck on my wrist to make sure I was seeing what I thought I was seeing. Indeed, it appeared that my mascara had turned. I could only imagine what my lashes had looked like over the prior few weeks! After all the hoopla about feminism and beauty, I debated simply not buying a new mascara. But then I'd be doing something just because other people said I should, which directly compromised my recent epiphany. I walked myself straight to the drugstore, bought a new mascara, and felt immensely satisfied by my purchase. People who mattered wouldn't mind.

N THE WAKE OF SO MUCH ONLINE DRAMA AND DEBATE, IT HAD been more than two weeks since completing my last BBCTG task. It seemed time for a bit more bridal beautifying. According to task #15, at some point "1–2 Months Before" my wedding, I ought to "use an at-home face mask or get a salon facial. (Don't risk an allergic reaction closer to your wedding day.)"

In the spirit of experimentation, I bit the bullet and spent thirty-five dollars at Target on a microdermabrasion and peel system and a conditioning clay mask. Thirty-five bucks was steep, but I was assured that I could return the products if my skin reacted badly. My next step: enlisting an unsuspecting amateur aesthetician.

Poor Michael was settling into an episode of *Weeds*, waiting for our Thai delivery to arrive, when I arrived home and accosted him with demands for assistance. I don't think he realized what he'd agreed to until he found himself following the microdermabrasion system's directions to apply "dermacrystals to clean, dry face (about the size of a quarter)." I assumed that the "about the size of a quarter" part referred to the scoop of dermacrystal goop, not my face.

As I stared at the ceiling of our TV room, Michael "gently massaged" my face for what must have been at least a few minutes longer than the recommended forty-five seconds. It must have been a good *Weeds* episode, because his fingertips started going numb around the time that my cheeks started tingling. Yowza!

"Shit, Michael! It's burning. Get it off!!" I shrieked.

He quickly, sloppily, applied "activator serum" to my face, and we both kind of freaked out when the ingredients started foaming. Apparently it was "normal to experience a warming sensation," but I'd had enough. I hauled my butt to the bathroom and gave everything a thorough rinsing. This took awhile since Michael had generously microdermabrased half of my neck and an inch of my hairline. He said I looked like a creature from the swamp.

My attempts to get Michael to help with the conditioning clay mask were temporarily thwarted by the arrival of our dinner. We were back to work soon after finishing our mango sticky rice. Michael finger-painted my face with the clay mask from Boots, which promised to clarify my skin "with a negative electrical charge to pull out impurities." It was olive green and slimy. Then it dried. Michael kept trying to make me laugh because whenever I smiled, green flakes of the dried mask sprinkled onto my T-shirt. I pondered whether we could find a way to actually test these flakes for their supposed "negative electrical charge," but it was almost midnight and my facial had already reached ridiculousness.

Michael headed to bed, looking bewildered by his new expertise. I washed all of the green goop off my face (at least I hope I did!). My skin felt really soft, but considering all that effort, I was more impressed by how empty my wallet felt.

I returned the products the next day, only to find out that, because they'd been opened, I could get only store credit, not my money back. Oh well. Finding ways to spend thirty-five dollars at Target wouldn't be too hard.

Even though task #15 had been a disappointment, and even though some of my online critics had taken issue with my decision to complete the BBCTG list, I knew I would keep having fun with it until the end. If modern feminism wanted me to stop asking permission, I could start here.

A S THE MONTH OF JULY CAME TO A CLOSE I FELT PROUD OF myself. I'd "come out of the closet" to my blog readers regarding my angst about weight loss and ended up finding closure on choice feminism—an issue that had haunted me for years. I'd experienced one of those rare *aha!* moments, realizing that, in my efforts to please everyone and be the best at everything, I'd held myself to impossible standards while also straining the connections I wanted to have with other women, whose own gifts and talents deserved celebration.

Deciding that I couldn't—and no longer *wanted* to—have it all felt so much more inspiring than the prospect of striving hopelessly to have it all for the rest of my life. All I had to do was be honest with myself about my values and ambitions, and then seek out people who helped me stay on course while distancing myself from those darned choice feminism enablers.

Had I solved the complex relationship between feminism and beauty? No. But I'd found peace regarding my own place within these debates.

SIX

August

MAKEUP FREE MONDAYS AND MAKING IT WORK AT WORK

If you're properly attired, you're hired. And if you're not, I don't care how "Qualified" you may be—it will be a case of "clothes, but no cigar."

MISS PIGGY

COMING OFF OF JULY'S "WHAT MAKES A GOOD FEMINIST?" drama and debates, I'd been giving some serious thought to going without makeup for a spell to see what would happen. This idea came about after reading through the comments that emerged in reaction to my essay about feminism and dieting. Several commenters had gone beyond discussions of weight and dieting to accuse me of committing feminist sacrilege by continuing to wear makeup and for working my way through TheKnot.com's BBCTG list. Yet just as many had said the opposite, that worrying about what anyone else thinks of me (even other feminists) would be, in and of itself, anti(choice)feminist. To diet or not to diet? To wear makeup or not to wear makeup? To embrace bridal culture or to shun it? It seemed that the answers to these questions were leading me toward a "double bind."

Defined as "a psychological impasse created when contradictory demands are made of an individual . . . so that no matter which directive is followed, the response will be construed as incorrect," the concept of a double bind is familiar to pretty much every woman in America (Madonna-Whore complex, anyone?). Sociologists concerned with gender inequality often use the concept of the double bind to describe the plight of women in the workplace. Because our culture continues to associate success and leadership with masculinity, ambitious women are forced to either challenge the norms of leadership or those of femininity. Some describe it as a choice between being respected and being likable. As Bart Simpson once famously muttered, "You're damned if you do and you're damned if you don't."

So what was *I* to do? In the wake of my entry into the debates surrounding choice feminism, wearing makeup seemed to be a choice that needed conscious deliberation. I hadn't gone without makeup for ages, but my no-mirrors project had already shown me that wearing much *less* makeup hadn't seemed to alter my life's course, and that it also saved time and money. More important, rather than try to meet anyone else's expectations, I wanted to base this decision on my *values*, particularly my commitment to challenge social inequality. I felt certain that makeup and fashion *could* be compatible with feminist ideals, but I also felt strongly that in order for this to be the case, their use should be rooted in creativity and pleasure, rather than fear of not living up to society's latest version of patriarchal perfection.

I spent quite some time contemplating my beauty routines and their meaning. In doing so I kept circling back to three words: *addiction*, *habit*, and *ritual*. Defined, an addiction is a condition of being compulsively occupied with or involved in something; a habit is a recurrent, often unconscious pattern of behavior that is acquired through frequent repetition; and a ritual is a detailed method of procedure faithfully or regularly followed, often as a religious rite.

I realized that for much of my life, my relationship with makeup had most closely resembled an addiction. I'd viewed makeup as a necessity, something I couldn't go without. The idea of not having it on hand made me anxious, so even though I applied it every morning, I also carried a small touch-up kit with me all day. This way of wearing makeup was one that reproduced social inequality. The beauty standards to which I held myself were exactly those that most reified hegemonic hierarchies of gender, race, sexuality, and class; my ability and willingness to spend a good chunk of each month's paycheck on new products and current styles was a manifestation of my class privilege; and, on a more individual level, my obsessiveness stole time and energy I could have used for more meaningful pursuits. This was an unhealthy addiction.

My decision to go without mirrors was the first time I'd battled the addiction. Yes, I still felt like I needed to wear makeup, but I'd eased up on the products I was wearing and no longer carried a touch-up kit with me. As my makeup practices became routine (and, frankly, boring), they entered the realm of an unconscious habit. Having a makeup habit seemed much healthier and more socially benign than a makeup addiction, but I decided I wasn't satisfied. I still wore makeup every day, without fail. Wearing less and worrying less were both good things, but I still found makeup compulsory and wore it in conforming ways. Also, if I wanted to wear makeup primarily for creativity, pleasure, and self-expression, I needed to wear it consciously. I needed my habit to become a meaningful-yet-not-obsessive ritual.

Using makeup for creativity and expression would have to wait until the end of my no-mirrors experiment, but growing comfortable wearing less—or none at all—would be an important first step. It was time to swing the pendulum again, even though it scared me.

Feeling frightened to go without makeup during a no-mirrors project might seem really weird, since I couldn't actually see myself. But even if I couldn't see it, I believed that my makeup helped me look more polished, more feminine, and prettier. Since cutting back on the number of products I was using, I'd even begun to feel (vain?) pride in my mirror-free makeup application skills. Hands down, the most frequent question women asked me after hearing about my no-mirrors project was "How do you do your makeup? It looks so good!" These compliments made me feel special and also had the effect of encouraging me to keep wearing makeup.

Leaving the house without any makeup scared me less than my earlier fears of leaving the house with poorly applied makeup; I'd prefer to appear as though I was rocking a new barefaced androgynous look than have my face resemble an application accident. I was also beginning to realize that makeup had been a security blanket. It probably had been my security blanket since my teenaged and young adult years of having bad skin, when I would have sooner left the house without brushing my teeth than without applying foundation, concealer, et cetera. I'll never forget the humiliation I felt when a Chinese foreign exchange student in my graduate program asked me, "My friend Kjerstin, what is wrong with your face?! It looks so hurt!" I started my second round of Accutane the next week. Recalling this history helped me understand why I felt more confident wearing my security-blanket's worth of makeup on my face, but I didn't have the same "this is really shaping how people view me" excuses I'd had back then.

Enter Makeup Free Mondays, a beauty movement promoted by BeautyBean.com, an airbrush-free beauty website dedicated to body-positive beauty. Alexis Wolfer, founder of BeautyBean.com, began Makeup Free Mondays (which I see as a delightful cross between Meatless Mondays and Casual Fridays) as a way to encourage women to feel more comfortable in their own (naked) skin and to stop seeing makeup as a requirement. This is exactly what I needed.

Still, the thought of going without makeup—especially at work—was terrifying. I'd spent the better part of the prior four years conducting research on how appearance shapes workplace discrimination. I was fascinated yet horrified by the demands of "aesthetic labor"—which includes a worker's appearance, style, and manners of behavior—in virtually every workplace. Different jobs, of course, had different expectations for appearance and style, but none were looks-neutral, and women and minorities generally faced stricter penalties than men for not conforming to aesthetic expectations at work. Add this to the myriad gendered, classed, and racialized stereotypes that influence how people interpret our looks and style choices, and it becomes clear that attractiveness is a moving target. Thanks to my graduate studies, I simply knew too much.

Remember back in Chapter One, when I wrote that attractive people are advantaged in the workplace? Well, this is generally true, but I may have oversimplified things a bit. In truth, the relationship between beauty and success in the workplace is fraught with complexity; in most workplaces and jobs, attractiveness is rewarded in hiring, respect, and promotions, but this isn't always the case. Sometimes it's actually more advantageous to be plain.

For example, studies reveal that unattractive women may be disadvantaged while working low-level positions, such as being a secretary, but in upper-level positions, and in fields that are historically male-dominated, good-looking women may be viewed as too feminine, less intelligent, and less competent (not only by men, but also by their female peers). In a study of attorneys, it was found that the very best-looking female attorneys were less likely to achieve partnership before their fifth year after graduation from law school compared with average-looking women attorneys. Many scholars believe that a "bimbo effect" exists, causing extremely good-looking women to be penalized in labor markets and be taken less seriously. I'd certainly observed hints of this in academia, with the opposite being true in the fashion industry.

In another interesting study, similarly complex patterns appeared regarding criminal sentences for crimes: Attractive female offenders, whose offense was not deemed to be appearance-related (i.e., burglary), received greater leniency than unattractive offenders. However, when the offense was perceived to be attractiveness related (i.e., swindling or con jobs), attractive offenders received *harsher* punishments than their unattractive counterparts! In other words, this body research suggests that if a woman's job is one in which she is seen as being able to unfairly "get ahead" by being beautiful, she'll be judged more harshly, as though she'd used her beauty to con her way into advantage. However, for jobs in which attractiveness seems unrelated to success, being beautiful might be a bonus, thanks to that darned halo effect.

Styling and makeup present another area of complexity. For example, the amount of makeup a woman wears impacts the extent to which she will be seen as likable, competent, trustworthy, and attractive. Researchers showed study participants photos of women that had been digitally altered such that the same woman would appear in different photos wearing four different levels of makeup, described as none, natural, professional, and glamorous. In the first study, subjects were first shown the images for 250 milliseconds. In a second study, a different set of research subjects looked at the same photos for unlimited amounts of time. The women in the photos were rated in terms of competence, likability, attractiveness, and trustworthiness. The researchers found that, when the faces were shown very quickly, all ratings went up with increasing use of cosmetics, regardless of the look. However, when research subjects were given unlimited time to view the photos, the results changed. As explained by one of the study's authors, "When they got to the more dramatic makeup looks, people saw them as equally likable and much more attractive and competent, but less trustworthy." Supporting this idea that too much makeup is detrimental for women, another study found a correlation between increased time spent on personal grooming and lower income.

Researchers have found a "Goldilocks effect" (yes, this is a real term) when it comes to breast size and how women are perceived in the workplace; breasts should be not too small, not too big, but *juuuust* right. In one study, participants watched one of four videos in which a female actor delivered a speech on a neutral subject. The only difference between the four videos was the size of the woman's breasts, which ranged from A to D cups (the researchers had the naturally small-busted actor stuff her bra with increasingly voluminous amounts of cotton padding). After watching one of the videos, participants were asked to assess the woman on a number of characteristics. Women were generally *not* influenced by breast size, but men perceived the woman more favorably on both professional and personal characteristics when her breasts were medium-size, i.e., neither too small (A-cup) nor too big (D-cup).

Knowing what this body of research predicted about beauty and the workplace was torturous for me. Wear makeup, but not too much. Medium breasts are ideal, so pad your itty-bitty-titties or mind your melons. Try to be as attractive as possible if you're in a low-status position, but downplay your attractiveness if you want to be taken seriously as a leader. Trying to navigate all of the potential variables was overwhelming, especially since I had three professional roles: graduate student, college instructor, and volunteer/activist at About-Face. Sometimes knowledge is power, but other times it's paralyzing.

In light of this, abandoning makeup once a week might provide a refreshing break from my overanalytical calculations . . . but would it come at a cost?

F OR MY FIRST MAKEUP FREE MONDAY, I WAS SCHEDULED TO teach two lectures. Raising the stakes even higher, I'd invited Lisa Wade, a well-respected sociologist and cofounder of the Sociological Images blog, to give a talk in my Sociology of Deviant Behavior class. Lisa was a role model of mine, and even though I suspected that she didn't give a fig about makeup, I wanted to feel like I was putting my best self forward when I spent time with her. I'd never imagined that I could be at my best without at least a swipe of mascara, some concealer, and pinched cheeks for a healthy flush. But instead of my normal mirror-less makeup routine, I left my condo that morning wearing only sunscreen and lip balm.

Of course, I had to decide what, exactly, counted as makeup. For example, was it fair to decide that my SPF15 makeup primer oughtn't count as makeup since it wasn't tinted? A sales rep at Sephora had promised me that this primer would help both "brighten" and "even out" my skin tone. Would it count if it enhanced my skin tone, even if it wasn't technically makeup? What about curling my eyelashes? Using an eyelash curler was obviously *not* makeup, but it wasn't exactly natural, either. What if I ate berries with breakfast and they "accidentally" stained my lips and cheeks in stunning shades of makeup-free raspberry-rouge and blackberry-blush?

I stared at the sheet hanging over my bathroom mirror and contemplated not washing my face, in hopes that the prior day's waterproof mascara was still clinging to my eyelashes. What would be less awful, greasy skin with dark lashes or clean skin with invisibly blond lashes? With a sigh, I went ahead and washed my face. I applied the sunscreen/primer, curled my eyelashes, looked longingly at my makeup kit, and then added some SPF30 lip balm to my lips. My face felt great, but not being able to see myself in the mirror made the whole process really anticlimactic (yet nerve-racking). I felt like a freak for missing the *scents* of my foundation and lip gloss.

What did I do with the five minutes I'd shaved off my morning routine? I must have been desperately craving contact with some non-makeup cultural symbols of femininity. I sniff-tested all of the perfume samples I'd collected over the past few years and decided to spray myself abundantly with something called Touch, by Tocca. It had smelled great in the sample sprayer, but not so much on me. According to the marketing materials, the core scent notes of the perfume should have been gardenia and balsam. Sadly, even though the sample sprayer smelled like gardenia (heady romantic floral), I just smelled like balsam (a resinous pine tree). I spent the next few minutes unsuccessfully attempting to wash the scent off my wrists and neck. Overall time saved: *negative* three minutes. Oops.

After all of this I felt really nervous to leave the house. I felt more nervous, in fact, than I'd felt at the beginning of my project when I hadn't been sure if I'd applied lipstick to my eyes and mascara to my nose. All I knew was this: I was barefaced and I smelled like a pine tree. Was I about to commit career suicide (i.e., the worst-case scenario)? Or was I about to experience a major body-image breakthrough?

What actually happened fell a bit short of a major body-image breakthrough, but certainly wasn't anywhere near career suicide. Simply, nobody noticed. Or, if anyone did notice, nobody said anything or acted very differently; not my students, not my office-mates, and not even Lisa Wade, with whom I had a lovely chat over coffee after her guest lecture. I guess this doesn't surprise me on a logical level, but on an emotional level I'm still suspicious that people were just being nice. Then again, maybe being nice is all that should count?

The next day I wrote up the whole story in a blog post, and promptly received the following comment from Lisa Wade:

I didn't even notice that you weren't wearing makeup! :)

An exclamation point *and* a smiley from Lisa Wade? Score! It felt awesome to know that a role model of mine was engaging with my project. Still, I knew that my questions about makeup—whether I needed it—couldn't be answered through just one Makeup Free Monday. I'd need to take this show on the road. Going without makeup while teaching in my own lecture hall was one thing, but my professional life extended across a variety of venues, including giving conference presentations at the upcoming annual meeting of the American Sociological Association, as well as my work in the About-Face offices. Also, I didn't know this yet, but my professional and personal lives were about to clash colorfully into each other, publicly and dramatically.

'D PLANNED TO SPEND THE REST OF MY WEEK TEACHING MY classes and prepping for my upcoming trip to Las Vegas for the annual meeting of the American Sociological Association, the biggest and most important conference for sociologists to attend each year. I was looking forward to meeting other graduate students and sociologists from across the country who shared my research interests. This year's ASA would also be a valuable opportunity for me to share and get feedback on my own. I was slated to give two presentations; the first would be about a research project I'd done on beauty standards and gender norms in sororities, and the second presentation would be based on a research project I'd done with my mentor, Abby, and my friend/colleague, Dave Frederick, that explored whether reading news reports on obesity causes people to express more fat prejudice. I would be presenting my own research, but Abby would be giving the other talk, which took some of the pressure off. Regardless, I had two PowerPoint presentations to create.

And so, on Tuesday morning, the day after my first Makeup Free Monday, I settled into my office at UCLA to get some work done. I'd made about an hour's worth of progress when a text message pinged on my phone.

"There's an article about you in the Bay Citizen!" wrote Jennifer Berger, the executive director of About-Face and a good friend of mine. This was exciting news, but not a huge surprise. A few weeks back, after my blog had been picked up by Sociological Images and Jezebel, one of the About-Face interns had drafted a press release explaining my project and my work with About-Face and had sent it out to a few local news groups. We were all hoping that any news coverage of my story might help bring some much-needed attention to the work that About-Face was doing. A writer from the Bay Citizen, a nonprofit news site in San Francisco, had been the only reporter we'd heard back from. I'd spoken with her on the phone for a few minutes, and we'd all crossed our fingers that she'd get the story approved. I clicked on the link Jennifer had provided in her text, pleased to find that the article ("Local Blogger Swears Off Mirrors for a Year") had been overwhelmingly positive about my project and had also included a great description of About-Face along with a link to the website.

"Yay!" I texted back to Jennifer. "Glad the press release caught some attention!"

I turned back to my work, but was quickly distracted by an unexpected flurry of e-mails to my inbox. Apparently, the Bay Citizen article had caught the attention of a slew of other news media. Within hours, I'd been contacted by several radio stations requesting on-air interviews and by reporters from the Huffington Post, Canada's *Globe and Mail*, and San Francisco's ABC news station. Was I going viral?

The next few days passed by in a blur of radio interviews and local media requests, broken up by my desperate and distracted attempts to prepare for my talk at ASA. On Wednesday, Jezebel ran an article titled "Can A No-Mirrors Campaign Change How We Think About Beauty?" and by Thursday I'd been interviewed on a handful of small radio stations. I was excited and flattered by all the attention, but felt overwhelmed by the near-constant bombardment.

Nothing shocked me more than hearing from a writer at *The New York Times* who wanted to pitch my story for their wedding section, Vows. With excitement verging on delirium, I called Michael immediately.

"*The New York Times* might want to cover *our* wedding!!" I shrieked with delight.

"Huh!?" he asked warily. "What, exactly, would that entail?" Michael had, up until this point, been excited and amused by my ten minutes of fame.

"Well, before we could even be considered we'd have to fill out this really long questionnaire," I explained. "Then, if we got picked, they'd send a reporter and a photographer to be at our wedding, and we'd end up in the paper and on the website. How cool is that?! Your mom is going to flip!"

I heard only silence from Michael's side of the conversation.

"Hello? Are you still there?" I inquired.

"I'm still here," he responded with a sigh. I heard him take another deep breath before continuing. "I'm just not sure how I feel about this. I don't want to rain on your parade or anything, but the idea of having a reporter at our wedding makes me feel really anxious. It's going to be stressful enough for me to recite vows in front of all our family and friends."

"Oh," I responded, gulping. I'd forgotten about Michael's dislike for public speaking. "Can't you just take a couple of beta-blockers or something?" I suggested obnoxiously. I figured we'd both be walking down the aisle under the influence of at least a few glasses of champagne anyway, so why not add an antianxiety medication to seal the deal before we sealed the deal? Then we'd both be happy, right?

"I really can't think about this right now. I'm about to go into a meeting. Can we talk about it later?" he asked.

"Okay," I agreed, realizing I may have been a bit overbearing. "I'm sorry. I didn't mean to stress you out."

"It's okay. I want to be supportive. Just promise me you won't agree to anything like that without talking to me first, okay?" he pleaded.

"Of course not," I promised. *He'll come around,* I told myself. Who could refuse *The New York Times?*

After hanging up the phone, I immediately went back to the *NYT* Vows website and started filling out the lengthy questionnaire. It started simply enough, asking for details about the wedding date and the ceremony venue, but quickly evolved into something reminiscent of a detailed curriculum vitae—for every member of my family as well as Michael's. Around the time I finished entering my father's occupational details, my enthusiasm crumbled. This felt like bullshit.

I'd been floating around in the clouds of bridal fluff, imagining myself to *finally* be the kind of person who ended up in the *New York Times* wedding section. Instead, I felt like a shelter mutt trying to fake a pedigree, all for the privilege of competing in some hoity-toity dog show. It felt fake, even though the prospect of having my wedding on those infamous pages tugged a bit at my heartstrings. But who, exactly, was I trying to impress? And why was I furiously filling out this questionnaire-cum-pedigree-chart when I had two important professional presentations to prepare for?! I'd jumped onto the bridal ballyhoo bandwagon once again and needed to get off at the next stop. I forced myself to turn back to my PowerPoint presentations, muttering, "Sanity comes first, sanity comes first, sanity comes first . . ." under my breath.

T HE NEXT MORNING I FLEW TO LAS VEGAS TO ATTEND MY CONference. I'd managed to finish giving a handful of radio interviews and was proud, but hopeful that the media attention might be settling down. I wanted to spend my time at the conference focusing on my research, not my no-mirrors project. Very few of my colleagues even knew that I was shunning mirrors, much less blogging about it, and I hadn't forgotten my advisor's warning that anything that resembled autoethnography wouldn't be taken very seriously by "the academy." For the next four days I wanted to keep my professional and personal lives as separated as possible. As my plane landed in Las Vegas, I promised myself that I would ignore any media requests that trickled in over the next few days and wait to deal with them until I got back home.

What I didn't know was this: In between the time my plane had taken off and the time it landed, Yahoo! had published an article about my no-mirrors project on its home page.

I suddenly found myself bombarded by a whole new level of media interest. Even though my first taste of press attention had been fun and flurrisome, I soon developed a new appreciation for that old saying about having too much of a good thing. My smartphone pinged and pinged and pinged with new e-mails, texts, and calls.

Gone were the polite requests from local radio shows and nonprofit and feminist news outlets. I'd no sooner unpacked my boring conference suits and hugged my friend Liz (my roommate for the conference) than I began to receive an onslaught of e-mails and phone calls from the big guns; producers from *Rachael Ray*, Anderson Cooper's new talk show, *Anderson Live*, *The Doctors*, *On Air with Ryan Seacrest*, NBC's *Today*, and ABC's *20/20* were all interested in having me on their programs.

I was flattered (okay, thrilled), but the timing was horrible. Of all the weeks in the entire year, that week was the one in which I most needed to focus on my research and connecting with other sociologists in the academic community. I thought I might be able to just put off getting back to the requests (this usually worked in my personal life!), but ignoring the e-mails and calls wasn't working; if I didn't answer quickly, they'd just try again, sometimes using a different e-mail address or phone number. I was in way over my head and starting to freak out.

A few minutes later I received a panicked and angry text from Michael. Apparently when one of the producers hadn't been able to reach *me*, they'd gone to the trouble of looking up *his* contact information. This person had called the main number for Michael's department at Stanford, asking to speak with him. I felt awful, and angry. That was just plain rude!

I'd no sooner apologized to Michael than I received a cryptic e-mail from my mom:

Good morning, my sweet daughter! Please don't take any of those awful Yahoo comments seriously. I hope you're okay. Call if you need to talk. I love you.

What's she talking about? Awful comments? What awful comments? I tried in vain to connect my laptop to the hotel's wireless network so I could read the article for myself.

"Here, I'm connected," Liz offered, handing me her laptop.

I entered my name into a search engine and prepared for the worst. My smartphone continued to ping.

I found the Yahoo! article and scanned it for trouble. First, I noticed with pleasure that the author had included a photo of me that happened to be my favorite from the engagement photos Michael and I had taken several months back. I really loved that picture. I thought I looked cute and even a little bit glamorous, wearing my favorite bright blue Tracy Reese jacket. The text of the article was similarly nice and balanced, with no outrageous critiques or accusations.

What's the big deal? I wondered.

And then I read through the comments, all 1,063 of them.

Plenty of them, particularly those written by women, were supportive of my project and kind, but the comments written by men were another story. Most of them dismissed my project by accusing me of being fat, ugly, stupid, or some combination of the three. Words like *heifer, fatso, dogface, feminazi, fugly* (aka *fucking ugly*), and *fucking stupid ugly-ass fat bitch* were scattered across the page. They even made fun of my favorite jacket.

I couldn't stop reading the comments, not even after my hands started shaking and the tears began to flow. It was like a horrible car accident I couldn't look away from. I knew that many of my role models in the Health at Every Size community had experienced this sort of public fat-shaming and had dealt with it gracefully, but this was my first time and I crumbled. When I reached the end of the comments I was in a state of shock. I'd spent so many years calling myself fat and worrying that I was ugly, and here, it seemed, was proof that my critical voice had been right all along. Sure, my body was healthier now than when I'd been in the midst of my eating disorder, and I was grateful for this, but it was still awful to be told I that was ugly, and therefore dumb and worthless.

Even the few kinder posts seemed to doubly confirm my fears of fat, such as when one man gallantly came to my defense by saying, "Plus-sized chicks are hot. It's a shame society makes women believe that you have to be a toothpick to be beautiful." Completely true, of course, but not how I usually defined myself. Speaking of which, my horrified reactions to being described as fat made me feel like a Health at Every Size phony; it had been easy to proudly endorse body diversity from the safe confines of my average-size (and, thus, infrequently bullied) body, but when it was my turn in the hot seat I wavered.

I wanted to call Michael, but felt too ashamed. Several of the comments had expressed pity for my future husband (i.e., "I feel sorry for the idiot who's marrying her. What a train wreck! Get out now!"), and I didn't want him to know this and feel ashamed, too. Instead, I called my mom, crying.

"I'm such an idiot!" I sobbed. "I never should have started this stupid project. I felt so confident, but I must have been delusional. Now I'm just humiliated. I feel like I just got put back in my place. Maybe I deserve this for thinking I wanted the media attention."

"Calm down, Kjerstin, it's going to be okay. Really," my mom soothed. "Don't let a bunch of anonymous bullies intimidate you. They don't know you, so those comments weren't even about you. To them you're just some woman—*any* woman—who did something without their permission. You struck a nerve, that's all. Trust me, confident women who don't apologize for themselves will always upset insecure and old-fashioned men. If you start apologizing for yourself now, they'll have won!"

She was right, and I knew it, but I wasn't yet finished with my pity party. I needed to wallow in sadness for a spell, licking my wounds. My mom listened patiently for a while longer as I cried it out. I knew that I needed to let myself experience all of my hurt, frustration, and embarrassment before I would be able to move past it.

There is beauty in the breakdown, I reminded myself. *Let go. Let go of control. Just ride the wave.* This mantra had helped me survive emotional anguish in the past, and I needed to call on it again now. The idea was simple: shame, fear, anxiety . . . all of these were as much a part of the human experience as pride, joy or pleasure. Running away from negative feelings—or trying to ignore them in hopes that they would just go away—never worked. But consciously sitting with them, getting to know them, and allowing myself to fully experience them—as awful as it seemed—made me feel stronger. I liked to envision emotional pain as an ocean wave: impossible to stop but exhilarating to ride. Okay, well, I wouldn't exactly describe emotional turmoil as exhilarating, but willing myself to fully experience it does make me feel more alive. This is what makes a breakdown beautiful to me.

And so I sat with my feelings for a while, and once I'd exhausted myself and grown bored of feeling "fully human," I was calm again. I was okay. It was time to summon up some anger.

My mom was right. Those comments weren't about me, they were about what I represented: a woman who hadn't asked permission. It wasn't personal, it was political; it was misogyny; it was patriarchy; it was fat-hatred; it was everything I'd ever wanted to fight against, both for myself and for other girls and women. Here was an opportunity to be a role model instead of another victim. I didn't want any of my blog readers—or *any* woman or girl, for that matter—to see me cave in to this torrent of cruelty by validating the insults as anything other than bullying. I turned to my Top Ten list for inspiration. I knew my naive three-year-old self would have been completely destroyed by this cruelty, which was exactly why I couldn't let other women absorb these messages without me putting up a fight. It was time to channel Miss Piggy's karate moves (HI-YA!). I still felt hurt, but I would fake it 'til I made it. I would be a role model.

I didn't know exactly how, but I was determined that those sexist, misogynistic bullies would not have the last word.

TRIED MY BEST TO PUT THE BULLYING OUT OF MY MIND, AND the next few days passed by in a blur of conference presentations, networking, and putting off making any decisions about the media. I tried my best to forget about the circus I'd stumbled into in my private life, and instead did my best to focus on my professional life. My presentation on Sunday went well, as did my coauthored talk on Monday.

Monday was my second official Makeup Free Monday, and it went well. In addition to ditching my makeup, I also ditched my contacts in favor of my favorite pair of cat-eyed glasses and felt completely in my element. I couldn't help noticing that at least half of the other women at the conference weren't wearing any makeup, either, and wearing my fun glasses made me feel like the chic geek I wanted to be. *Sociologists rock,* I thought. It occurred to me that I'd felt more pressure to be fully made up and fashionably chic when spending time with my hip and trendy college students than I was feeling with my more down-to-earth colleagues. I knew this had to do with my belief that my students were less likely to take feminism seriously if I looked like a stereotypically angry-and-ugly feminist.

Helping my students think critically about gender inequality had always seemed worth it to me, but at what cost to my own sense of authenticity?

That night, after Liz and I enjoyed a few free cocktails at the casino, I drafted the blog post I'd been mulling over ever since reading the Yahoo! comments. I'd needed a few days away from the situation to collect my thoughts and gather confidence.

In it, I addressed some of the more thoughtful critiques of my no-mirrors project and thanked my readers for their support. Next, I set some ground rules for civil debate: "I WILL be deleting any bullying (i.e., "you are UGLY/FAT/STUPID/CRAZY") comments left on this blog . . . As I like to tell my students, it is fine (in fact encouraged!) to critique ideas, but not people. In particular, I will not tolerate misogyny or fat-hatred, and especially do not want my readers to see these types of comments and feel threatened, bullied, or insecure by proxy." I didn't want to seem ashamed or apologetic, so I closed with my all-time favorite Miss Piggy quote: "Beauty is in the eye of the beholder, and it may be necessary from time to time to give a stupid or misinformed beholder a black eye!"

I reread my post one time before uploading it to my blog. I fell into bed emotionally exhausted but proud of myself. I couldn't control what was written about me on the rest of the Web, but I could control the content on my own website. When other women visited, they would see no hate and no shame.

ONCE THE MEDIA FLURRY—AND ITS ACCOMPANYING ONLINE bullying—began to settle down, I was finally able to catch my breath and think about all that had happened that month and what it had meant to me. August had begun with my decision to explore how wearing (or not wearing) makeup was shaping my life, particularly my professional life. I'd decided that my choices mattered, and therefore deserved a closer look. My resulting commitment to Makeup Free Mondays had led to tangible progress, particularly when I learned that my professional environments allowed ample flexibility for this (at least in the direction of wearing *less* makeup . . . wearing *more* might have had the opposite effect!). Yet this step back from vanity was accompanied by an unexpected step *toward* it, as I found myself enjoying my moment in the media spotlight (at least until those trolls had their say!). I felt conflicted about liking the media attention and terrified that my professional colleagues would judge me for spending time on a mostly nonacademic project. Then I felt conflicted about feeling conflicted. Was I shallow and vain to enjoy the attention? Or was the pressure I felt to behave modestly just another gendered double bind? Would a man in a similar position have felt so conflicted? Would a man in a similar position have been subjected to the same flavor of online abuse?

These questions would remain mostly unanswered, but one thing felt certain: Whether I enjoyed the attention or not was less important than how I used it. Being the target of cruel, sexist, and misogynous Internet bullying had been awful, but it had incited a sense of social responsibility. Standing up for myself might not have been the most "ladylike" thing to do, but it had been the right thing. HI-YA!

SEVEN

September

MIRRORS FOR SALE(S)!

Many a man thinks he is buying pleasure,
when he is really selling himself to it.

BENJAMIN FRANKLIN

SEPTEMBER WAS SHAPING UP TO BE THE MOST HECTIC month of my project. I simply had too much going on, including putting my condo on the housing market, wrapping up final lectures and grading for my two summer classes, celebrating my bachelorette party, traveling to Louisville for a future-in-laws-hosted engagement party, and moving all of my things from L.A. to San Francisco permanently, all while wrapping up numerous final wedding details.

September also marked the sixth full month of my project. The halfway point—Day 183—was fast approaching and would fall on September 24, exactly one week before my wedding. With so many months behind me, I felt confident that I'd finally transitioned to life without mirrors; things that had formerly been challenging were no longer so, or were at least easier to manage. *I've totally got this!* I thought to myself. I knew that my wedding day might pose some internal challenges, but I felt certain that the tough stuff was behind me and that avoiding mirrors would be smooth sailing from here on out. How very naive I was.

Deciding to sell my condo in Los Angeles had been difficult, as the housing market in L.A. was less than ideal at the time. I felt bittersweet about leaving the place where Michael and I had met for the first time, even if I was leaving it to move toward a future together with him. Michael and I knew that our choices were to either (try to) sell the condo or to rent it out while we waited for the market to bounce back. I was wary of managing tenants from across the state and anxious to have my mortgage debt behind me since my employment prospects were uncertain, so we decided to put the condo on the market to see what happened. We figured that we could always rent it out if it didn't sell.

I met with the realtors who would be managing the sale. They introduced themselves as Patty and Chad, but I immediately renamed them Barbie and Ken in my mind. Both were gorgeous blond Hollywoodesque types, with long limbs, ice-blue eyes, and almost-too-perfect teeth. Dressed in pastels that highlighted their "I spend all of my weekends at the beach" tans, I couldn't help wondering if they had coordinated outfits for effect. I was a bit dazzled, but snapped out of it in time to talk business.

"Your home is lovely!" Patty/Barbie began, while walking through my living room and kitchen. "I don't think we'll even need to stage it," she continued. I was flattered, but suspected her tone might change once she saw my bedroom and bathroom. I was right.

"Why is the bathroom mirror covered with this . . . What is this? A sheet?" Patty/Barbie asked, bewildered.

I began to explain my no-mirrors project, apologizing profusely for the covered mirrors, when I was interrupted.

"Oh my gawd! I heard about you on the radio! Are you the girl they interviewed on the Ryan Seacrest show?!" Patty/Barbie squealed.

Embarrassed, I confirmed that, yes, that had been me.

"Well, that's wonderful! Our new client is a *celebrity*!" Patty/Barbie exclaimed with a smile. I knew she was mostly just trying to flatter me, but I hoped her enthusiasm would spill over into the marketing of my condo.

"Will you be willing to uncover all of the mirrors for showings? We're hoping to have your first open house next Saturday, the eleventh," Chad/Ken asked cautiously.

I assured them that this wouldn't be a problem. I'd be in Kentucky on the eleventh anyway, and moving back to San Francisco soon after that.

"Oh good!" Chad/Ken responded, clearly relieved. "We don't want buyers thinking that a vampire lives here! Well, maybe one of those kooky Twilight fans would like that, but I wouldn't count on it," he snorted. Patty/Barbie giggled along, and I tried to do the same.

In addition to uncovering the mirrors, Barbie and Ken also recommended that I stage my second bedroom, which was now unoccupied since my last roommate had moved out a few weeks ago. Being on a strict budget, I was looking forward to this creative challenge. To make a "bed," I inflated a queen-size air mattress and then placed it on top of four identical decorative storage boxes for height. A small bookshelf from my closet became a side table, and a desk lamp became its reading light. A naked air mattress sitting on top of four storage boxes wasn't going to fool anybody, but I knew I could disguise the getup with a mountain of pillows and the right bed linens.

For more inspiration, I looked up "how to stage a home" online and stumbled across a wealth of tips and information, including this one:

> *Decorate using mirrors instead of paintings or photographs on the walls. Mirrors help bring in more light, and a large mirror can make small rooms look larger.*

Versions of this last tip came up again and again in my research about home decor. It seemed that, to realtors and interior designers, mirrors offered both aesthetic and practical advantages over other decorating options. Not only were mirrors more aesthetically "neutral" than paintings or personal photographs (which a buyer may find distasteful), but they also helped reflect light throughout one's home, and a large mirror could make rooms appear more spacious.

This made sense to me. Since beginning my year without mirrors, I'd noticed how frequently mirrors were used to decorate stores and restaurants. Restaurants, especially, seemed to love adorning their walls with humongous mirrors, probably to give the illusion of having a dining room twice the actual size. For this reason, I'd often found myself forced to sit at restaurants with my back against a (mirrored) wall. I'd also noticed that covering the wall-to-wall mirror in my bathroom had made it look much cozier. I loved cozy, but I knew that in real estate listings *cozy* was just a euphemism for *itty-bitty-teeny-tiny*. Chad/Ken was right to insist that I leave the mirrors uncovered for any showings.

But then I stumbled upon a more specific tip for using mirrors to sell homes.

*Place a mirror in the entryway of your home so your buyers can
literally see themselves living in your home.*

This idea seemed reasonable enough—that is, until I read another article that insisted that sellers ought to use a "skinny mirror"
for this purpose. In his article "Skinny Mirrors: You Look Great,
and the House Does, Too," Pat Kennedy, real estate agent and
contributor to *The Washington Post*, explained that it isn't enough to
make your house look great; you want potential buyers to like how
they look inside of your home. Described as "an interesting form of
subliminal marketing," Kennedy insisted, "We don't want our listings to make people look fat!"

Had I read that correctly? I needed to make sure my home didn't
"make people look fat" or else they might not want to buy it? This
didn't sit well with me, but I couldn't help giving it some thought.
Skinny mirrors, those beloved and hated mirrors that are concavely
warped *just subtly enough* to make one look slightly slimmer, but
not to such an exaggerated extent that we doubt the veracity of
what we're seeing. Sure, funhouse mirrors had been showing us our
outrageously stretched out or squished down reflections for years,
but we know when we're looking at a funhouse mirror. The beauty
(or ugliness) of a skinny mirror is in its subtlety; the effect is slight
enough that we believe—or want to believe—that what we're seeing
isn't warped at all.

Skinny mirrors have haunted retail shoppers as an urban myth
for decades, crystallized in our cultural history through an episode
of *Seinfeld* in which Elaine buys an expensive dress at Barneys because she looked great in the store's mirrors, but is then horrified to
find out that the dress looks awful on her everywhere else. She becomes convinced that Barneys had used skinny mirrors to dupe her,

and tries to return the dress, accusing the store of "false reflecting." Cher Horowitz, the fashionista protagonist of the popular 1990s film *Clueless*, expressed similar skepticism about mirrors while choosing an outfit for an important date, explaining to her friend, "I don't rely on mirrors, so I always take Polaroids!"

Those who wish to see themselves skinnified (or who want their potential home buyers to do so) can buy their very own "The Skinny Mirror" for $69.95 from FunHouseMirrors.com, an online retailer that apparently specializes in false reflecting. The marketing copy for The Skinny Mirror reads: "This mirror . . . is known as: The convex mirror, The woman's mirror, The diet mirror, The 'Wow, I look good' mirror and The 'I will have that dessert' mirror!" and guarantees that "the further you stand back the skinnier you get!" I found this mildly disturbing, thanks to the blatant sexism and the "I can eat dessert only if I'm skinny" attitude. But then I read the advertising copy for another product, called "The Fat Mirror," which was basically touted as a weight-loss product. The Fat Mirror was described as "The 'I shouldn't have eaten that whole pie' mirror, The 'I think I should start exercising' mirror, and The 'What do [you] mean a large doesn't fit' mirror!" It sent shivers down my spine to imagine women buying The Fat Mirror in hopes that seeing themselves looking chubbier than reality would help them stick to extreme and unnecessary weight-loss measures. Why pay $69.95 for a distorted body image when you can get it for free just by turning on your TV or flipping through a few pages of *Vogue*?

It's easy to laugh at the idea of a conspiracy of "false reflecting" by the retail garment industry, but it may not be terribly far from the truth. After all, in addition to the blatant advice offered by the realtor I already mentioned, an entire subfield of "environmental psychology"—not to mention millions of dollars spent on market research—has toiled to understand the environmental conditions under which people will spend more money at retailers. These researchers examine how different types of lighting, scent, music, and other aspects of interior decor shape our buying habits. These are the folks who advised grocers to put milk and eggs in the back of your local Shop 'n Save. These are the folks who advised fast-food owners to paint their walls and logos in warm colors, such as red, orange, and yellow (colors that have been found to increase appetite), and to play loud music and offer only uncomfortable chairs (so customers eat faster and leave sooner). These are also the folks who advise casino owners to banish all clocks and windows, to keep fluorescent lights turned bright, and to provide free drinks while people gamble, so that we're more likely to lose track of time (and money).

To think that potential uses of mirrors would be ignored by retail strategists would be naive. Indeed, Forever 21 has been accused of using tilted mirrors, positioned such that a shopper's head and shoulders look proportionally bigger than her stomach and hips, in order to increase clothing sales. Because Forever 21 gives only store credit for returned merchandise, shoppers have accused the company of intentionally creating the same type of "false reflections" sales that Elaine complained about on *Seinfeld*. I'd experienced these types of mirrors myself from time to time; in them, my head always looks a smidge big, and my legs appear lengthened. It can be disheartening to find out later that what you thought to be a flattering outfit is far from it.

But this isn't where mirror manipulations end. Taking a different approach entirely, Chico's, a plus-size retailer, removes mirrors from its fitting rooms entirely, forcing customers to venture back onto the sales floor—and into the strategic hands of enthusiastic sales clerks—in order to see themselves in the garments. I remembered my first time trying on clothes without a mirror, at Ross. The bored sales associate who told me I looked "fine" might have missed out on an opportunity for a big sale! As Julia Roberts would say: Big mistake. Big. Huge! (I've always wanted to say that.)

All this impromptu research about the ways that clothing retailers (and house sellers!) manipulate mirrors to trick customers into larger purchases made me feel almost relieved that I was currently immune to most of such trickery, and would be for another six months. Yet with several very special occasions looming in the upcoming days and weeks—including my bachelorette party, an engagement party, a bridal shower, my birthday, and my rehearsal dinner and wedding—I had retail on my mind. I wanted to shop. Even though I wouldn't be able to see myself in mirrors for these events, I hoped that once my project was over I'd be able to look back at the photographs and feel satisfied with how I'd put myself together.

T HE END OF THAT WEEK WAS THE KICKOFF OF MY BACHELORette party. A few hours before we were slated to begin, I traipsed off to a hair and makeup appointment with Sarah, the bachelorette hostess. Sarah and I have been close friends since the first week of graduate school, when we immediately clicked and soon ended up spending all of our free time (and homework time) hanging out. We'd spent a year as roommates, played on the same dodgeball team, and always "got" each other when life threw us curveballs. We'd been friends long enough to have a few "us" things, including a favorite Dave Matthews song, a favorite mouthwateringly sexy men's cologne (which both of our husbands now wear), and a love for going to get our makeup and hair professionally done together before big events, like birthdays and, now, my bachelorette party. It felt funny to realize that I was getting my makeup professionally done for my bachelorette party and not my wedding, but I couldn't resist enjoying something that had become a tradition for Sarah and me. Besides, she treated!

At the salon, I asked my hair stylist and makeup artist to go "Miss Piggy" on me, requesting bouncy curls and big lashes. It felt odd to be so fully styled without mirrors, but I watched Sarah being beautified across the way and figured that if I looked half as great, I'd be in pretty good shape for an evening of debaucherous girl time.

From there, Sarah and I headed back over to her place to join the other women getting ready. I brought several party-dress options; I wanted to gather my friends' opinions before choosing (trust! Huzzah!). Both Hanna and my friend Lisa (who, like Hanna, is extremely low-maintenance) were accosted by the rest of us, and Sarah and I enthusiastically chose their outfits, styled their hair, and applied their makeup; it felt like the cool-girl slumber party I'd never been invited to in middle school. In true little-sis style, Hanna ended up wearing the slinky dress I'd found at Nordstrom Rack. I opted for an even slinkier one I'd bought at Ross a few months prior for twenty bucks. It was bright blue with black trim, *super* short, and had cutouts at the waist and back. Paired with my favorite sky-high leopard-print stilettos and a bright pink tiara (a gift from my friends, to be paired with an embarrassingly bright pink feather boa), I felt adequately coquettish and ridiculous.

Once ready, we took cabs to a restaurant in West Hollywood, a self-proclaimed "Birthday and Bachelorette Party Headquarters" that was famous for a weekend drag queen burlesque show. I was looking forward to really letting loose with my girls, and the bawdy and colorful show didn't disappoint. The cocktails started flowing and we were soon hootin' and hollerin' through several boisterous acts by a set of incredibly talented and glamorous performers. It was turning into a perfect girls' night out. (Note to any bachelorette party organizers who are feeling inspired by this story: Unless the gay club you're considering has specifically identified itself as a "Bachelorette Party Headquarters," don't go there; it's obnoxious to flaunt girlie wedding bullshit in front of folks who, at the time of this writing, do not yet have marriage equality nationwide. An exception can be made if there are *two* brides, and they're marrying each other.)

Just before the last act, the MC called out to the audience, asking whether anyone was celebrating anything that evening. Apparently, every table in the house was celebrating some sort of event, as the entire restaurant suddenly began screaming and squealing. I found myself being pushed and pulled up onto the stage, along with a few more brides-to-be and birthday girls. Once we'd been introduced by the MC, it was announced that we were about to compete with one another in a "booty-shaking" contest. *Gulp.*

The rules were simple: Each contestant would take the stage for thirty seconds apiece to "shake her booty" along to the MC's choice of cheesy pop music. I knew I was moments away from feeling completely ridiculous, and possibly embarrassed, but the energy in the room was contagious. (Frankly, if the crowd had included a lot of heterosexual men I probably would have declined; nothing creeps me out more than being leered at by sloppy drunk men, which is exactly why I'd requested this venue for the party; the only men in the place were in drag, and they'd already strutted *their* stuff on stage.)

I watched the first two contestants bump and jiggle their way through choppy clips of Christina Aguilera's "Dirty" and Britney Spears's "Toxic." I was frankly impressed and intimidated by their moves, and glad I hadn't been first. (I later learned that the second contestant was actually a well-known *adult film actress*, which may explain some of her excellent performative skills.) I was relieved to see that the crowd was friendly and seemed to be rewarding enthusiasm over skill.

While watching the other contestants, I had a few moments to strategize, and also took a second to say a prayer of thanks that I'd chosen to wear a modest (i.e., very full coverage!) pair of undies under my short party dress. And then it was my turn.

LMFAO's "Sexy and I Know It" started thumping from the speakers, and I began dancing while my closest friends shrieked and screamed. I attempted my signature chicken dance and booty shake move, swung around the stripper pole once, and finished with a classic "drop it low" move (followed by a painfully geriatric attempt to "bring it back up" whilst wearing stilettos). For the first time in my life, I was glad to see a stripper pole; without it I would have fallen on my ass. It was exhilarating and scary at the same time.

I felt the vibrating thump of the bass below my feet and heard my friends cheering me on. Thirty seconds felt longer, and I remember having flashbacks to times in high school when I'd practiced "dancing sexy" in front of the mirror in my bedroom. Back then I'd self-consciously admired my body while practicing what I thought sexual confidence *ought* to look like. This time, in the surprisingly safe space of a drag queen burlesque show, I experienced a taste of what sexual confidence *felt* like. My memory of a table crowded with highly educated avowed feminists screaming their lungs out to encourage their friend's booty dance, well . . . that vision will stay with me forever.

Thanks to my friends' loud cheering, I actually *won* the contest! It turned out that the prize was awarded based on the crowd's enthusiasm, rather than on our dancing talent (though I'd like to think that my chicken dance had something to do with it!). My table had the most—and the loudest—people, so it was quite a coup. The adult film actress looked pissed, but I didn't care.

As the evening wound down, I found myself thinking that I felt completely beautiful. I'd had no idea what I looked like, but hadn't spent the night wondering or worrying about it. Instead, I'd unselfconsciously enjoyed myself in the moment, feeling comfortable, excited, and in good company. I'd spent the entire day feeling utterly connected to my girlfriends and sister, and this made me feel deliriously happy and lucky. This feeling of connectedness, along with the bodily confidence I'd surprised myself with during my thirty seconds of booty-dancing fame, made me wonder what it meant to *feel* beautiful. It wasn't a concept I could easily articulate or analyze in my inebriated state, but I knew I wouldn't forget the feeling. *The next time I feel like this I'm going to figure it out. I need a recipe for this feeling!* I promised myself. *Next time.*

THE NEXT MORNING I WOKE UP WITH A HANGOVER. I DID *NOT* feel beautiful; I felt like barfing. This shouldn't have surprised me considering the prior night's libations. I wanted to bury myself back into bed and hibernate indefinitely, but I needed to spend a few more hours with Hanna and Laila, who had traveled by plane to be at the party. Fighting nausea and a not-so-mild headache, I put on my best "I'm in horrible pain" face and asked my friends, "So . . . how's everyone *else* feeling this morning?" I was hoping for a unanimous declaration that we should stay in bed and watch HGTV.

Of course, everyone else felt just fine. *I'll be all right,* I thought. *I'll just tough it out for the next six hours and rest after I drop everyone off at the airport. What's the worst that could happen?*

"So . . . how do you guys want to spend your last afternoon in Los Angeles?" I asked. We decided to drive to Santa Monica to combine two fun things: shopping and beaching. We showered, dressed, and hit the road. It was a fifteen-minute drive, but we made an early stop to get breakfast. The prospect of solid food made me feel queasy, so we settled on smoothies. With a sixteen-ounce Orange Carrot Karma in hand, I began to feel better. I had renewed confidence in my ability to enjoy the next few hours. Onward!

My only request for the day had been that we visit Sephora so I could have help picking out some wedding-day makeup. On my Bridal Beauty Countdown to Gorgeous list was the instruction to "Meet with your makeup artist for a trial run. If you're not hiring a pro, get a makeover at a department store counter and purchase anything you need now (so you have time to practice)." I figured having my sister and close girlfriend in town and at my bridal disposal presented a unique opportunity to experiment a bit with makeup under the watchful eyes of two people whose taste I respected and who would also be physically present at my wedding to help replicate any makeover tips we gleaned from the pros. I figured I should get a long-wearing foundation and maybe some waterproof eyeliner.

Sephora has been a favorite shopping spot of mine for years, but I hadn't been in one for months. After all, it's basically a maze of mirrors wherever you look. I hadn't felt up to the challenge so had been avoiding the store, but the clock was ticking for me to take care of my makeup plans for the wedding.

The minutes after our arrival are a painful blur in my memory, but what I recall most clearly is being affronted by the overwhelming and overpowering scent of what seemed like a gazillion-billion perfumes and colognes. Walking into Sephora, I felt as though I'd mistakenly boarded an elevator filled with fifty great-aunts who had bathed in Chanel No. 5, Shalimar by Guerlain, and Opium by Yves Saint Laurent. My nausea returned and threatened to become vertigo. *You can do this!* I told myself. *You LOVE Sephora!* I was determined to make it through.

I swallowed a gulp of fresh air and marched in, breathing through my mouth. I found a sales associate whose makeup didn't look too ridiculous and announced, "I'm getting married in three weeks and I need help picking out a foundation to wear on my wedding day!"

She smiled widely, revealing lipstick-stained teeth (yikes!), and said, "Oh, congratulations! Let me show you some products I like." I followed behind her as she headed toward a makeup display. We must have walked past eight or nine mirrors on the way. I tried to ignore anything shiny in my peripheral vision, but it was still impossible to avoid all of the mirrors. I'd glimpse one and look away, only to find myself facing yet another one, having to look away again. It was dizzying. I forced myself to stare straight ahead, like a carriage horse wearing blinders.

With my imaginary blinders up, I didn't notice that both Hanna and Laila had meandered off onto their own paths. Suddenly it was just me, the saleswoman, and a store full of mirrors. *Gulp.* We arrived at our destination, and the saleswoman reached for a few bottles of something that looked outrageously expensive.

"Here, I'm just going to color-test you. Hold on one second," she said, as she delicately dabbed a bit of foundation onto the back of her hand. There were two colors, indiscernible to me, but apparently one had "cool undertones" while the other was "neutral." It occurred to me that I hadn't explained to this woman that I wasn't going to be able to look at myself in the mirror. *Shit.* I felt my pulse increase and couldn't bring myself to speak. The room felt oddly overheated, and the back of my neck went clammy.

I stayed perfectly still as the sales associate delicately brushed a line of each of the foundations onto my cheek. The lines of liquid foundation felt blissfully cool compared with the feeling of my reddening cheeks. *Say something!* I thought. *Now!* My eyes darted from side to side, hoping to catch a glimpse of Hanna or Laila. No such luck. But then my luck *really* ran out.

"Oh, you definitely have cool undertones," she said, as she reached for a handheld mirror. "Here, let me show you . . ."

As I cleared my throat to protest, I felt my stomach lurch. The room went blurry, and I knew it was too late to explain. Bile rose in my throat.

Don'tpukeinSephoradon'pukeinSephoradon'tpukeinSephora! *OMGOMGOMG!* I screamed silently to myself as I ran out of the store, hand covering my mouth.

I felt fresh air hit my face the moment I passed the entrance, but the relief was temporary; there was nothing I could do to stop what was happening.

I saw a large trash bin on the sidewalk a few dozen yards away and broke into an awkward sprint, my hands covering my mouth as though they could levee the oncoming flood. A few feet from the garbage, it started. Vomit. But it wasn't just any vomit. Bright Orange Carrot NOT-SO-Karma smoothie spewed from my mouth, spurting through my fingers. To my increased horror, once I finally reached the garbage, I saw that it was topped with some kind of roof thingy, so I had to wedge my head sideways in an attempt to aim. It was impossible; orange puke was everywhere, running down the garbage and all over the ground.

Onlookers scattered. I heard a child shriek, "Eeww! She's throwing up, Mommy!"

Yes. Yes I was. I was throwing up bright orange puke outside of

Sephora, with tears welling from the pain and humiliation. I finally stopped heaving, but didn't know what to do with myself. My hands were covered in sticky vomit, and I didn't have even a single sheet of tissue in my purse. I wanted to look around for help, but couldn't bear to face the stares I knew I'd encounter.

In a few seconds, I heard Hanna's voice behind me. "Are you okay?" she asked cautiously. I turned to look and saw that she and Laila were only a few feet behind. They both looked at me with pity and concern, and immediately went into awesome-friend/sister mode. Hanna had already grabbed a handful of tissues from Sephora, which she handed to me, while Laila ran off to a neighboring Chipotle to plead for a glass of water on my behalf. She came back with the water, as well as news of a public restroom nearby.

I followed Hanna and Laila to the restroom, where I managed to wash my hands and splash water on my face before rushing into a stall to throw up again. Thankfully, nobody was around to watch the spectacle that time, but it still felt awful. I was glad Hanna had seen me barf plenty of times since childhood. It also helped to know that she saw ukky bodily functions on a daily basis in her job as a medical assistant. She was unfazed, which helped me calm down, too. When I came out of the bathroom stall, Hanna had taken off one of her layered T-shirts, and she offered it to me.

"You have puke on your shirt," she explained, and I looked down to see that my tank top was, indeed, splattered in orange. Tie-dye it was not. Good to know. I washed up for a second time and changed.

Twenty minutes later the three of us were walking ocean-side near the Santa Monica Pier. I didn't feel up to venturing down to the beach, but we found a bench with a view and sat for a while in silence, soaking up the sun as it set over the ocean.

The salty air flowing in with the tide was the best thing I'd breathed all day. As I filled my lungs with deep, calming breaths, I recalled the oppressive perfume cloud I'd walked into at Sephora. Yes, I'd been hungover and already nauseated, but I also knew that my time away from my (formerly?) favorite store had changed it for me. Sephora no longer smelled like inspiration, and its flashes of mirrored light no longer looked like glittered glamour. Rather, for the first time, I'd recognized it—viscerally—as part of the invisibly oppressive "gilt cage" Mary Wollstonecraft had written of more than two centuries ago. The same dream was still for sale, but I wasn't buying it anymore.

THE SECOND FRIDAY IN SEPTEMBER MARKED THE END OF SUM-mer school at UCLA. I was relieved to wrap up both of my classes with final exams that my students could take online. Since the grading of my exams would be completed automatically through the testing webpage, my work was mostly done. All I had left to do would be to calculate final grades, send them out for students to re-view, and then manage all of the inevitable grade-grubbing and requests for extra-credit assignments that would be pulled at the last minute, before I submitted my *final* final grades to the UCLA registrar. Luckily, all of these things could be done remotely and electronically, rather than face-to-face; with no more in-person lec-tures to give, I was finally free to make my way back to San Fran-cisco. I couldn't wait. I'd missed spending time with Michael, and we had a wedding to plan, after all!

But there were a few events on the calendar that I had to get through before that could happen. First of these was a party—well, actually, two parties—to be hosted by Michael's parents in Louis-ville, Kentucky, where Michael had grown up. After learning that

Michael and I would be getting married in California and that our wedding guest list would be limited, Michael's parents offered to host an engagement party at their home to give their friends and extended family the opportunity to join in on the celebration, even if they couldn't make it all the way out to the West Coast. Although we knew that most engagement parties take place fairly soon after the engagement, it had been impossible to find an earlier weekend that worked, so we decided to bend the wedding etiquette rules a bit in favor of inclusiveness. Michael and I started calling it our wedding *pre*party. Adding to the festivities, Sherry's friends decided to throw me a traditional bridal shower on the Monday following the engagement party, so it would be quite the weekend!

The Ackermanns had chosen a festive 1950s Hotel de Cuba theme for the event, instructing their guests to wear their festive finest and stocking up on expensive back-channel-imported cigars and an armory stockpile of rum. The guest list for the party—which, other than my immediate family and grandparents, was primarily composed of friends and family on the Ackermann side—was notably larger than our entire wedding list. Sherry's party-planning skills were notorious, and it was sure to be epic. I was incredibly excited, despite my post-teaching exhaustion.

I would be traveling from Los Angeles to Louisville via a two-hour layover in Las Vegas. I was disappointed that my layover hadn't been routed through Chicago's O'Hare International Airport, as I'd recently read about a new technological innovation for displaying product advertising in "smart mirrors" in public restrooms. The restrooms in O'Hare were among the first places to implement these mirrors, which reportedly welcome consumers with digitized brand advertisements appearing on the surface of the mirror, much like the screen of a smartphone. As the consumer approaches the mirror, the advertisement migrates to the top right-hand corner, and the rest of the screen becomes a fully functioning mirror.

A CNN article interviewed Brian Reid, the founder and president of the Huntersville, North Carolina, company that manufactures and markets these smart mirrors. Apparently public bathrooms in airports had been selected because they are high-traffic. People use them right before boarding a flight and right after landing, and those travelers just about always stop to look at themselves in the mirrors above the sinks, Reid explained. So why not use these perfectly-functional-but-not-income-producing mirrors for advertisements? I wondered how people would react when seeing an unexpected advertisement as they looked at their own faces. I laughed out loud when I read Reid's explanation: "Well, it is an unexpected sight. . . . And some people do think, 'Gosh, is there no sacred place?' But we hope people realize that we have purposely chosen not to be around the toilet. We're over by the sink."

Yes, you read that correctly; this marketing middleman wanted consumers to be thankful that his company hadn't put their promotional smart mirrors *inside bathroom stalls.* Since I was shunning mirrors, I had selfish reasons to be relieved by this, but even if I hadn't been trying to avoid my reflection, I'm sure I would have found the smart mirrors placed inside toilet stalls to be ridiculous—not to mention intrusive. Still, I would have loved to watch people's reactions to encountering these smart mirrors for the first time.

Product advertisements in airport bathroom mirrors are just one application of smart mirror technologies. Indeed, the *smartest* smart mirrors are actually able to recognize the people or items that are being reflected in them, so that product advertisements and other digital content can be customized. For example, some department stores have begun installing smart mirrors in their dressing rooms. These "personal shopper" mirrors move eons past The Skinny Mirror by recognizing the articles of clothing being tried on by the shopper and then offering advice on matching accessories. The mirror scans the garment tag and then instantly displays items in the store that complement the garment. However, it was unclear whether these smart mirrors were programmed to know whether or not the garments complemented the wearer!

Using similar personalization technology, researchers have also developed an innovative voice-controlled mirror that offers new ways for consumers to control and personalize their media content, as well as technologies that help monitor and improve health. The "Magic Mirror," as *The New York Times* calls it, provides "motion sensing technology to read physical cues from a user, voice recognition to detect verbal cues, and an RFID [radio frequency identification] tag reader to recognize objects in the mirror's proximity," according to medGadget. One blogger described it as "a giant wall-mounted reflective iPad with a webcam."

The Magic Mirror might, for example, recognize a box of over-the-counter medication, or a bottle of prescription medication, if they were tagged with an RFID chip. The Magic Mirror could then display important information, such as directions for use of the medication, a schedule of when it should be taken based on one's calendar, doctor information, and the day of your next appointment with your physician. Of course, the mirror would also be wired to recognize consumer products so that it could offer customized coupons and promotions for these products, or those of their competitors.

Getting back to reality, my layover in Las Vegas was uneventful. I did visit one of the restrooms in my terminal, but the only magic I found there was some woman's left-behind ten-dollar poker chip, which I quickly blew through at a few of the penny slot machines while I waited for my flight.

I arrived in Louisville, Kentucky, later that evening, along with my mom and dad, who drove there from St. Louis. Michael flew in later that evening from San Francisco. After a few hours of catching up, we all went to bed. If Sherry's party-planning reputation held true, the next day we'd all be busy from dawn until dusk; we needed to be well rested.

There was much to do the next morning, so once breakfast was over we were all quickly swept into the party preparations. From wiping down a few hundred bar glasses to polishing the silver and setting out plates and napkins, we were all put to work. I laughed out loud to see what appeared to be a borrowed funeral-home-lobby sign in the Ackermanns' entryway that read WELCOME TO HOTEL DE CUBA! The caterers arrived and quickly took over the kitchen. A one-man Cuban drum band was setting up shop in the living room. Tiki torches lit a pathway to the house, and tropical plants and small potted palm trees lined the borders of the room, which was quickly converting to a dance floor.

"Oh! Make sure you don't take the price tags off those trees!" Sherry announced from across the room. "I'm taking them all back to the store tomorrow!" Hearing this, I felt a surge of camaraderie with my future mother in-law. It also reminded me that I needed to take a trip to T.J.Maxx to return the bed linens I'd bought to stage the second bedroom in my condo.

Once the bulk of preparty tasks were completed, I ran upstairs to get dressed and do my hair and makeup. In my attempts to stay on the Hotel de Cuba theme, I'd brought along two bright floral dresses for the trip. The first, which I'd bought at Nordstrom Rack the week before, was a one-shoulder-strapped blue-and-yellow number with a knee-length A-line skirt. The other was strapless in bright pinks and purples, with a poofy shorter skirt. I'd had this second dress for ages but hadn't found the right occasion for its debut. I'd initially planned to wear one of these dresses to the party and use the second one for the bridal shower on Monday afternoon. But my choices didn't stop there; on my way out the door to the airport, I'd decided at the last minute to also bring along my "Little White (reception) Dress" I'd bought on eBay (aka Wedding Dress #3). Since most of the guests at the party weren't able to go to the wedding, wearing this dress for both events seemed like a good way to get more bargain for my buck.

I turned my head from side to side as I peered at each option, but my eyes kept coming back to the delicate ivory embroidery on the bust of the reception dress, not to mention the glimmering silk shantung fabric of the all-the-rage-those-days bubble skirt. My mind had made itself up. Reception dress it would be!

I carefully climbed into the dress and tried to tug it up over my hips. It wouldn't budge past my thighs. *Whoopsie!* I thought. *I'm supposed to put this on over my head.* Moments later the dress was on but still unzipped, and I did my best to fasten some removable padded bra cups into the bodice using double-sided tape. When I'd first tried on the dress several months back, the bust area had gaped open whenever my posture was less than perfect, à la Gwyneth Paltrow circa 1999 in her infamous pink Ralph Lauren Oscar dress. Not wanting to flash my wedding guests with every shrug, I'd found a pair of removable bra cups that promised to "add a full cup size" to my bosom.

Once the cups were in place, I zipped the back of the dress as high as I could manage without help and slipped a button-down blouse over the whole ensemble to protect the white dress from makeup spills and smears. It was uncomfortably warm upstairs, and I was under two layers of clothing, so I was glad I hadn't managed to zip the dress higher than my lower back. I quickly applied my usual makeup routine sans mirrors in the bedroom, and then headed over to the bathroom where Mandy was getting ready. After helping me with my eye makeup, Mandy pronounced me "ready for action!"

"Could you help me zip this up the rest of the way?" I asked as I unbuttoned the blouse.

"Of course! Oh my gosh, that is the most beautiful dress! How cute!" she exclaimed.

But then she couldn't get it zipped past my midback.

"I think the zipper is stuck," she muttered.

"Oh, it always sticks at that seam," I replied. I wasn't too worried. I'd struggled to get the zipper past that very point when I'd first tried the dress on. It took some muscle.

"Here, I'll help," I offered. I took a deep breath and then blew all of the air out of my lungs while sucking in my gut. I used my hands to coach the fabric tighter around my front so it could reach closer together in the back. "Try now!" I choked, forcing a last bit of air from my near-collapsing lungs.

"Damn, it's still stuck!" she exclaimed. "I don't want to break the zipper!"

Feeling a pang of anxiety, I asked Mandy if she could go get my mom to help.

A few minutes later, my mom arrived on the scene.

"Oh, you look so cute!" she exclaimed. "And my goodness! Those bra cups certainly do runneth over, don't they?" she added with a singing chortle. I smiled with an exaggerated shoulder shrug, and the three of us began to battle with the dress. I tried to limit my breathing to shallow gasps of air, stolen in between zipping attempts.

"Are you sure this dress is the right size?" my mother finally asked a few moments later. I wasn't the only one who had started to sweat. "I don't want to break the zipper!"

"It fit a few weeks ago!" I insisted. "Seriously, just pull that zipper as hard as you have to. It won't break, I promise!"

As I felt my torso shrinking into submission, I imagined that I was Scarlett O'Hara being laced tightly into her corset by Mammy before the grand party at Tara. A few seconds later I was, indeed, zipped. Mandy scampered downstairs to join Sherry in greeting their arriving guests, and I attempted a sigh of relief; the air went out easily enough, but it didn't come back without effort. I hoped it wouldn't come to smelling salts.

My mom gave me a slow once-over as I spun around to give her the full view. "It looks a little tight, but not too bad," she said. "It's a beautiful dress, but are you comfortable? Can you move easily? That's the most important thing."

"Comfortable enough!" I responded, and it was true. Sure, it wasn't exactly my favorite pair of elastic-waistband jeggings, but I ought to be able to get through the next few hours. "It feels fine," I confirmed with determination as I slipped on a pair of matching white silk peep-toe heels.

"Well, that's good. The first guests are arriving, and I'm sure they'll all want to meet you!" she exclaimed. "You're the belle of the ball!" We headed downstairs together to join the festivities.

When Michael saw me, he broke into a huge grin and said, "You look amazing, sweetie!" It felt great to hear that; I needed an extra boost of confidence before meeting the rest of the raucous Ackermann tribe. I giggled a bit when he wiggled his eyebrows at my unusually cleaving cleavage. He handed me a freshly made mojito, and I took his arm to meet the folks he'd been speaking with when I came up.

Over the next few hours I must have met at least fifty people, all incredibly nice and welcoming. Unfortunately, all was not well with my dress. I could feel the bodice jutting into my rib cage, and the bra cups kept threatening to rise up through the low neckline. I was constantly tugging at my dress or slipping into the bathroom to reposition my breasts so that they fit into—instead of under—the bra cups, which seemed to have their own travel itinerary for the evening. The embroidered fabric of the dress rubbed against the skin below my armpits, and I began to feel overheated and sweaty thanks to the packed crowd. To make matters worse, I quickly realized that I couldn't sit down. I'd committed a cardinal clothes-shopping mistake—I'd forgotten to try sitting down in my dress. Even though the bubble skirt appeared loose and poofy when viewed from the outside, a constricting inner lining seemed stretched to the breaking point every time I attempted to rest my feet. I finally ended up half sitting, half leaning on the arm of Michael's chair. It wasn't the most comfortable place to rest my bum, but I needed a break from all of the standing and mingling.

My mom came up and asked me if I felt all right. "I hate to tell you this, but one of your bra cups is showing again," she began. "It's coming out near your armpit this time!"

After a deep sigh, I said out loud what we'd both been thinking: "This dress isn't working, is it? Tell me the truth."

"Oh, I'm sorry, honey, but it really isn't," she confirmed. "It looks nice enough when you're standing completely still, but whenever you move it fights you. It's just too tight, and those bra cups are causing

more problems than they're solving. You know what they say: You should wear the dress, and not the other way around, no?"

"Ugh! Why didn't you tell me this earlier?" I asked.

"I tried to! I asked you if you felt comfortable and whether you could move around. Sorry, but I think this one is on you," she said.

She was right. It was time to wave a little white flag of defeat. As I hurried upstairs to change into one of my other dresses, I felt relieved, but also terribly embarrassed. I'd wanted to look elegant and fashionable when I met all of the Ackermann clan, not as though I'd stubbornly (or moronically, or tackily, or—egads!—whorishly) stuffed myself into a too-small dress. As I slipped dress number two over my head, I tried to remind myself that "people who matter don't mind, and people who mind don't matter." I knew that this was true, but I still felt bad about possibly giving off the wrong first impression to Michael's family and their friends.

Twenty minutes later, I was feeling much better. After suffering from the constriction of my *too*-little white dress, I'd opted for the strapless number I probably should have chosen in the first place: no straps, no lining, no constriction, and heck, no bra (much less one that threatened to jump out from the dress each time I gesticulated or went in for a hug).

But I still had a bone to pick with Michael. I found him on the dance floor doing some version of "the sprinkler" with his dad. I cut in for a dance, which gave us the opportunity to chat.

"Why did you say I looked great when my dress didn't fit?!" I demanded. "It was really important to me that I look nice for this party, and apparently my dress was too small!"

Michael looked sheepish. "I didn't really notice that it was too small. I mean, I saw it the first time you tried it on, and it looked good then. But tonight I was mostly looking at your boobs," he admitted, a bit guiltily. I rolled my eyes as he led me into a spin. Oh well, at least *he* hadn't minded!

But how had this happened in the first place? The answer—and its lesson—was clear: I'd gone against my commitment to "practice trust" and paid the price. Instead of listening to my mom, who had suggested that I make sure I felt comfortable in my dress and could move around easily, I'd put my own opinion first and made a mistake. Sure, the repercussions hadn't been fatal (indeed, the fact that the Ackermanns' guests hadn't seemed to notice gave support to my mantra about those who matter not minding . . .), and to be honest I may have made the exact same decision if I'd been able to see myself in a mirror that night, but this was a solid reminder to accept help when offered and to listen to people worthy of my trust.

THANKS TO MY RECEPTION DRESS FIASCO, I KNEW WITH CERtainty that Wedding Dress #4 was the right choice for my wedding day. To clarify, I'd already committed to wearing it back when my mom had bought it for me, but a small part of me had still been drawn to Dress #1. That part of me had changed its mind. The prospect of having some kind of wardrobe malfunction, or not being able to comfortably sit down at my wedding, was a deal breaker. I shoved Dress #1 into the back of my closet and felt relieved that I'd taken my mother's advice.

My first dress fitting was scheduled for the Wednesday after I got back to L.A. I was determined to move back to San Francisco by the end of the following weekend, which meant that I needed to find a seamstress who could complete the alterations on my wedding dress quickly, and hopefully cheaply. Waiting to get it altered in San Fran-

cisco would be cutting it too close, even for me. Besides, with a bustling garment district in L.A., I figured I'd have a better chance at
finding a seamstress or tailor who could work within my budgetary
and timing constraints.

After scoping out different seamstress and tailoring options online, I'd landed on what seemed to be the right mix of positive reviews alongside claims of reasonable prices and fast turnover. Several
of my friends had spent well over $500 simply on the tailoring of their
wedding dresses, and I didn't want things to get out of hand. All I
wanted was a simple bustle so I could walk around without the train
dragging behind me, and—if possible—for the currently straight-
across neckline of my strapless dress to be converted to a sweetheart.
Even though the dress was a bit long, I would save at least a few hundred bucks simply by wearing extra-high-heeled shoes; I'd found a
great pair of nude patent-leather wedge platform shoes for thirty
bucks at T.J.Maxx. I brought these with me to my dress fitting to
make sure the seamstress didn't insist on bringing up the hem.

I'd asked my friend Lisa to accompany me to my fitting and act
as my eyes for the occasion. As I mentioned earlier, aside from
Hanna, Lisa is probably my most fuss-free and practical friend.
Raised in a small town in Wisconsin, Lisa had a love for cheese, an
easy smile, and rarely wore makeup. I knew that when it came to
wedding dress alterations, she would be wholly unimpressed by unnecessary fanciness. Therefore, I trusted her to let me know once I'd
reached my good-enough-is-good-enough standard.

I also wanted a friend with me for moral support, in case my
wedding dress ended up being too tight. According to the scale I had
at home, my weight had been mostly stable since mid-April, but the
too-little white dress incident had really thrown me for a loop. I told
myself that it would be okay no matter what as I carefully loaded my

dress into my car on the way to Lisa's apartment. But I didn't know how I would react if my wedding dress refused to zip up mere weeks before my wedding.

Lisa climbed into my car and we drove to the seamstress's storefront, which happened to be only a few blocks from her apartment. We parked and walked into a bit of chaos. The front area of the seamstress's shop was probably smaller than my bedroom, and filled with bolts of fabric, several half-dressed dress forms, and at least three sewing machines, one that looked to be at least a century old. Posters of Marilyn Monroe decorated the walls, and a portable three-piece screen divided a small changing area from the main room. A huge mirror leaned against the nearest wall. I peered at it from an angle, wondering how many other brides-to-be had passed through its view.

After peering around the screen and not seeing anyone, I called out, "Hello? Is anyone there?"

We heard the frantic yipping of what sounded like a pack of small dogs as a woman emerged from a door in the back of the room. She was a petite and busty brunette with tanned skin, dramatic coal-rimmed eyes, and indiscernibly ethnic features.

"Hi! I'm Jenny! Are you Kristen?" she asked, speaking so quickly that I almost didn't understand her.

"Yep, that's me! Actually, it's pronounced *Keeeeerstin*," I responded, reminding her, "I'm the bride that can't look into the mirror."

"Yes yes yes! That's right! And you need the alterations done real quick, right?" she asked energetically.

I nodded, then asked where I should go to try on my dress. "Do you have anything we can cover the mirror with?" I asked.

"Oh, you can just get changed out here!" Jenny suggested.

"Right here in front of the store windows?" I asked, confused.

The sidewalk was bustling, and I didn't want the passersby to become lookers-in.

"Oh, sorry! We can move the screen so nobody can see you," Jenny explained, reaching for the screen. It was at least three times her size, so Lisa stepped in to help out before it slipped and crushed her.

I asked Jenny if she had a bathroom where I could wash my hands before handling my wedding dress. I'd heard nightmare stories of women unknowingly smudging their dresses with dingy handprints during the alterations process.

"Actually I have a litter of Pomeranian puppies in my bathroom, and they aren't exactly house-trained yet. There's poop all over the floor!" she explained with a high-pitched laugh. Lisa and I shared an eyebrows-raised look with each other as Jenny continued. "Puppies! They're adorable!" she squealed. Perhaps noting our wariness, she explained, "I wanted my kids to witness the miracle of life! You know how it is."

Actually, I didn't know. And frankly, I didn't want to find out. Puppy poop and wedding dresses didn't sound like a good combo. What the hell had I gotten myself into?

I had a travel pack of wet wipes in my purse, which I hoped would do the trick. I handed the pack to Lisa, who raised her eyebrows at me in a "What the hell is up with this lady?" look. We were dealing with quite a character, to say the least.

Once the screen was up, blocking the windows, I began undressing while Lisa took my dress out of its garment bag. I slipped into my giant platform wedges and said a little prayer of hope that the dress would fit. Lisa gathered all of the layers together to slip the dress over my head while I covered my face with my hands to avoid getting any makeup on the fabric. I took a deep breath, let it all out, and held the dress up under my armpits while Lisa started to zip.

The dress zipped easily. Sweet relief.

"Okay, so what are we doing here?" Jenny asked. "The hem is good, and it fits you perfectly around your waist and bust. What do you need me for?!" she joked.

I explained the bustle and neckline I was hoping for, and Jenny nodded her head.

"I can get this done in a day or two, no problem!" she promised. The total bill would be under a hundred dollars. Despite my concerns about Jenny's state of mind, I knew I had no choice but to trust that everything would work out.

I dropped Lisa off with a hug of thanks, and then had to rush off to my next appointment.

I was going to get eyelash extensions.

Yes, you read that correctly: eyelash extensions.

Eyelash extensions were all the rage in L.A. at the time, according to my students. And I'd recently stumbled upon an online coupon giving a steep discount to first-time clients at a "lash bar" a few blocks from my apartment. Since I still had a habit of walking out of the door with waterproof mascara on my nose, the possibility of not needing mascara for the next two or three weeks was tantalizing. For thirty-five bucks, I'd have gorgeous, low-maintenance eyelashes for both my wedding *and* my honeymoon. I was excited, but also nagged by the fact that this was more of a want than a need. But maybe it wasn't so bad. After all, the only reason I was doing something so high-maintenance now was so that I could be *low*-maintenance later. That kind of canceled things out, right? Besides, the coupon wasn't refundable. *Maybe I'll keep this decision to myself,* I thought. *Eyelash extensions probably won't even be noticeable, since people are already used to seeing me wearing mascara.*

These second thoughts came to me as I sat in the small waiting room of what appeared to be a hair salon that had closed for the evening. Apparently the "lash bar" was just an after-hours thing.

Just as I was about to chicken out and write off the thirty-five dollars I'd spent as the price I'd paid for a moment of weakness, a door opened and out walked . . . Bambi. Well, obviously the client leaving the room wasn't actually a cartoon baby deer, but her eyelashes were gorgeous! Thick, long, dark, and yet somehow natural-looking. Ooooh! This was going to be awesome!

The lash aesthetician (lashthetician?) called me in. She looked to be a natural blonde, and yet, like her previous client, she had amazingly gorgeous, thick, dark lashes. I explained that I was getting married in two weeks and wanted to give my lashes a boost. After describing my whole no-mirrors project thing, the lash lady promised to be careful and said, "Oh, well then this will be especially perfect for you! When I'm done with your lashes, you won't need any eye makeup at all, not even on your wedding day!"

That sounded great to me!

I was told to lie down on the lash lady's table and warned that I would need to keep my eyes closed for almost a half hour. The woman taped some kind of lower-eyelash patch onto my face, which covered my lower lashes to the root. "We don't want to glue your eyes shut!" she explained. My eyes immediately began to water.

The patches were positioned to cover every bit of my lower lashes, which meant that they were seriously close to my eyeballs. Even with my eyes closed tightly, it felt a little ticklish. Tears began running down the outsides of my face. I wanted so badly to rub, or at least wipe, my eyes, but I forced myself to lie still as the woman got to work. *Just a few more minutes,* I imagined.

Just then, I heard a doorbell ring. "Oh, that's my other client! Be right back." I was alone for about five minutes, but then heard footsteps coming into the room. I couldn't help myself and removed the lower lash patches for some relief.

"Hey Kjerstin, my other client can't wait very long, so I'm going to do you both at the same time, okay?" It wasn't so much a question as an announcement. I gritted my teeth in annoyance, but responded positively. "Oh, it's okay. I understand!" I was at this woman's mercy and couldn't afford to be difficult. She placed the patches back on my face and got back to work. I could hear her wheeled chair rolling across the wood floor as she shifted between her other client and me. *Trust. Trust. Trust,* I chanted inside of my head. It seemed like forever before she was done.

"Ta-da!" shrieked the lash lady almost forty-five minutes later. I felt the lower-lash patches being untaped from my face and winced as I felt a few of my lower lashes being pulled out along with them. I opened my eyes and raised my hand to give everything a good feel.

"How long *are* they? I can feel them touch my eyebrows!" I said, alarmed. It didn't feel like just a "boost."

"Well, they're kind of dramatic, but it's for your wedding!" the lash lady explained.

I must have looked nervous, because she quickly promised to "trim them a bit."

I lay back down and closed my eyes. As I listened to the lash lady *snip, snip, snip* away, it was all I could do to stay completely still and pray that my eyebrows weren't being sacrificed. When she was done, I opened my eyes and noted with relief that my eyelashes were no longer tickling my brows.

"There you go. Perfect!" exclaimed the lash lady. I thanked her, wearily and warily.

On my walk to the car, I put my glasses back on and realized that, despite being trimmed, my lashes were still long enough to hit my spectacles when I blinked. I pulled my glasses a bit lower on my nose and drove home.

"Who does crazy shit like this two weeks before their wedding when they can't even look at what they've done?!" I muttered to myself. It was past dark, and I needed dinner and sleep. I'd overanalyze myself tomorrow.

T HE NEXT DAY I MET WITH ABBY FOR MY WEEKLY DISSERTA- tion status-update meeting. I was feeling pretty good about it. In the past several months I'd completed several interviews and knew that I had an interesting paper to write for my first chapter. We caught up for a few minutes and then began to discuss my dissertation plans. I'd just finished explaining what I thought was a pretty sharp idea for my first dissertation chapter when Abby interrupted me.

"I'm so sorry, but . . . ah . . . are you wearing fake eyelashes?" she asked. I cringed.

"Oh no, are they that obvious?" I asked. "I thought my glasses would kind of hide them."

"Not really . . . They're kind of, like, wow!" she said, blinking her hands open for effect. Apparently my eyelashes resembled the fingers on jazz hands.

"Oh, this is really embarrassing," I said, truly embarrassed. I attempted a weak explanation: "I found this coupon online for eyelash extensions, and I thought it would be a way to not worry about wearing mascara over the next few weeks . . ."

"Well, you definitely don't need to wear mascara, that's for sure!" Abby joked. I felt my academic credibility dwindling with every

spidery blink. Clearly my "lash look" was more Tammy Faye than
Bambi.

Once I was home that night I wanted desperately—more desperately than I'd ever felt since the start of my project—to dig out my
old magnifying mirror from the back of my closet so I could go to
town with a nice long and obsessive stare. I resisted, screaming on the
inside. Instead, I found myself morphing back to my scab-picking,
nail-biting, ten-year-old self. Warnings from the lashthetician be
damned, I couldn't keep my hands away from my eyelashes, and I
didn't care.

I picked and tugged for hours while I watched TV. Lash by lash,
my fingers searched relentlessly for little bits of glue and any uncovered faux-lash roots. It was soothing and satisfying, as most OCD/
trichotillomanic quirks are, at least in the moment. I banished my
usual "Stop this, you're a freak!" thoughts and just went with it. The
rest of the world faded away, as I thought about nothing other than
my determination to remove each and every lash, one by one. It was
a low moment. Sure, I wasn't obsessively counting calories or berating myself for not going to the gym, but compulsive behaviors like
this show up only when I'm under a lot of stress and not coping well;
I couldn't have stopped if I'd wanted to.

By the time Benson and Stabler had thrown the bad guys in jail
for the third or fourth time, I was done. A pile of spidery lashes lay
in my lap, and when I ran my fingers along the lengths of my lids, I
no longer felt anything foreign. I didn't feel much at all, actually.
Along with all of the faux lashes, I'd pulled out the majority of my
own natural ones. My eyes were almost completely lashless. *This is
not good,* I thought, still fighting the urge to pull out all the natural
lashes that remained. I didn't trust myself to resist, so I took a sleep-

ing pill and went to bed. If there was beauty in this breakdown, I hadn't yet found it.

T HE NEXT DAY I AWOKE WITH A MAJOR "WHO THE FUCK cares?" attitude. Finally. Paying money to have a perfect stranger glue fake lashes onto my face had been a stupid idea from the start, and if I'd trusted my instincts or paused for a minute to ponder, "What would Gloria Steinem do?" I never would have considered it. Compulsively pulling out most of my lashes hadn't been the most productive coping mechanism, but it had done at least one thing: It had pushed me to an edge, and then I'd fallen off of it. I was too exhausted and defeated to care about looking perfect on my wedding day. I was over it. SO FUCKING OVER IT.

This ended up being a good thing; my final dress fitting was scheduled for that afternoon. I didn't feel nervous at all; I felt brave. Carelessly, recklessly brave.

Lisa took the bus from campus to my place, arriving forty magical minutes early. We caught up for a few moments, but then realized we were both really, *really* hungry. Looking a little bit miserable, Lisa hesitantly suggested that we could wait until after the fitting and then enjoy a proper meal together. The unspoken assumption was that I probably wanted to be a little bit starving when I tried on my dress. You know: empty stomach = littler stomach = tears of joy when said stomach looked less chubby in my wedding gown. Except, of course, something about that equation was totally dumb. I mean, if a little food in my tummy was going to prevent my dress from fitting, shouldn't I want to know now, rather than on October 1? After all, I was planning to enjoy food on my wedding day. If anything, I needed to make sure that my dress had room for an expanding mid-section.

Emboldened, we quickly ventured out to the nearest burger joint. If you didn't know this already, Los Angeles is a burger city, so I never found myself far away from a fix when I developed this particular craving. On this day, we landed at the nearest dive, and I opted for the Burger of the Week, which was innocently described as a Cheesesteak Burger. And sweet potato fries.

I don't know what I was expecting, but when my meal arrived I realized that I'd essentially ordered the innards of a huge Philly cheesesteak piled on top of an already huge hamburger. It was two sandwiches in one. A chimera sandwich, if you will. Well, I won't bore you with the details of how amazingly delicious this was, but let's just say I managed to eat every bite. Since it took me both hands to eat my monster burger, Lisa ended up downing a hefty share of the awesome sweet potato fries, but I was okay with that. A girl has to prioritize, no?

Lisa and I were both super nervous about handling my dress with burger juice on our hands, and the burger stand didn't have a restroom. We cleaned up as best we could using paper towels and wet wipes. Then we headed over to see crazy Jenny, running a few minutes late.

The first thing I noticed once we arrived was that the neckline of my dress looked a bit wonky. Let's call it a Monet neckline; it looked decent from across the room, but kind of sloppy once I saw it up close. I knew that Jenny had actually cut the fabric in order to make this alteration, so there was no way to undo it. Bummer. I asked Lisa if she thought it looked okay, and she shrugged. "It's fine. Don't worry about it." *At least it looked fine from a distance,* I thought. My next thought surprised me: *Besides, who cares?* Indeed.

The moment I started thinking "Who cares?" things went extremely well. The dress felt amazing on my body; after a decent belch, the gown zipped up over my full-term food-baby without complaint. Lisa did all of the required oohing and aahing, which made me feel quite bridal, despite my full gut and absent eyelashes. I wiggled my hips, chicken dance–style, and squealed with excitement. It was one of those epic true bridal moments, hamburger grease and all.

On my drive home I decided it might have gone so well *because* of the full belly and hamburger grease, and especially because of the "Who cares?" How lovely to know that a bride-to-be can say "Oh fuck it" and then get exactly what she wants. Despite the craziness that it took to get there, I wouldn't have had it any other way.

THAT SUNDAY WAS THE FIRST OPEN HOUSE FOR MY CONDO. IN preparation, I carefully removed all the curtains covering the mirrors. *No vampires live here!* I said to myself, satisfied. I was pleased with how everything looked, but now that my room was filled with reflective surfaces again, it felt a bit dangerous. To avoid seeing myself, I spent most of the day in my office at UCLA, but once back at home I had to implement different strategies. I forced myself to adopt a slouching, stare-at-the-ground posture to avoid making eye contact with myself, but it wasn't comfortable and certainly didn't feel very bridal. This wasn't going to work. I didn't want to go through all the effort of covering the mirrors again, so I had to figure out another way to get through the next twelve hours. I opted for the simplest strategy I could think of: I took my contact lenses out and kept my glasses off. My blurred vision wrapped a fuzzy cocoon around me. Sure, I probably saw more reflections of myself than usual, but they looked to me like blotches of color. As with other areas of life, good enough would be good enough!

I DROVE BACK TO SAN FRANCISCO THE NEXT DAY, AND MY MOM arrived a few days later. A former coworker of hers, who was also a friend of mine, was getting married exactly six days before my wedding, and we were both excited to go to the event together. I decided to take advantage of the opportunity to do a trial of my wedding hairstyle, which had been chosen by my blog readers in a poll, and really see how well my chosen updo would hold up for a long event.

My mom liked the look, which was good enough for me, but a lot of pieces had fallen out by the end of the night; I'd have to request extra hairspray for my own event. But more important, my mom's close scrutinizing of my hairstyle had led her to notice my lashes, or lack thereof.

My mom was probably the only person on the planet who would notice a change in my eyelashes. Blushing, I mumbled my horror story about the extensions and prepared myself for a lecture. But she just laughed. "I wish I could have seen how they looked! Maybe they weren't as bad as you thought."

"I saw the look on Abby's face, and that's all I needed to know!" I responded. "But I wish you'd been there, too, so you could have warned me *before* that!"

Staying in my condo by myself over the past few days had revealed to me how much I'd come to rely on my friends and family to be my mirrors when I needed it. Maybe that whole "practice trust" thing had finally kicked in? I hoped so.

Now all that was left to do was to get married.

EIGHT

October

MY BIG FAT MIRRORLESS WEDDING

*Family faces are magic mirrors looking at people who
belong to us, we see the past, present, and future.*

GAIL LUMET BUCKLEY

O N THE AFTERNOON OF SEPTEMBER 30, IN THE MIDST OF all the chaos that shows up on the day before one's wedding, I found myself alone in my apartment for a spell. Michael had left to help pick up family and friends from the airport, and my mom and Aunt Sarah were off shopping for last-minute table decorations. I was waiting for Hanna and Peter to pick me up at my apartment so we could all drive down together. I was really looking forward to spending this hour-long drive with my siblings. By some odd miracle, Hanna was running late for the first time in her life. Then again, she was with Peter, who had probably never been *on time* to anything before. I should have been mad, but instead I was relieved.

With my mom and aunt in town for the past week, I hadn't had any time to myself in days. Constant socialization is torture for an introvert, even a closeted one like me; I'd compare it to not being allowed to sleep. Time alone is when I regroup and recharge. Because of this, having an hour and a half all to myself felt amazing, especially since it occurred just before all of the weekend's official events would start. I had a moment of calm before the storm.

I sat quietly on my bed for a few minutes. I closed my eyes and took a few deep breaths. I'd planned and anticipated this weekend for months. Every detail had been carefully contemplated, from the wording of our vows to the color of my toenail polish (blue, to finalize my collection of old, new, and borrowed items). Yet I realized that if I wasn't careful, it might all pass by in a blur. This worried me. I wanted to feel *present* at my wedding, to enjoy the events as they unfolded and to consciously fill my memory bank with special moments.

I was in the middle of one such special moment: alone with my own thoughts of what was about to happen. I really wanted to look at myself in the mirror. I needed to reconnect with myself, and looking at myself in the mirror had been my means to this end for years. *Oh no, you don't!* I chided myself. *Not gonna happen. Not now, not tomorrow. Hold yourself together!*

Easier said than done. I was on the brink of a major life transition, and I wanted to consciously honor this moment for myself. If I couldn't do it my usual way, I'd need to find another. Journaling was my second drug of choice.

I wrote a list of all of the special moments I wanted to remember. I started with the very moment I was in, and added several more: driving to the rehearsal dinner with Hanna and Peter; getting ready with all of my bridesmaids, my chosen family of amazing girlfriends; feeling my dad's steady hand as I walked down the aisle; seeing all of my grandparents, all alive and well, smiling at me on my way to the altar; making eye contact with Michael before our vows; enjoying every delicious bite of food and sip of wine during the reception.

As I wrote each thing, I imagined myself pressing the pause button on an internal remote. I wouldn't be able to remember every moment of the weekend, but I promised myself that the ones on my list wouldn't pass by on fast-forward.

Just as I finished up the list, my phone rang. Hanna and Peter were parked outside. It was time to go, and I was ready.

THAT EVENING'S REHEARSAL DINNER WAS A WONDERFUL OP-portunity to spend time catching up with friends and family. The speeches were epic and the food was wonderful. Sherry and Doug had really outdone themselves to make it a welcoming and festive event. We all laughed at the thorough roasting that Michael's groomsmen gave him. On the other side of the spectrum, my brother, Peter, gave a heartfelt speech that brought tears to my eyes and really brought down the house. It was the perfect kickoff to what was sure to be an amazing weekend.

THE NEXT MORNING I WOKE UP EARLY TO THE SOUNDS OF MY sister and the hairdresser setting up in the other room. I'd asked Hanna to take the first turn getting her hair styled, since she's a morning person. Next would be my high school friend Honora, who also didn't mind the early hour because she was on central time.

I drifted back to sleep for what felt like mere seconds before the doors to our bedroom banged open loudly. Mandy, who had arrived for her own hair appointment, took a running leap and landed in bed with us.

"Happy wedding day!" she shrieked. "Michael, you have to leave. Now! You shouldn't look at Kjerstin until later." Michael, still fast asleep, barely even moved.

Where did she find the energy? I wondered. It was barely eight a.m., and we'd been out past one a.m. I was surprised and relieved that I wasn't completely exhausted. I got up, threw on a pair of baggy jeans and an old tank top, and checked the clock, realizing that I still had time to kill.

Finally, two hours later, it was my turn to sit in the hairdresser's chair. Feeling brave, I told her, "The same thing as my trial, but with more hairspray and bobby pins. Can we do it with an Audrey Hepburn poof thing going on at the crown?"

"No problem, I'm on it!" she said, armed with a can of hairspray and a teasing comb. I settled into the chair and tried to relax. With impeccable timing, Hanna opened a bottle of champagne and poured a glass for everyone.

The hairdresser had just finished dousing my head with hairspray when I realized we had only an hour left before it was time to head over to the ceremony venue. I needed to get started on my makeup. I would be putting on my usual basics—foundation, blush, cream eye shadow—and makeup maven Mandy would help out with the finishing touches.

When Mandy had finished, I stood up and started gathering my makeup. I saw a flash of myself in the mirror as I turned around to leave. It happened so fast that it barely registered in my brain, but I remember my head looking unusually big, as though I were a living Bratz doll. *Hmm, must be my hair!* I thought with a stab of anxiety. It was too late to change anything (and I *had* asked for big hair!), so I tempered my panic by chanting "good enough is good enough is good enough is good enough" over and over in my head.

"Is my hair, like, *crazy* big?" I asked Mandy.

"Naw, it's good!" she replied. "Besides, remember what they say down south: The bigger the hair, the closer to God!"

"Well, as long as it doesn't look like a mistake . . ." I murmured, sighing.

"Not at all. You're the bride. Own it!" she countered. She had a point there.

And so I decided to put my unusually big head out of my head. As long as it didn't look like an accident (and Mandy swore that this was not the case), I would own it. Besides, what better time to be closer to God than on my wedding day?

THE ENTIRE WEDDING PARTY—BOTH BRIDESMAIDS AND groomsmen—loaded onto the shuttle taking us to the ceremony site, a small winery in Woodside, California. Even though tradition warns that grooms oughtn't see brides before the wedding, we decided to be practical. Michael's parents had generously offered to pay for shuttle transportation to and from the ceremony site, and it seemed wasteful to book separate shuttles for the men and women in the wedding party. Besides, I was wearing a pair of jeans and a tank top, so I probably looked like my regular self (save for the extra eye makeup and Bratz-doll head!).

When we finally pulled up to the winery, our wedding photographers, Geoff and Lisa, were there to greet us. Seeing these two made me feel immediately more relaxed; I trusted them completely. The ladies and gentlemen split in different directions to get ready; Lisa came along with us, and Geoff tagged along with the guys.

All of our hair was already done, but we still had to get dressed and touch up our makeup. When we got to the room, Mandy started helping me apply extra eyeliner as the other bridesmaids covered up the full-length mirror in the room. At first they attempted glamour by trying to drape it in silk pashminas. When this didn't work, they opted for the practicality of paper towels and masking tape. Good enough is good enough! Once this was done, they all disappeared into the bathroom to put on their dresses and get ready in front of the bathroom mirror, which would remain uncovered.

Reminding myself about my old, new, borrowed, and blue, I wrapped my great grandmother's pearl necklace around my wrist to wear as a bracelet, fastened the new pearl necklace Sherry had made me around my neck, wrapped my bouquet in a lace hanky I was borrowing from Laila, and admired my dazzling Tiffany Blue–painted toenails.

I headed to the bathroom so I could put on my wedding dress without flashing any unexpected visitors. I was careful to avoid seeing myself in the mirror as Hanna and Laila helped lift the dress over my head. I tiptoed back into the main room, barefoot and holding up the skirt of my dress in both hands. Hanna helped zip me up, and then, with Liz's help, held me steady as I stepped into my monstrously high heels. I heard the rapid clicking of Lisa's camera and looked up at her with a smile.

"How do I look?" I asked the group. This was one of those bridal moments, and everybody knew it; squeals, clapping, and oohing and aahing ensued.

"How do you *think* you look?" asked Laila.

"I think I look great!" I replied as matter-of-factly as I could muster. I felt *gorgeous*. Everything—all of the shopping, tailoring, beauty routines, and pampering, not to mention the soul-searching— that had brought me to this prototypical bridal moment was etched into my memory, and as I stood among my closest friends, I felt exactly how I'd always hoped I would on my wedding day: confident, feminine, glamorous, and—most important—loved.

I'd had my doubts in the weeks preceding my wedding, but right then, looking at myself in a mirror was suddenly not an option; I felt so good that I had nowhere to go but down. Suppose my hair wasn't exactly what I'd had in mind, or maybe my eye makeup looked trampy, or perhaps my dress actually fit kind of weird? Any of these things—and who knew what else—might have been true. But so what? A quick glance in the mirror could have given me only one of two outcomes: Either I'd look exactly as amazing as I felt, or I'd look worse. The first couldn't make me feel any happier, and the second would only add unnecessary and unproductive stress.

Did I believe—or even *want* to believe—that I looked perfect? No. I wasn't delusional, just practical. I believed in all of my heart that I looked good enough, and good enough was exactly how I wanted to feel.

There was only one thing left to do: I applied a swipe of strawberry lip gloss—the same one that I'd worn when Michael swooped in for that first kiss—and grabbed my bouquet. It was time to get hitched.

BEFORE I KNEW IT, THE GUESTS WERE ALL SEATED AND IT WAS time for the ceremony to start. We hurried outside, clomping up the gravel path in our teetering heels, to line up at the entrance of the ceremony site. Despite the beautiful view, it was surprisingly chilly. And windy. It was so windy, in fact, that my chapel-length veil began to blow around, out of control and into my face. I felt it smearily sticking to my lip gloss and feared that my voluminous updo was on the verge of becoming unhinged. I made my second executive decision of the day (the first having to do with my poofy hair).

"I'm ditching the veil!" I announced as I hastily unpinned it by feel.

Why had I wanted a veil in the first place? I wondered. Wedding veils have traditionally been associated with modesty and (virginal) purity, neither of which really applied to me. Worse, the groom's *removal* of the bride's veil is said to symbolize his taking possession of his wife, either as lover or as property. No thanks. Unveiling *myself* felt more aptly symbolic.

I heard the beginnings of our recessional music and took a deep breath. One by one, my bridesmaids and their escorts disappeared to walk down the aisle. And then it was our turn. I looked up at my dad, who asked, "Are you ready?" I nodded, smiling, and gripped his arm more tightly.

As I walked down the aisle, I did my best to smile and take in the view of my loved ones smiling back with support and encouragement. I looked down the aisle and locked eyes with Michael. He smiled at me, and then I watched with amusement as his face contorted into an awkward grimace. He was crying, but seemed to be fighting it with all the muscles in his face. Before that moment I'd never seen him cry. I remember thinking, *Dang, Michael is an ugly crier!* It wasn't the most romantic of thoughts, but in truth I found the grimace endearing. I couldn't help laughing, along with many of our guests, who had seen the same thing. The ice broke, and Michael wiped his eyes, laughing at himself.

My dad and I reached the front row of guests, and I turned to my mom, linking arms with her so that she could join us for the remaining few yards to the altar. And then, before I knew it, I was standing in front of Michael. Both of my parents hugged me, and my dad gave Michael a sporting high-five. The patriarchal handoff was complete!

I felt Michael squeezing my hands, and I smiled at him. "You are so beautiful!" he whispered as we turned to our pastor and waited for the ceremony to begin. As he said it, I knew it was true. How did I know? Because I'd already felt it. In that moment I decided this: If I *felt* beautiful, I was.

Twenty minutes later we'd recited our vows, exchanged rings, and shared a strawberry-lip-gloss-flavored kiss to the sounds of cheering guests. It was a done deal; we were married!

AFTER THE CEREMONY, IT WAS TIME TO GET THE PARTY started. Michael held out his hand to me for our first dance. We'd done our best to avoid any overtly mirror-themed things for the day, but the song for our first dance broke this rule; a beautiful cover of "I'll Be Your Mirror," originally by the Velvet Underground, had simply been too close to home for us to pass up. No phrase could better capture our relationship, our promises to each other, and our hopes for our future together.

Some might scoff at the idea of wanting my life partner to be my mirror. I'm sure plenty of choice feminists and body image avengers will be deeply bothered by the prospect of a modern woman look- ing to another person (a *man*, no less!) for feedback on herself. In fact, it may be more *en vogue* to tackle self-awareness, self-esteem, and self-improvement without care for what others think, but this hasn't always been the best choice for me. As someone with a history of spewing self-hatred at my "real" reflection in "real" mirrors, it felt wildly liberating to reject my anorexic inner voice in favor of the assurances (and sometimes thoughtful critiques) of a trustworthy and truly decent person. Finding a loving and supportive partner who already sees the best in me, and who pushes me to be more self-accepting—while helping me stay on path when I behave in contra-diction with my values and ambitions—has been priceless. If I'm good enough for Michael, I'm good enough, full stop. Being able to offer him the same is pretty awesome.

I was surprised to find out that Sherry and I had chosen to wear almost identical ivory faux fur jackets that evening. The rest of the evening went by in a blur. I remember eating a lot of my wedding cake (which had, unfortunately, toppled over during dinner) and urging my friends to "try all of the different wines!" I danced with each of my grandfathers, which was so special. Our photo booth, which came with a myriad of props, was a hit, and by the end of the night almost everyone was in some form of costume. It was joyful and epic, if I do say so myself.

I didn't look in the mirror all day, and I didn't miss it. I was proud of myself, but to be honest, it was probably the easiest day without mirrors that I'd had so far. After all, the real goal of my project wasn't simply to avoid mirrors, but to more fully experience everything else going on in my life. And, as you may have noticed, on my wedding day I simply had better things to do!

A FTER THE WEDDING MICHAEL AND I SPENT A WEEK AT HOME recovering and catching up on sleep and work. Then we were off to Hawaii for our honeymoon. It felt a lot like our recent camp-ing trip, only better (particularly because we were sleeping in real beds). There were no mirrors, no scales, less makeup, less anxiety, and less stress. I felt better and more self-accepting than I had in ages. Had marriage instantly solved my crisis of identity and body image? I suspected not. Rather, saying good-bye (aloha?) to my iden-tity as a bride-to-be—and all the bridal pressures that came with it—lifted a huge burden from my shoulders and psyche. I could return to my usual self.

It was during these days that I began to give more thought to what it meant to *feel* beautiful. How is feeling beautiful different from looking beautiful? In its most obvious sense, looking beautiful is on the outside, and feeling beautiful is on the inside. Looking beautiful is something most people want, but it doesn't actually guarantee happiness, and striving to look beautiful can cause a lot of misery, as I knew from firsthand experience. Even if we reach a point where we are, somehow, objectively beautiful, it can't possibly last. We age. We go out of style. We end up staring wistfully at a few old photos because we're convinced that at *that* moment—and perhaps never since—we looked beautiful (if only we'd known then . . .).

Before giving up mirrors, I'd never imagined I could feel beautiful without knowing what I looked like. I'd assumed that feeling beautiful was the hyperconfidence I sometimes experienced after getting a haircut or spending extra time on my makeup. But that was just what it felt like when I'd conflated my looks with my self-esteem on a good day. On a bad day, conflating looks with self-esteem had been disastrous. I knew that I'd probably looked less conventionally "beautiful" since starting this project, but in being so I'd managed to better separate my looks from my self-esteem.

Recently, I'd felt beautiful on two distinct occasions: on the night of my bachelorette party and again on my wedding day. One day I took a notebook to the beach and began to journal about the experiences. I hoped to more clearly articulate exactly what beautiful had felt like, and also figure out whether the feeling had required particular social or environmental contexts.

First I made a list of the multiple feelings that had combined to create "beautiful." The list included feeling joy, calm, confidence, pride, and peace, with a side of creativity. I decided that there was a tinge of vanity involved in feeling beautiful, but that it was the generous sort of vanity—the kind that allowed me to feel unique and special, while leaving space for every other person on the planet to also be unique and special. I couldn't have made this list before my no-mirrors project. Giving up mirrors had given me the opportunity to recognize the feeling of beautiful. With less knowledge of my body's appearance, I'd begun paying more attention to my body's feelings, both physical and emotional, and I'd developed a more acute sense of these things.

But what did my bachelorette party and wedding have in common that helped this happen? Could I analyze the context of these events to better understand this feeling of beautiful? Even more ambitious: Could I tease out some conditions that must be met in order to experience it?

I gave these questions all the analysis I could muster while balancing a mai tai in the sand. I was pleased with what I came up with. It was a very honest analysis.

First: I felt beautiful when surrounded by people I loved who really knew me, loved me, saw the best in me, and whom I felt comfortable around. In both cases I'd been surrounded by my sister and closest girlfriends throughout the day.

Second: The events themselves had helped me feel unique and special. I questioned whether this was because I'd been the center of attention (which I knew I enjoyed a bit, thanks to my guilt-ridden enjoyment of the prior month's media attention), but after some thought I realized that this was only a small part of what made me feel special. But the much larger part, in both cases, had been a sense of pride for the creativity and organization that I'd put into *planning* the events. It gave me enormous pleasure to see my friends and family having just as much fun as me, and made me feel more connected to them. I wasn't sure if "planning the event" was a specific condition, but I suspected that "pride in an accomplishment" was.

Third: I couldn't deny that, on both occasions, I'd spent more time than usual engaging in beauty rituals (note, *not* beauty addictions or beauty habits). I was kind of disappointed to realize this because I'd hoped that feeling beautiful would have had nothing to do with my appearance. You know, inner beauty and all that. But I had to be honest with myself. Somehow these rituals were, themselves, meaningful, even if I didn't know what I looked like. Perhaps the key was that I'd engaged in them in a *social* context, alongside my sister and closest girlfriends, rather than by myself in front of a mirror. Clearly, my loved ones made for the best mirrors, reflecting love rather than looks. Or perhaps I'd simply internalized some of our culture's conflation of beauty routines with femininity. I was okay with this possibility; I was seeking authenticity.

Fourth: A glass or two of chilled champagne never hurt!

I knew I didn't have any more bachelorette parties or weddings in my future, but after reviewing my lists I felt confident that, by spending time with my favorite people, by acknowledging my unique gifts and accomplishments (no matter how weird—or perhaps especially the weird ones!), and by establishing rituals that made me feel womanly, and by always keeping a chilled bottle of champagne waiting in my fridge for impromptu celebrations, I would have plenty of future opportunities to feel beautiful. And if I felt beautiful, I was.

OCTOBER 21 MARKED OUR LAST DAY IN HAWAII. NEITHER MIchael nor I felt ready to leave paradise, but there was no getting around it; the honeymoon was over. It was time to go home and get on with our lives.

With this in mind, we arrived at the Kauai airport in grumpy moods. Four hours in cramped seating would be a quintessential reintroduction to real life. In an act of desperation, I asked the woman at the check-in counter if there was any chance of us being upgraded, explaining, "We're on our honeymoon!" with more excitement than I felt. I'd never actually pulled off an upgrade in my life, so I didn't think it would amount to anything, but when we arrived at our departure gate we were called up to exchange our tickets for business class. Score! Suddenly our vacation wasn't yet over after all! Apparently there are a few airlines out there that still do nice things just because they can.

We boarded our flight at the earliest possible moment, excited to settle into the luxury awaiting us. Complimentary champagne provided the perfect opportunity to say a quick toast to our amazing honeymoon, and to rest of our married lives.

I snuggled into my seat and began watching the first of what I hoped would be several cheesy chick flicks. Next to me, Michael did the same with what I presumed to be a bunch of dude-esque action films. Time flew by, with complimentary mai tais flowing as fast as we could drink them. Everything seemed great, but then, a few hours later, I noticed that Michael seemed to be fidgeting uncomfortably in his seat. He was also wearing his sunglasses, which I found strange.

"Hey, are you awake?" I asked, whispering. Maybe he was having bad dreams or something.

"Shhhhh," he hissed. "I'm not really asleep. I'm pretending to be asleep."

"Huh? Why? What's wrong?" I whispered back, alarmed.

He exhaled deeply before responding, "I just did something really embarrassing, but I can't tell you about it until we're off the plane. I'm just trying to avoid eye contact with the flight attendants."

I rolled my eyes as though annoyed, but the suspense was killing me. *What in the world had he done?*

Once we'd landed in San Francisco and were waiting for our bags, I started badgering Michael to tell me what had happened.

"And why are you wearing your sunglasses inside?" I teased. Really, this was getting weird(er).

He wouldn't tell me until we were back in the privacy of our apartment. His cheeks were flushed from embarrassment as he explained.

"Okay, so I was watching a movie, and shortly after Liam Neeson finished rescuing his daughter and saving the Western world from evil, the plane hit some turbulence. Every time my seat belt tightened, I felt like I was about to pee. I'd been holding it in until the movie was over. . . ."

"Okay . . ." I responded, gesturing for him to get on with the story.

He cleared his throat and continued.

"Okay, so as soon as the turbulence was over, I headed for the first-class lavatory. It was just as small as the regular ones in the back of the plane! Anyway, I had to lean back a bit to pee, since I'm tall. It was a long pee, and at some point I looked over and caught a peek of myself in the mirror. I must have had beer goggles, because I was, like, fascinated by how cool I looked, with my tan and my new sunglasses. I remember thinking that I looked like a cool surfer dude, like Keanu Reeves in *Point Break*. No, better than that—like *Patrick Swayze* in *Point Break*!"

This made me laugh. The last time Michael had attempted surfing he'd come home with a concussion from hitting his head on the surfboard. Patrick Swayze? I love the man, but no.

"Get to the point!" I urged. I'm an impatient listener.

"Okay, so I was ogling myself in the mirror, wearing my sunglasses and feeling really good. But after I finished my business, I turned to flush the toilet and realized that I'd been peeing on the floor the whole time! I was standing in a pee puddle!" He looked so ashamed, but I had to laugh.

"Oh my gosh, no way!" I exclaimed. "How did that happen?"

"I was too busy admiring myself in the mirror to notice," he admitted. "I tried to clean it up with paper towels, but the puddle had already spread under the door."

"Oh no!" I said. This was worse than I'd imagined. "What did you do?"

"I thought I might get away with it by acting like nothing had happened, but when I opened the door one of the flight attendants was already trying to clean up. She was wearing rubber gloves and dabbing at the carpet with a bunch of cocktail napkins. I was frozen. I didn't know what to do or say. I started to offer to help, but she just glared and told me to sit back down . . . and *stay seated*." Michael cringed while describing his chastisement; he wasn't used to getting into trouble. My mouth was agape with shock.

"Anyway, I went back to my seat and put my sunglasses back on. I pretended to sleep for the rest of the flight. I was too embarrassed to look anyone in the eye!"

I promised him that his secret was safe with me (at least until I ran out of interesting things to blog about!) and we tried to laugh it off. But seriously, yuck! You'd think that by that time he would have learned a lesson or two from my own mirror mishaps. I supposed he'd had to learn his own lesson the hard way!

NINE

November, December

PEACE ON EARTH AND GOODWILL
TO MY BODACIOUS BOD

Never believe in mirrors or newspapers.

TOM STOPPARD

M Y MOTHER AND MOST OF MY FRIENDS HAD WARNED ME
that I would feel depressed in the aftermath of my wedding. I'd mourn no longer being the center of attention. I'd feel a gaping hole in my life where the drama and excitement of endless wedding planning had formerly resided.

Apparently the post-wedding slump is a common phenomenon, and there's an unofficial name for it: postnuptial depression—or PMD, for short. The condition (if you can call it that, since there is no mention of it in medical literature) reportedly affects one in ten newlywed women, though I wasn't able to scare up any numbers for newlywed men. Yet the partners of PMD sufferers are certainly affected: An article in *Time* magazine suggests that between 5 and 10 percent of PMD-affected newlyweds have "strong enough remorse, sadness, or frustration to prompt them to seek professional counseling." Although the very term "postnuptial depression" seems to locate the problem as residing within individuals, I imagined it as a *cultural* affliction, aggravated by the wedding industry; as eloquently described in *One Perfect Day*: "If we brides are led to believe that our wedding day is truly the most amazing, romantic, and important day of our lives, then it can only go downhill from there." What could be more depressing than that?

I could see why my friends and family were worried. As a lover of grand projects, I'd thrown myself into wedding planning with gusto, and seemed at times to revel in the drama. I enjoy few things more than solving problems, and my wedding to-do list was basically an inventory of potential crises to be solved ahead of time. Indeed, my mother suggested that the sudden *absence* of wedding stress might itself be stressful.

I was prepared for all of this, but it didn't happen.

Instead, I felt surprisingly calm and quietly satisfied. I felt like myself again, but better, which made me realize that I hadn't felt like myself in a while. The calmness and life-finally-feels-right centeredness that I experienced in the weeks and months following my wedding proved something that I'd suspected: Being a bride-to-be had been toxic. The cultural pressures of wedding hoopla had caused me to go (maybe just a little itty-bitty bit) insane.

Before becoming engaged, I'd always battled a tension between my values and my behaviors. From biting my nails to indulging in the latest fashions, my life had involved progressive self-improvement as I worked to eliminate behaviors and patterns that didn't fit who I wanted to be. I'd figured out ways to balance my shallower, more girlie side in *normal* life, but being a bride-to-be had thrown everything off-kilter.

Avoiding mirrors had restored a great deal of this balance, but with my wedding behind me and my no-mirrors project ongoing, I was boosted even further in the direction of my values. While planning my wedding, avoiding mirrors had helped me become a calmer and less appearance-obsessed version of *bridal* Kjerstin; now that the wedding was over, avoiding mirrors was causing me to be a calmer and less appearance-obsessed version of *regular* Kjerstin.

I found myself at peace with my body—*ridiculously* at peace with my body—in a way that I hadn't felt in months, if ever. Did I miss wedding planning? Sure, sometimes. But the moment that gaping hole opened up, I found other projects with which to fill it. The most obvious of these were my dissertation research and volunteer work with About-Face. Deciding to bring my focus back to the work that so clearly engaged my values and ambitions made me feel balanced again. I was back on a path that felt less scripted and more authentic.

But getting back to work wasn't the only thing on my mind. Feeling so calm and in balance—feeling so *well* and at ease with my body—made me want to turn some attention to my physical and mental health. Returning to my Top Ten Ways to Be Kjerstin list, item 4 reminded me that to be my healthiest I needed to "focus on healthy behaviors, not numbers on the scale." It was time for a Health at Every Size check-in.

As I've mentioned before, the Health at Every Size (HAES) movement fights to disentangle body size from health. It argues (with tons of supporting scientific evidence) that bodies come in a variety of different shapes and sizes, and that *behaviors* are more indicative of a person's health than weight or BMI. Randomized controlled clinical trials show that HAES approaches to health are associated with statistically and clinically relevant improvements in

physiological measures (e.g., blood pressure, blood lipids), health behaviors (e.g., eating and activity habits, dietary quality), and psycho-
social outcomes (such as self-esteem and body image), and that
HAES achieves these health outcomes more successfully than
weight-loss treatment and without the contradictions associated
with a weight focus. These are the main tenets of HAES:

> *Self-Acceptance:* HAES accepts, respects, and celebrates the
> natural diversity of body sizes and shapes; there is no in-
> herently wrong or bad body size or shape.
>
> *Normalized Eating:* HAES rejects externally imposed rules
> for eating, in favor of eating in a flexible manner that
> values pleasure and honors internal cues of hunger and
> fullness.
>
> *Physical Activity:* HAES supports finding joy in moving one's
> body and becoming more physically vital.

HAES saved my life, and had kept saving it over and over again,
any time I felt anorexia creeping back in. When I'd finally decided
to enter a recovery program to deal with my eating disorder, I was in
poor health. My bones were slowly disintegrating, and my kidneys
were showing signs of irreparable damage. Yet my BMI was in the
"normal" category. I remember thinking, *Okay, I'll get treatment so
I'm not so obsessed and miserable, but I won't gain weight. I don't need
to. I'm at a healthy weight. . . . Probably not even thin enough to be really anorexic . . .*

My body disagreed, and I certainly was anorexic. I had to accept
that *my* healthy weight didn't fit into current official BMI standards.
In other words, at five-feet-five and 155 pounds, I was *technically* a
smidge overweight (BMI of 25.8), yet healthy, or fat and fit, if you

will. And I was not alone in this designation. According to a 2008 study from the Albert Einstein College of Medicine in New York, more than 50 percent of "overweight" adults and 30 percent of "obese" adults are metabolically healthy. This means that they have no insulin resistance, diabetes, high cholesterol, or blood pressure issues, and no increased death risk compared with metabolically fit "normal weight" people. Conversely, nearly 25 percent of normal weight people were found to be metabolically *un*healthy and at greater risk of death. In other words, it's healthier to be fat and fit than it is to be thin and unfit. And trust me, when in the throes of anorexia, I was both malnourished and *un*fit, despite my "normal weight" BMI. This is where HAES stepped in to save my life.

While in treatment, and in the still-recovering years after, I slowly learned to eat a variety of nourishing foods in response to feeling hungry, and to stop when I felt full. Rather than eating what the latest diet books were suggesting, I started eating based on what tasted good and what made me feel energized and adventurous. Of course, I also learned that there's no such thing as "perfect" eating, and that for the rest of my life I will probably need to be more mindful about food than most people, to ensure that I don't fall back into old habits.

I learned to exercise for the joy of being active, or for the pride of finishing a race, rather than as punishment for eating too much or as a get-out-of-jail-free card for a planned binge. I began to focus on making my body stronger and more flexible instead of thinner, and I found out that a mere twenty minutes of moderate exercise in the morning could improve my outlook (and my writing!) for two days!

I discovered that sleep is medicine, and that sleep deprivation makes me feel really negative and bitchy. I gained a little weight when I stopped restricting food, and then I gained a little more when I finally found an antidepressant that helped me feel like my best self. And I had to be okay with that. It took some adjustment, and a lot of patience, but I finally realized that I'd rather be happy and healthy than thin, sick, and miserable. Of course, this is not what our culture teaches us to think. Most people, myself included, were taught that it's impossible to be happy unless we're thin, and we believe it; rather than being fat, women have expressed preferences for being mean, stupid, losing limbs, being run over by a truck, and even death (assuming that the truck didn't kill you first, I guess).

Anyway, the weeks after I returned from my honeymoon felt like a perfect time to reconnect with my body, by checking in with my eating, by getting back into a regular exercise routine, and by catching up on sleep. I began by focusing on one healthy habit each week, ranging from "get more rest, activity, and nourishment" to "drink more water" and (Michael's favorite) "have more sex." For each week, I intentionally emphasized welcoming more of these good things into my life, rather than trying to avoid bad things. So, for example, I'd tell myself things like "Eat more vegetables," instead of "Eat less junk food." I'd already spent too many years of my life trying to get by on less of what my body needed; now it was time for more. Little did I know how important these healthy behaviors would soon turn out to be.

ON THE SECOND DAY OF NOVEMBER, I RECEIVED A PACKAGE IN the mail. I knew what it was and that I probably shouldn't open it. The package contained the electronic files of my wedding photos (YES! YES! YES!), which I'd been planning to *not* look at until the end of my no-mirrors project (NO! NO! NO!).

Back when I'd established the rules of my year without mirrors, my readers had decided by vote that I could look at my wedding photos if I wanted to. But then Hanna promised to throw me a huge party at the end of the project if I could resist.

I loved my sister, and didn't want to disappoint her. As an added bonus, Hanna and her boyfriend, Nick, were known for throwing amazing parties. So when she challenged me to stay away from my wedding photos, I knew that I ought to try my hardest. Besides, I'd been feeling so at peace with my body and happy with my newly rebalanced life in general that it seemed plain foolhardy to risk back-tracking on all of my progress over a bunch of photos that would certainly be waiting for me at the end of my project.

Resisting these photos would require the utmost self-control and determination. To make matters worse, Michael was out of town for work, so I didn't have the option of asking him to hide the package from me.

I was very good for two hours. I tried to hide the package from myself by shoving it out of sight in a random drawer of my bathroom dresser. And yet, surprisingly, I managed to "find it" again only a few hours later. I held the thick yellow envelope in my hands and sniffed it, smelling the scent of paper and packing tape. I traced the edges of the tape with my right index finger, noting an upraised tape edge near the envelope seal. At first I tried to smooth the raised edge down, to restick the tape and reseal the package. But it wouldn't stick. Suddenly this bit of unstuck tape became my obsession. The asymmetry was intolerable. If the edge wouldn't stay stuck, I would have to remove it from the package entirely. I was compelled.

And so I picked at the tape with my nails. Soon enough, the of-fending piece was off. But then there were others. I wasn't *opening* the package, I was *fixing* it, I justified to myself.

But then, suddenly, the package was open. The only acceptably symmetrical tape pattern was one without tape at all. I decided to just . . . open the box . . . a little bit. I could do this without looking at all the photos, right?

But then I caught that first glimpse of a forbidden photo, covering the customized DVD case of our wedding slide show. I saw brightly colored flowers contrasted against the white of my wedding dress, and my curiosity took over. (Oh heck, it had taken over from the moment I started picking at the tape.) I took out the DVD case and held it up to the light.

I look pretty awesome! I thought, taking in the fascinating site of myself dressed in white, dolled up to the max, holding hands with Michael. *Wow, my hair really* was *big!* I noted, with amusement. But Mandy was right—I'd pulled it off.

But I felt guilty about this peek. Hanna was going to be so pissed at me! I forced myself to stop snooping. The DVD remained in its beautiful case, and I willed myself to go to bed early just to avoid the temptation. I couldn't sneak more peeks if my eyes were closed.

THE NEXT DAY I MET UP WITH HANNA FOR LUNCH. OVER A healthy feast of vegetarian bolanis from Costco, I casually mentioned that the wedding photos had arrived. I was fully prepared to guiltily confess my peek at the DVD cover. Instead, Hanna asked me how they looked. I gave her a look of confusion and reminded her that I wasn't supposed to be looking at my wedding photos until my no-mirrors project was over, an agonizing five months away.

"Oh, right. I forgot about that," Hanna said nonchalantly. "Whatever. You should look."

Whatever?

Of course. Whatever!

Suddenly *whatever* made sense. My sister's nonchalance was the encouragement I needed. Why choose to hold myself to higher standards than what my sister, or the bulk of my blog readers, expected of me? Indeed, what better way to get an extra body-image boost than to see photos of myself on a day when I felt particularly gorgeous and loved? I believed that looking at my wedding photos would make me feel happy, so that's exactly what I did.

I went home after lunch and threw myself a little wedding photo viewing party. It was just me, a mug of tea, two cats, and over a thousand beautifully captured memories. It was the best party I'd been to since, well, my wedding! I saw—no, not just saw, actively and intentionally *looked* at—photos of myself for the first time in months. It couldn't have been better: My makeup was lovely, my dress fit beautifully, my hair—big as it was—looked elegantly chic. Most important, I looked just as happy as I'd felt.

While looking at these photos I felt surrounded by wonderful memories. As fun as it was to see photos of myself for the first time in ages, I took just as much pleasure in seeing everyone else having a good time. I relived snippets of time throughout my entire wedding day as I went through each and every photo in chronological order: my bridesmaids covering the mirrors; the smell of my dad's aftershave as he walked me down the aisle; the hilariously teary grimace on Michael's face as I walked toward him; an image of my beautiful mom and handsome brother laughing together during the ceremony; the laughing spins on the dance floor that I'd taken with my grandfathers; my toppled wedding cake, which had tasted so much better than it looked; and finally, the end of the evening, the moment that Michael and I shared alone in the moonlight, staring at our friends and family celebrating the night away. Looking at these photos hadn't turned into an exercise in determining how great or awful

I'd looked; it was about remembering how happy I had been. It made me happy all over again to relive it.

I still felt a bit guilty, but only because I hadn't had the patience to wait until Michael returned from his business trip before diving into the photos. I'm sure he would have preferred to look at them together, but I was glad I'd had the time to do this alone. If Michael had been there, I would have felt self-conscious about my reactions, and I was glad that they had been unfiltered. I wondered if I would feel the same way about seeing myself in a mirror for the first time again.

Of course, seeing photos of myself did have some impact on the way I felt about my looks. It was a pleasure to see myself looking happy, loved, and glamorous; it relieved any lingering sense of paranoia about what I'd looked like on that day, or in general. I had evidence that I still looked like me (albeit, me in a big white dress with lots of makeup, poofy hair, and sparkly jewelry), and that was nice. I gave myself permission to stare until my tea went cold. It felt indulgent, but not in a naughty way. It was more like self-care, a way to check in and assure myself that absolutely nothing irreparably bad had happened as a result of giving up mirrors.

SEEING MY WEDDING PHOTOS, COMBINED WITH THE CALM confidence I'd already been feeling, made me feel additionally relaxed and brave. Having the wedding behind me took a major edge off my concerns about appearance. I found myself skipping my makeup on more days than just Mondays and picking increasingly comfy clothes, even on days when I was scheduled to work at About-Face. Some might accuse me of teetering on the edge of "letting myself go," but it didn't feel that way. I wasn't letting myself go, I was letting myself back in. I was taking more risks and feeling more forgiving of myself.

Leading up to the wedding I'd been too scared to use my usual prescription Retin-A as part of my skin care routine. I've known for years that this is a great way for me to keep my skin clear (and wrinkles at bay—bonus!), but it also makes my face peel and flake like crazy. The only way to deal with the flakiness and peeling had been to notice when it was happening and then exfoliate my face in the shower using a washcloth, followed by gobs of moisturizer for the next day or so. It scared me to worry about having a flaky face on my wedding day, so I'd stopped using it full-stop when I did away with mirrors. In other words, I'd wussed out.

As soon as I got back from my honeymoon I'd started using it again, applying a pea-size dab to my face on Sundays, Wednesdays, and Fridays. Almost immediately, my face started getting flaky again; every time I washed my face I could feel the surface skin peeling away under the pads of my fingertips. But it didn't bother me anymore. I wasn't about to be the center of attention at a wedding. Instead, I felt blessed to once again be just another normal imperfect woman in a very big and overpopulated world. So instead of worrying about it, I began to just exfoliate as best I could each night, using a washcloth, and then slap on some moisturizer before heading to bed. *No wusses here!* I thought to myself.

Next, in an act I consider to be pure genius, I finally solved my never-ending struggle to find perfectly fitting jeans that didn't cut into my midsection. My solution was (drumroll) maternity jeans. Yes, you read that correctly: maternity jeans. I'm sure a lot of women would absolutely cringe at this idea, but let me tell you this: They're all missing out. Big-time. Don't knock it until you try it, folks. Here's the thing: My body is not the perfect hourglass all those "built for curves" jeans are designed for. I have a rounded tummy. That whole "tiny waist, wide hips, round booty" thing makes sense on me only if you think my waist starts directly below my boobs. Because of this, even my best-fitting jeans have always felt like they're cutting me in half every time I sat down at my desk to start writing. I'd get the dreaded muffin top and struggle to keep the back of my pants from sinking down into plumber-butt when I kneeled or sat down. All that fidgeting and frustration to get comfortable—especially since I was never actually able to get comfortable—was stupid. I was fed up and tired of trying to fit my body into my jeans, instead of finding jeans that fit my body.

I remembered the freedom of my three-year-old self, and thought, *Damn, I wish I were still a little kid so I could wear elastic-waistband jeans! Those were so cool and comfy, I didn't even have to zip or button them, I could just pull them right up and then go out to play.* Despite the current jegging trend, I still hadn't been able to find a pair of jeans that felt as good as that, until I decided to think outside of the box, realizing that millions upon millions of women in America get to wear elastic waistband pants during pregnancy. I went to the nearest Gap Maternity location with Liz, and was overjoyed to find that Gap's size 10 maternity jeans with a "demi panel" were the most comfortable jeans I'd ever worn in my entire life. The best part? According to Liz, as long as my shirt covered the elastic "demi panel," they looked exactly like *non*-maternity jeans. And so, in the months after my wedding, wearing my elastic waistband maternity jeans became my secret weapon for feeling comfortably at ease all day, every day, especially days spent sitting in front of my computer. I felt like a genius, and stopped caring so much about the labels on my jeans. I felt outrageously comfortable; that's all that mattered.

O N THE THIRD WEEKEND IN NOVEMBER, MICHAEL AND I
won a lottery. Okay, okay—not the kind where you get rich,
but we were (kind of) randomly selected to participate in a national
health study, specifically the National Health and Nutrition Examination Survey, or NHANES. Only 520 residents in all of San
Francisco County were chosen, and 70 percent of those were Asian-
American (called "oversampling"), so the fact that Michael and I,
über-Caucasians, were picked was extraordinarily unlikely.

For the past fifty-two years, the NHANES has been conducted
yearly by the National Centers for Disease Control and Prevention
(CDC). NHANES is the nation's most comprehensive study on the
health and nutritional status of Americans. I'd run across numerous
academic articles citing NHANES data in my own research, so the
opportunity to actually become a data point for this study was totally
intriguing to me!

When we were asked if we could be interviewed in our home,
and then to come to the study site to participate in numerous medical tests, I didn't hesitate for a second. Michael acquiesced, even
though this wasn't exactly his idea of a fun Sunday afternoon. But I
pointed out to him that, in addition to the pure coolness of the experience, we would be receiving a lot of (free) medical tests and would
be paid a few hundred dollars for our time and participation.

Early on Sunday morning, Michael and I drove to the local examination site. Four portable trailers had been set up on a land plot
in downtown San Francisco, just a few blocks from About-Face.
Once we arrived and showed our IDs, we had to change into medical scrubs before being guided through the maze of trailers, which
were set up with dozens of stations for medical tests.

In addition to collecting the usual boring data on our height, weight, body temperature, and blood pressure, we also had our hearing tested, our grip strength tested, and we reported on twenty-four hours' worth of food intake (down to every tablespoon of buffet food we'd sampled at Whole Foods the night before), as well as numerous blood tests. I received a full body scan and had various odd body measurements taken, such as the length between my shoulder socket and my elbow. I peed in a cup, spat in a vial, and swabbed my privates for a self-administered STD test. Fun stuff, right?

Well, I thought so, too, until the very end when I was handed a printout called the "Preliminary Report of Findings."

Now, this preliminary report didn't include everything I'd been tested for that day, but it did list all of the results that could be ascertained within hours. I learned that my blood pressure and heart rate were within the normal range, my oral health was deemed adequate, my hearing was also normal, my muscle strength was excellent (!), and all of the measures taken in my "Complete Blood Count" were within the normal-to-excellent range. In other words, I'd just received a clean bill of health. Almost.

My "body measurements" (i.e., BMI and waist circumference) were flagged as a concern. With my weight of 159.8 pounds and height of five feet, five inches, my Body Mass Index (BMI) came in at 26.5, so I was labeled "overweight" by current medical standards (though I knew from my research that this BMI would have been considered "normal weight" just a few years before). But there was more: My waist circumference was measured at thirty-six inches, one inch above the recommended maximum. (Apparently they hadn't followed my tip about measuring my waist immediately below my breasts!) Because of these two measurements, the report warned me that I had an increased risk of health problems such as type 2 diabetes, high blood pressure, and cardiovascular disease.

Okay, so those are the facts of the story. Here are the feelings: It completely sucked. It threw me into a tailspin.

Given my background, that seemed likely. I'd embarked on a serious (and very public) self-acceptance project in which I hadn't seen myself in the mirror in months, and I'd conquered an eating disorder almost a decade prior. Add to this the fact that I knew that I was at a healthy weight for my body, and—here's the kicker—I was also intimately familiar with recent research published by the CDC (yes, the exact same CDC running this study!) that found that the "overweight" BMI category actually had the *lowest* mortality rates (yes, that means lower mortality rates than the so-called "normal" BMI category). In fact, on the basis of the CDC data, my BMI of 26.5 was basically at the sweetest sweet spot for long-term health. Knowing all of this stuff, I should have been in a pretty good position to not care too much about the warning I received from NHANES.

So what happened? I read the report and "felt fat." (Yes, I know that "fat is not a feeling," but y'all know what I'm talking about!) Suddenly my normal blood pressure was replaced by a warning that my thirty-six-inch waist was putting me at risk for high blood pressure, and my excellent grip strength didn't feel so excellent anymore. Despite everything, my first thought was, *I need to lose some weight.* How had I come so far, only to find myself right back at the beginning?

STRUGGLED FOR SEVERAL DAYS TO BANISH URGES TO GO ON A crash diet.

Just ten pounds! I thought to myself. *That's all I'd need to lose to get*

into the "normal" BMI category! If I can just get back to my usual 155,
and then lose another five, I'll be fine!

Despite all of the progress I'd made in the past year, and despite
the sense of calm that had washed over me since the wedding, it was
hard for me to deal with the fact that I'd gained some weight.

The fact that I'd gained a few pounds wasn't even a complete
surprise. My two-week honeymoon had been a bit of a free-for-all of
amazing food and drinks. Other than a few hikes, my exercise routine had also taken a two-week vacation. I'd been okay with this,
wanting to relax and enjoy our vacation without stressing out about
food or exercise. I knew it was likely that I would put on a few pounds,
so I'd intentionally *not* stepped on a scale in the weeks following our
return to normal life. I wanted to give my body time to sort itself out
through my focus on healthy habits, imagining that it would settle
back to my usual weight. Obviously it wasn't quite there yet.

I'd faced panic-inducing episodes of weight gain before, and I
knew I was at risk of diving into a crash diet. People recovering from
eating disorders often talk about being triggered by certain events or
situations. Being *tsk-tsk*ed by the NHANES report was a trigger for
me. All of my people-pleasing urges rushed in, as I imagined rapidly
losing the weight and earning an A+ on my next health exam. *I don't
fail tests,* I thought to myself. *I want a retest. Next week. Same place,
same time!* It was bad.

I knew from past experience that, unless I wanted to end up in
the hospital with kidney stones, I would have to "fake it 'til I made
it" by following HAES principles. HAES helped me the most at
times when I feared that my body was out of control. Not trusting
my body was always the first step down the wrong path. So, on Monday, the day after I'd received my NHANES report, I wrote a blog
post about my struggles and asked for support being patient with my

body, to trust that as long as I treated it well it would settle into a healthy place. Thanks to my prior research on resolutions, I knew that putting this goal into writing would make it a pact, and that sharing my plans with other people would provide social support for the attempt.

I T TOOK ME TWO FULL WEEKS OF INTENTIONAL PATIENCE, MODerate exercise, and careful *non*-dieting before I started to feel better, before my confidence and calmness returned. I didn't lose any weight, but that was okay. Weight loss has never been part of HAES, and besides, the NHANES report had essentially noted that I was in good health. Most important, I allowed myself to enjoy Thanksgiving, my favorite holiday. I've heard people claim that "nothing tastes as good as skinny feels." I hate this phrase, and disagree completely. I've had both, and Thanksgiving tastes way better than skinny feels. I promise.

Did I eat a lot on Thanksgiving? Oh yes, indeed; having the flexibility to enjoy special food on special occasions (without guilt) is an important element of normal eating habits!

My reaction to the NHANES report had been a bit like the moment I'd realized that my first wedding dress was too tight; in both cases, a voice inside my head had sprung out of hiding to tell me that I ought to lose weight. It wasn't my rational voice, and it certainly wasn't the voice of my three-year-old self; it was my dormant anorexic voice. I had to accept that it might always be there.

People say things like "Once an alcoholic, always an alcoholic." I think that eating disorders are similar. Even if a person "recovers," he or she has to recommit to recovery time and time again as our culture and media deliver onslaught after onslaught of unhealthy messages and beauty standards. I reminded myself that feeling like an activist would be much more empowering than feeling like a victim. *Be a role model.* I needed to turn my fear into anger and my body shame into righteous outrage.

Even in my post about needing support for body image struggles, I'd refrained from sharing my experience with NHANES with my blog readers because I was ashamed to admit my weight gain. (I kept thinking of how horrified Michael's mom might be if I announced to the world that I was "overweight.") But I decided that sharing my weight and measurements, and struggles with being "diagnosed" as overweight, might help other women feel braver, too. I wrote out every last bit of the story, including my height, my weight, my BMI, my waist circumference, and how ashamed and panicked I'd felt when I read the report I'd been given. I promised to be brave and unapologetic about my unique body. It was a major "you go girl!" moment.

O

VER THE NEXT SEVERAL WEEKS, LIFE GOT CALM AND HAPPY again. I developed a solid routine for regularly working on my dissertation. I dove into evaluation data analysis for About-Face, and also gave a presentation about my research findings to their board of directors. I was living a purposeful life, and it felt nice. The holiday spirit seemed alive and well in San Francisco, and Michael and I were excited to make plans for our yearly St. Lucia's Day brunch.

St. Lucia's Day is a traditional Scandinavian holiday. When I was growing up, my family invited our friends and neighbors to our home to celebrate the occasion over a potluck brunch. Each year, a little girl was chosen to be St. Lucia. She would dress in a white gown with a red sash and wear a wreath of candles in her hair as she welcomed the guests for brunch. Traditionally, the eldest daughter in the household would carry out these St. Lucia duties, but I'd grown tired of picking candle wax out of my hair post-brunch, so we began to pass the tradition along to a different neighborhood girl each year. Of course, as soon as it was no longer her daughters' hair, my mom ordered a wreath decked out with battery-operated fake candles. As a teenager I rolled my eyes at my family's St. Lucia's Day brunch tradition, but as soon as I no longer lived at home with my parents, I'd begun to miss it.

This year, Michael and I would be cohosting our first St. Lucia's Day brunch in San Francisco. I'd planned out the menu (mostly foods from Ikea!), and we'd invited all of our friends. The party would be held on the morning of December 18, and we were flying to Louisville for Christmas two days later. After spending Christmas Eve in Louisville, we would drive to St. Louis to spend Christmas Day with my family.

Everything was shaping up to be a perfect holiday season.

And then I ruined my hair.

The hair saga started with boredom. In those weeks before Christmas, I'd begun to feel that itch to mess with my hair, the urge to do something different. For all of my adult life I've been searching for that perfect haircut and color combination that perfectly expresses *me*. Alas, some days I feel retro punk and androgynous, while other days I like to channel classic (über)femininity. I am alternatively a student and a teacher, a reader and a writer, a fashionista and a stays-in-her-PJs-all-day slouch, a glamazon bombshell and a Makeup-Free-Mondays all-natural kinda gal. My multiple personae are easy enough to accomplish with a varied wardrobe, but not so much with my hair.

On that Tuesday before our St. Lucia's Day brunch, as I imagined what I might like to look like for the upcoming holiday season, I decided that I'd been feeling too natural, too slouchy, and not sufficiently glamorous or edgy. I wanted to show up at my in-laws' home looking chic and modern. My solution? I decided I ought to put Gwyneth Paltrow's hair on my head.

It didn't even seem all that risky. My hair is naturally light-ish blond and pin-straight, so to achieve Gwyneth Paltrow's sleek platinum locks, I just needed my hair to be lighter. We were on a tight budget, but no worries; that's what Walgreens is for! (Gwyneth *obviously* colors her own hair from seven-dollar boxed dye, too, right?) I left the drugstore with two boxes of "Very Light Beige Blonde."

In hindsight it's obvious, of course, that I may have been feeling more than a bit overconfident. I thought, *Hey, this should be easy.* It's not like I was giving myself highlights, right? All I had to do was mix the dye, cover my hair with it, set a timer, and then wash it out when the timer went off. Mirrors would be wholly unnecessary.

Once home, I followed the directions exactly, sans mirrors. Once the timer went off, I washed the dye out, dried my hair, and then eagerly peered at the ends (which I could see without mirrors). It looked fantastic! Pale buttery blond, just like the hair color I'd had as a little kid. Perfect!

Then I showed Michael. Well, to be more specific, I accosted him in our TV room, flipping my (supposedly) Gwyneth Paltrow–esque hair and posing for imaginary paparazzi.

"Ta-da! Surprise! What do you think?"

"Whoa! Wow, it looks cool!" Michael paused. "I mean, it's what you meant to do, right? It's kind of . . . bright."

"Yeah, well, I wanted to lighten it."

"Yeah, well, it's definitely lighter. Were you going for a kind of a punk thing?"

My heart sank. Punk? Uh-oh. And Michael is color-blind, so if he was seeing a problem, there was definitely a problem.

"Okay, what aren't you telling me?"

"Well, it's kind of different colors. It's really yellow near your face." Michael can see yellow. *Gulp.*

After more quizzing, I learned from him that the hair near my scalp was bright yellow, "like, neon." This wasn't predictable, but it was explainable: A while back I'd gotten highlights for the wedding, and my hair had grown since then. The highlighted parts, the ends that I could see, were perfect, but my roots were apparently neon yellow.

You'd think that at this point I'd wave a neon yellow flag of defeat and consult the experts, but I was too cheap for that.

Instead I thought, *Hmmm . . . Maybe I didn't leave the dye on long enough to lighten my roots! That's it!*

So I did what any sensible and extremely cheap woman would do: I brought out that second box of hair dye and colored my hair again.

Unsurprisingly, per Michael, my hair looked even worse after round two. *Shit.*

I finally waved that neon yellow flag of defeat. It was time to seek help from a pro, and I needed to do it before we went to Louisville.

I told Michael that I wanted to get my hair fixed at a salon, but he suggested that I wait until we were back in the Midwest for Christmas since it would be less expensive. "You've already spent twenty dollars messing it up. We can't afford for you to pay another fifty dollars, or whatever it would cost, to have it fixed here."

"Fifty dollars? Try two hundred!" I shot back. Immediately regretting this uncontrollable urge to correct people. This was not in my best interest.

The whole reason I'd bothered to color my hair in the first place was because I'd wanted to look chic and glamorous for my mother-in-law. I knew that she read my blog and that she'd have read that I'd gained weight. I felt embarrassed about this. I kept remembering that night when she'd told me she was proud of me for deciding to lose weight. Obviously I hadn't. I was scared that she would disapprove of or be embarrassed by me. I thought she'd always be disappointed that her perfect son had married the chubby girl. I didn't think I could explain this to Michael. All I knew was that I *had* to get my hair fixed before we left.

"What!?! You've got to be kidding. Two hundred dollars? Jesus, that's completely ridiculous," he responded.

I began to panic, my voice rising. "Michael, I *HAVE TO* get this fixed right away. I can't go walking around town with neon hair. I'll look like a crazy woman!" I pleaded.

"Yeah, well, maybe that would give people a warning. If you think it's okay to pay two hundred dollars on your hair, you *are* crazy!" he said, voice rising to meet mine. He continued, landing a blow where it would hurt the most. "You don't even have a job! I'm the only one with a paycheck. Maybe if *you* were making some money, too, we'd have enough in our budget for something like this. . . ."

I was so furious and hurt that I began to cry. I yelled back, "You *know* I applied for scholarships and didn't get any! Money is tight *everywhere*, including at school. It's not my fault that we're in a fucking recession." I glared at him. I was pissed off.

And I wasn't finished.

"Oh, and it's not like I'm sitting around watching TV all day; I'm working my ass off to finish my dissertation! What do you want me to do, anyway? Quit school? Ask you for permission every time I want to buy something? I'm not some traditional housewife begging for pin money."

"Oh for crying out loud!" Michael retorted. "Don't pull that sexism crap on me. It's not fair."

"You're damn right it's not fair!" I shouted back. "I'm in the midst of a crisis and you're being a jerk!" With that, I stomped out of the room and slammed the door. Of course, in our small apartment I had nowhere to go to be alone except for my bathroom.

I retreated there to sulk and mutter snappy retorts to myself. I glared at my covered mirror and wished I had a folding chair to crash into it. Seven years of bad luck? Whatever. Bring it on. I was pissed.

After a few minutes, Michael knocked on the door. When I didn't answer, he spoke through it.

"Look, I'm sorry I brought up all of that money stuff. I've just been really anxious about making ends meet on my fellowship salary." He sounded apologetic.

"Okay, I'm sorry I freaked out at you," I said back. "I just don't think I can handle waiting a few weeks to fix my hair."

I heard him sigh, and after a long pause, he told me it would be okay. "I don't understand why this is such a big deal, but I know you're really freaked out. Maybe it's the no-mirrors thing. Go ahead and make your appointment. We'll figure it out."

I knew that this was a fight without a real winner; the issues laid bare would come up again. Nevertheless, I was relieved.

THE NEXT DAY, AFTER WORKING FROM HOME TO AVOID SHOWing my hair-oops to the world, I arrived at the nearest hair salon wearing a fuzzy pink beret that I hoped looked casually chic and not at all like I was hiding a bad dye job. I sat down in the waiting area and flipped through a magazine, twirling a strand of hair around my fingers. Minutes later I met my new stylist/savior, Nikki, an energetic curly-haired brunette who immediately put me at ease. Apparently she'd seen worse (whew!), and she told me that I was actually lucky: Since my hair was so light, she wouldn't have to bleach out any dye before darkening it back to my natural color.

Confession: I hadn't yet found a way to tell Nikki about my no-mirrors project. I know, I know. I should have. But I already felt like such a huge moron for ruining my hair. I didn't want to seem like a *crazy* moron. So I sat in Nikki's chair, directly facing a huge mirror, attempting to hold a conversation by looking at *her* through the mirror while avoiding eye contact with myself. It was horribly awkward, and I'm not sure I didn't seem like a crazy moron anyway. I didn't allow myself to stare, but it was impossible to avoid seeing glimpses of my neon hair in the corners of my peripheral vision. Trying to avoid looking at these bits was like attempting to read *around* the highlighted portions of a textbook. Doable, but not easy.

Before I left the consultation, Nikki took pity on me and applied a neutralizing toner to take things down a notch before the full repair, which we scheduled for the following Monday. I was bummed that she didn't have any openings before our St. Lucia's Day brunch party, but at least I wouldn't be headed to Louisville with highlighter head.

Two days later, I returned for the full corrective color appointment, which involved over two hours of skilled labor. Facing multiple hours in the salon chair, I fessed up to Nikki about not being able to look in the mirror. I felt sheepish for not explaining things earlier, but Nikki was cool with it, and maybe even a little bit impressed. She kindly spun the chair away from the mirror, and we spent the rest of the time chatting about our lives while she did her thing. While washing dye out of my hair (my fourth color application in five days!), Nikki assured me that everything looked good. I believed her. After a luxurious twenty-minute blow-dry, Nikki snapped two photos for her portfolio, and I was on my way. I walked home with a bounce in my step, hair swinging. Michael confirmed that my hair was, indeed, fixed. Hooray!

L ATER THAT EVENING, MICHAEL CAME TO ME AND SAID, "HEY, we need to talk."

It sounded serious, and I was nervous.

"Okay, here's the thing. I know that you've been doing amazingly with your body image lately, so I don't understand what happened the other day. You completely freaked out about your hair. I don't even understand why you bothered to color it in the first place. What's going on?"

It was time to fess up. "It's your mom," I admitted. "I'm terrified of looking bad when we visit next week. I can't explain it, but whenever I'm worried about my looks, I keep wondering what your *mom* would think. Like, do I meet the Sherry standard? Every time I'm about to see her I want to buy cute new clothes, get my hair cut and colored, my nails done, and diet."

He looked surprised. "You know that's crazy, right?" he asked.

I didn't know what to say, so I stayed silent. It didn't feel crazy at all. It felt real and important. I was also kind of worried that reminding Michael of his mom's discerning tastes might cause him to adopt them himself.

But that didn't happen.

"Look, I know that my mom does things differently than you,

but she loves you and she thinks you're great. She says it all the time," he began. "You've built something up in your mind about her that just isn't true. Moreover, I don't understand why you would care so much about what she thinks of you anyway. It doesn't make sense to me. She's just one person! So she said she was proud of you for wanting to lose weight. So what? Hundreds of online bullies said much worse, and you managed to take it in stride and fight back without compromising your values. But now I'm watching you fall apart because of things you *think* my mom *might think* about you."

He was right, but it only made me feel more confused. I understood the logic, but I still felt as though Sherry cared a lot about my looks, and that I should care about her opinion of me. It was as if a part of me *wanted* Sherry to judge me. Michael was right, this wasn't making sense. My anxiety increased.

"You know what the worst part of this is?" he continued. "You're supposed to be an advocate for women and body image, and I feel like you've built my mom up to be, like, an enemy of everything you stand for. That's just not fair. She didn't have plastic surgery to spite other women; she just wanted to feel better about herself. I would have expected you to relate to that and be empathetic, but instead you're using it to justify your own insecurities."

Everything Michael had accused me of was right. I felt so confused. There had to be some reason for my behavior and anxieties, some explanation for why I'd created an enemy out of a woman who, for the most part, had been nothing but kind to me.

I started to cry and said the first thing that came into my mind: "It's just not fair!"

"What's not fair?" Michael asked.

It all came out in a rush.

"It's not fair that your mom gets to go on diets and have all of this

plastic surgery and spend money on clothes and makeup and haircuts, and she doesn't even feel bad about it! She just thinks of what
she wants to do and then she does it. She doesn't care what people
think. I don't think your mom knows what angst *is*. It's not fair!" Oh
shit, I could tell that I was on the verge of an epiphany, but I wasn't
sure I wanted to have it.

"So what?" Michael asked, not giving up. "Why is it important
to you that my mom feel guilty about these things? What possible
impact could that have on you, and why would you even want that
for her?"

"Look, I don't *want* her to feel bad. I just feel like it's unfair. I
wish *I* could do all of those things, too!" I exploded with emotion. "*I*
want to go on a diet! *I* want to spend money on cute clothes and
pretty things and two-hundred-fifty-dollar salon visits! *I* might want
to have plastic surgery someday, too. I know these things would be
bad for me, but I don't know how to stop wanting them. It torments
me to see your mom just enjoy it all, without feeling the guilt and
angst that I have."

I was really crying by this point, the sniffly-snotty-gulpy kind of
crying. I felt so pathetic, and freakish, and ugly—on the *inside*. I was
an insecure, spiteful, and jealous person. I was a hypocrite. I'm not
sure if Michael understood everything I was blabbering on about,
but he hugged me as I cried.

Two things were clear. First, Michael was right that his mother
couldn't possibly care as much about my looks as I'd insisted (and
even if she did, she couldn't possibly be judging me as harshly as I'd
been judging her!). Sherry hadn't been an unavoidable trigger for
my body image anxieties; she'd been an excuse for them. Part of me
clearly didn't *want* to give up my insecurities, and painting her in my
mind as a judgmental person I needed to impress had given me an

excuse to hang on to them. She didn't have any power over me that I hadn't given her. This meant that I could take that power back . . . if I chose to.

My second realization was more surprising: I was *jealous* of Sherry. I believed her to have a carefree and confident life, without doubts or regrets or angst. I wanted that for myself, but instead of trying to learn from Sherry's self-assuredness by asking her for advice or guidance, I'd judged her as though she didn't deserve it. It had been easier to point fingers at others than at myself. Worst of all, I should have known better. I'd learned long ago that the anorexic voice that told me I wasn't good enough was the exact same voice that whispered critiques of *other* women in my ear. It was a dangerous cycle: Just as my perfectionism rendered other women a threat deserving of cynical assessment, the very act of judging other women only fed into my own insecurities. I couldn't point this critical voice at others without being scorched myself, and vice versa.

Once I'd calmed down, I knew what to do: If I wanted to take power back from the fictional version of Sherry that I'd built up in my head, I'd have to get to know the *real* version. I needed to talk to Sherry and to keep an open mind while doing so. I'd made some harmful assumptions, and it was time to challenge them.

THAT EVENING I WROTE DOWN A LIST OF QUESTIONS I WANTED to ask Sherry. The prospect of what I was about to do made me feel nervous, but I calmed myself by going into research mode. I'd conducted dozens of interviews before, asking women about their experiences with body image and beauty culture. I'd be okay if I could just stop thinking of Sherry as my mother-in-law and see her as another interesting woman with a unique story to share.

In the morning I read my list of questions out loud to Michael over breakfast. He seemed a little squeamish. This surprised me. After our conversation the night before, I'd expected him to be excited by what I was about to do.

"Why do you look so nervous?" I asked. "You're not the one calling her!"

"I don't know," he said, sighing. "I just can't imagine asking her stuff like this. I don't really talk to my mom about the surgeries anymore. Every time she has a new one it terrifies me. She could go under anesthesia and never wake up . . ." His voice trailed off while he seemed to think more about it. "I never know what to say, especially *after* the procedure. I know she wants me to call her to ask how she's doing, and to compliment her 'new look' once she's recovered . . . but I worry that acknowledging any of that stuff would just encourage her to start planning the next one. I couldn't live with myself if I acted okay with all of it and then something horrible happened."

It surprised me to hear him say this much, but I knew that these issues were particularly fresh on his mind; at that very moment Sherry was recovering from a partial face-lift she'd had a few weeks prior.

"Well, is there anything you want me to ask her about?" I offered.

"No, it's okay," he said. "But I think it's good that you're talking to her, for both of you. I think it will make her happy to hear from you while she's recovering from this lift thing." I hoped so.

Later that day I called Sherry. I asked her how she was feeling and if I could interview her for my blog. I explained that I wanted to know more about her experiences with cosmetic surgery, and that I thought my blog readers would be interested in the topic as well. "It's something I've never interviewed anyone about. Most women try to hide it, but you don't. I think that's really interesting and cool," I explained, truthfully. I did respect Sherry's openness about her procedures; when women, particularly celebrities, deny having work done, it leaves the rest of us mere mortals feeling particularly disheartened by our inabilities to measure up.

I was grateful that Sherry didn't hesitate before agreeing to be interviewed.

"Well, first, it's nothing I'm ashamed of," she began. "I'm not ashamed to tell people I'm having it done, and then afterward they won't be shocked about it. They'd know anyway, and nobody would want to say anything. I want people to feel comfortable around me, including after a procedure. I don't want them to feel like they can't mention it or for people to act like they don't notice. Since I'm not embarrassed, telling people is more about making them feel comfortable."

I went ahead and asked the toughest question next: "So, what cosmetic procedures have you had?"

"Well, I had maxillofacial surgery on my jaw almost twenty-five years ago. It was for my bite—I was wearing down my teeth. But it also changed my look. Then I got breast implants about twenty years ago, but I removed them with my cancer surgery. The radiation and surgery had really deformed my left breast, so they did reconstruction. Since then one of 'em shrunk up again, but it's fine. I don't care."

"Ummm . . . what do you mean, 'shrunk up'?" I asked.

"Well, radiation treats your boobs like the oven treats a roast: When you cook them, they shrink and harden a bit. It's not the same piece of meat after it comes out of the oven, right? It's like that with radiation, even after the reconstruction surgery and new implants."

It was an apt comparison. "Okay, I get it now," I said, before asking a question I'd just thought of. "Did having breast cancer change the way you think of your body?" Her answer surprised me.

"I feel like I'm supposed to say yes, but it just didn't. I was relieved about my breast reconstruction, but I mostly just tried to get on with my life. I survived cancer, but I don't think of myself as a cancer survivor. It's not my identity. It happened to me, but didn't change the direction of my life," she explained, before adding, "By the way, I saw my oncologist today and got the green light for another six months!"

That was good news indeed! "That's fantastic!" I exclaimed. "Congratulations and thanks for sharing the news! Michael is going to be so happy to hear this."

"Yeah, it feels good," Sherry confirmed, in what was surely a great understatement.

She stopped after this, and I took it as a cue to get back to my questions. "Okay, so getting back on topic, what other procedures have you had done?"

"I had a brow lift and I got my eyelids done. That was several years ago. And then just a few weeks ago I got a lift for my lower face and neck. It was called a something-a-plasty, but I don't remember the exact word! I'm still healing from that."

"How are you feeling?" I asked.

"Well, everything feels really tight and swollen right now, but I think it'll look great in about a month. I'm excited for you to see it when you visit for Christmas!"

"Cool!" I said, not knowing the correct response. I was curious, of course.

I thought about Michael as I asked the next questions: "Having surgery can be dangerous, and I know that the recovery is painful. Have you ever thought, *Gosh, this isn't worth it?*"

She responded confidently, "No, I've always been pleased with my results, and I don't dwell on the procedure. I just think of the outcome. Frankly, after all the surgeries I had with my cancer, and on my feet—my foot bones got destroyed by the chemo—well, I'm used to medical procedures, and at least these are ones I *want* to be having!" She had a point there. After hearing this, part of me wondered whether choosing to have elective cosmetic surgeries was a way for Sherry to feel in control of her body again after her cancer. I decided to not bring it up. Nobody likes being overanalyzed without asking for it first.

"I know that Michael thinks you already look beautiful, and he worries about you when you have surgery. How have your other family members reacted?" I hoped Sherry's response would help Michael understand his mom better.

"Well, after my brow lift my dad told me that I didn't need to be doing all this stuff to myself. I actually didn't tell my parents about this last procedure because I didn't want them to worry about it. Their health isn't great. I wasn't planning to tell the kids for the same reason. I don't want them to worry, either. But I'm not afraid that they'll try to talk me out of things, since that's pretty impossible once I've made my mind up." I hoped Michael would feel less responsibility for his mom's decisions after learning this.

She continued: "Doug, my husband, knows that I'm very hard-headed and that I'm not gonna let it go. After listening to me for months, he just says, 'Oh, go ahead and do it if that's what you want.' Since he's busy and not particularly happy about my surgeries, I don't ask him to do anything for me while I'm recovering. I even took a cab on the morning of my surgery. He was there for me with my cancer, but I do this on my own. I'm very independent." *So Sherry definitely knows that her family doesn't want her to keep having cosmetic surgeries,* I thought, *but it's not as though she doesn't care about their feelings.* I'd have to think more about this later.

Instead, I asked, "So I've got to ask: Have your surgeries made you more confident about your looks?"

She responded with certainty: "Absolutely. I'm very vain about my personal appearance and how I look. I like my face; I don't want to change my nose or eyes or features, but I like to look younger. I love my husband very much; it's not like I'm going out to find a new man or anything like that! But youthfulness is important to me, and I think about how other people see me."

She paused for a second before sharing something that really surprised me.

"I don't know exactly how to say this, but my mom never once gave me a compliment on my looks. I was painfully thin my whole life. We'd go shopping together, and she would sigh and complain that 'oh, the clothes won't fit you.' Nothing I ever did looked good enough for her. Nothing. I had buckteeth, the whole deal. They paid for braces, thankfully. Anyway, I always had low self-esteem, starting from my mother's comments, I think. It wasn't intentionally mean or spiteful, it was just the way she was raised. She just never made it a point to help me feel pretty. The first time she told me she loved me, I was forty or something. Anyway, I was always out looking to prove that I could be pretty. And then, once I realized I *was* pretty, I just kept going with it!" She laughed at this last comment, as I scribbled her words into my notebook. I didn't want to miss a word of what she was telling me.

"Wow, I didn't know that," I exclaimed in surprise. I knew Sherry would be happy to talk openly about her opinions and experiences, but I'd not expected this story. I imagined Sherry as a little girl and felt a surge of emotion. "So did this change how you approached being a mom?"

She took a deep breath. "When Michael's sister, Mandy, was born, I didn't want a repeat of what my past was. I mean, I think that's a big part of why I am the way I am. When Mandy was a little girl, I made sure to tell her all the time how pretty she was, and how beautiful her curly hair was. I didn't want the first person to tell her she was pretty to be some guy trying to get down her pants. I wanted her to already have that confidence coming into adulthood, from her family. All girls deserve to feel pretty and loved, even if they have flaws."

I was practically speechless. I'd run out of my planned questions, so I just stammered my thanks and promised to send Sherry a copy of my blog post before I published it.

I sat for a while after we hung up. I read over my notes and filled in a few spots I'd forgotten to write up. And then I just thought for a while, journaling.

Everything had become so much clearer: Sherry's surgeries, her concern with appearance, the proud way she always complimented Mandy's outfits, hair, and makeup. I reflected back on the night when Sherry had called herself "lucky to have two tall children," and realized with shock that she hadn't been saying this to my mom, or to me, but for the benefit of Mandy and Michael, who were walking a few feet away, within earshot.

I'd been right about Sherry not feeling guilty about having plastic surgeries, but I was wrong to have assumed that she made her decisions thoughtlessly. It seemed this way only because she'd dealt with her issues long ago; she knew herself well enough now to feel certain about her choices, despite the costs and risks. Didn't every woman deserve to know herself this well? Sure, Sherry had made different decisions from those I hoped to make for myself, but she'd led a very different life from mine, and had different values, and different things to prove to herself. (What had my mom always told me? "People always do the best they can with what they have." I wouldn't forget it again.)

Sherry wasn't perfect. No parent (or mother-in-law) ever could be. But she'd tried her hardest to keep the past from repeating itself, and it warmed my heart to know that Mandy would continue this tradition with her own kids someday. Oh, and that lack of angst I'd been jealous of? I decided to go ahead and stay jealous of it, but admit it to myself. If I wanted to learn how to be confident in my own authentic decisions, it wouldn't hurt to have a stubbornly self-assured role model for inspiration.

It fascinated me to realize that, despite having reached a place of calmness and body-confidence, I was still vulnerable to triggers and excuses. Whether they appeared in the form of an automatically generated health report or an imagined monster-in-law, it would be up to me to recognize them for what they were. As it had for years, my commitment (and recommitment) to Health at Every Size, along with a willingness to test my assumptions, promised to pull me through these times.

The lessons I'd learned from my conversation with Sherry (and the meltdown that had preceded it!) felt like the final pieces to the puzzle I'd been working on since the beginning of my project. The most important piece was the reminder to recognize my feelings of jealousy and criticism toward other women for what they were: remnants of a destructive disease and perpetuators of a dangerous culture. I'd learned to ignore my anorexic voice when it picked on me, but I needed to apply this same reaction when that critical voice turned to others.

A second puzzle piece fell into place when I realized that my mother-in-law had earned every right to feel content and confident in her choices, even if they were different choices from those I hoped to make. Both of us had embarked on quests to make peace with our bodies, but we'd taken different paths. Her confidence was built from self-knowledge, and her choices were shaped by her unique history, values, and priorities. If I wanted that same assuredness for myself, I would have to get more comfortable with what *I* wanted (since I couldn't have it all) and who I wanted to be (since I couldn't be it all). I'd done a great job of identifying my values and goals, but I'd done a shitty job of letting go of the things I'd have to give up. My panicked freak-out about my hair had made this utterly clear; in its wake, I finally felt ready to mourn the losses of "it all" and move on.

TEN

January, February, March

GIVING BACK AND RESOLVING TO STOP
LIVING ON THE SURFACE OF MY BODY

We look into mirrors but we only see the effects
of our times on us—not our effects on others.

PEARL BAILEY

Januarʏ 1 arrived quickly, but I was prepared with a fantastic New Year's resolution. In my love for both mantras and lists, I'd come up with a fancy catchphrase for my resolution, along with a list of specific goals that would help me achieve it. My resolution was to "spend less time living on the surface of my body."

I'd been mulling over this mantra for a while. Giving up mirrors had made me painfully aware of how much time I'd spent focusing on my looks, whether in front of a mirror or not, and I'd decided that spending time worrying about my looks—or what was happening on the surface of my body—was less valuable and meaningful than spending time focused on how it actually felt to live *within* my body, or time spent contributing to and engaging in the world *outside* of it. By trying to "spend less time living on the surface of my body," I was committing to spend more time in these other realms. This seemed fairly easy to do while avoiding mirrors, but I was less than three months away from the end of my project and I wanted to strengthen these skills so I could continue on this path once mirrors were back in my life.

Now, before you start wondering if I'd forgotten all of the tips I'd learned for setting successful resolutions (i.e., the fact that vague and complex resolutions, like "Spend less time living on the surface of my body," were bad), have no fear. I made a list of a few simple and specific goals that would set me on track for success.

Under the category of focusing more on the experiences of living *inside* of my body, I resolved to (1) run a half marathon before the end of the year, (2) experiment in the kitchen, and (3) have more sex (realizing with a laugh that items 2 and 3 could be accomplished at the same time). My recent focus on following Health at Every Size had inspired these goals. It had been more than two years since I'd trained for a road race, and I knew it would feel amazing to reconnect with my inner athlete. Enjoying delicious food was similarly in line with HAES, and the tenet regarding "joyful movement" had always seemed to me like code for sex.

Under the category of contributing to and engaging in the world *outside* of my body, I resolved to (1) increase my volunteer work with About-Face and (2) connect with more body-positive organizations in the San Francisco Bay Area. As for increasing my volunteer work with About-Face, while planning my wedding I'd felt unable to give more than the bare minimum of the work I'd committed to (i.e., analyzing data once per quarter and presenting the results at board meetings). Now that my wedding planning was in the past, I wanted to step up my engagement; it was time for me to start giving media literacy workshops again. Connecting with other body-positive organizations in the area felt like a natural next step.

ONE OF THE FIRST DECISIONS I MADE TOWARD COMPLETING my New Year's resolution was to put off the whole half marathon thing for the time being. I knew from experience that this would be a huge commitment once I began training, so it seemed best to revisit it during the summer (or fall . . . or winter . . .). Cooking, too, could wait. Not so for the "have more sex" resolution. Let's just say that Michael really wanted to support me in this goal.

It seemed timely. I didn't want to overanalyze things too much, but there was no way to deny the truth: Michael and I had been in a serious slump in the romance department. We were pretty crazy for each other when we first started dating—holding hands all the time, smooching in public, lots of smooching in private, and frequent "You're so hot I can't help it!" butt-pinches whenever we could get away with it. During our year and a half of long-distance dating, we spent hours on the phone most nights when apart and hours in the bedroom when together. It was awesome.

But all that romance took time away from other things— important things—including time for work, time with friends and family, and time getting exercise. Since moving in together, we'd both been able to reinvest in all of these other things, which felt great. Our lives had more balance, and it was phenomenal to finally share a home. But for some reason—or perhaps for many reasons—this reshuffling of our lives had dampened the romance. We just weren't lusting after each other the way we used to, and it was a bummer.

I feared that some of this might be related to my no-mirrors project. I'd been so much less focused on my looks (which has been wonderful for my body image and confidence!), but in doing so I'd also spent the majority of my days comfortably hanging out in a T-shirt and slouchy jeans, wearing minimal makeup, and with my hair always in a ponytail. At bedtime I changed into elastic-waistband PJ pants that came practically up to my ta-tas, worn with (what else?) a huge old T-shirt. Did Michael still find me attractive? Amazingly, yes (not that he wouldn't prefer a slightly less schlumpy wife!). But I didn't feel very sexy. I wondered: At what point does feeling comfortable with both yourself and your partner start to kill the romance?

My lowered libido came as a surprise to me. I really thought that focusing on how I felt instead of how I looked would have made me feel sexy all the time. But I may have underestimated the extent to which primping and grooming helped me feel attractive and sexy. Despite feeling increasingly comfortable with my body, I hadn't been feeling particularly amorous. I was rarely "in the mood" lately, and it didn't help that Michael had been too exhausted after work to put much effort into "setting the mood."

For example, a few weeks prior, Michael and I had gone to dinner at our favorite sushi restaurant. I even dressed up (i.e., changed out of my PJ pants) for the occasion! After complaining for thirty minutes about the exhaustions of my day, I felt a glimmer of that wanting-to-snuggle-and-kiss kind of feeling. So I leaned over the table, looked longingly into Michael's eyes, and said, "Any interest in giving me a full-body massage when we get back home?" (I even suggestively wiggled my eyebrows.) He perked up and said, "Ooooh, that sounds fun!" But once we got home, Michael's energy dropped faster than a sake bomb. He haphazardly scratched my back for about five minutes and then started bargaining for "payment up-front." I know that sounds awful, but by this point we both exploded into giggles and exchanged some tickles (I also gave Michael a "full-body massage" by scratching his left biceps). But that was the extent of it. Bonding: check. Sexy-time: uncheck.

So, did we still adore each other? Absolutely! Did we still find each other attractive? Yep. (I still found Michael crazy-handsome, and he seemed to think I was somewhere between cute and gorgeous, depending on the day.) Did we have a healthy and respectful relationship? Yes. Were we having fun and enjoying time together? Absolutely! (Just not so much in bed.)

I shared these concerns in a blog post, asking my readers for advice, and was shocked (and delighted) when I received an e-mail from Abby, my PhD advisor. She wrote to tell me about a story she'd recently heard at temple.

"The rabbis were talking about why there are mirrors in the tabernacle or holy of holies or some sacred Jewish space, and the answer is that mirrors are holy because during the time that the Jews were enslaved in Egypt and the men were so exhausted from hard labor that they had no interest in romance/baby-making, the women would use mirrors to make themselves beautiful and get their husbands into the mood. Thanks to their ingenuity, the Jewish people continued to reproduce during this trying time. So, this provides Talmudic support for your hypothesis that mirrors can help make women feel sexy!"

This was such a treat to read. First, I loved hearing any story in which women save the world. I think we do it a little bit every day just by being who we are, but it's great to see these heroic (heroine-ic?) roles being recorded in our religious and cultural artifacts. Second, I liked learning about reasons to appreciate mirrors. In less than three months they'd be back in my life, and I wanted to feel excited about that. This story reminded me that spending time in front of a mirror wouldn't have to be accompanied by insecurity and it didn't have to represent a departure from living in accordance with my values. I hoped that by the time I returned to mirrors, I'd have learned enough to bring the good stuff, like this, back with them.

I read Abby's e-mail to Michael, who then suggested that our first step once my project was over ought to involve attaching a humongous mirror to the ceiling above our bed. I told him I'd have to think about that (ummmm . . . probably not). In the meantime, we started scheduling some in-between-the-sheets dates to get back into the habit of "joyful movement."

As for my resolution to begin giving media literacy workshops for About-Face, I gave Jennifer the heads-up on this and was immediately scheduled for three workshops in the coming months, including one at the annual University of California San Francisco Young Women's Health Conference. I was excited but also nervous: I hadn't given a workshop in ages and hoped I'd be prepared.

I wasn't sure exactly how I ought to connect with other body-positive women's organizations in the Bay Area, but I trusted that I'd be able to figure this one out within the next year.

THE BEGINNING OF 2012 BROUGHT WITH IT MORE TO PLAN than just resolutions. I was quickly closing in on the end of my no-mirrors project, and I needed to decide exactly how I wanted my year to end. I'd been putting this off for a while in an effort to stay focused on enjoying the final months of the project, but by the end of January I knew I needed to start brainstorming.

For the most part I was feeling excited to look at myself in mirrors again. This wasn't to say that I was no longer reaping the benefits of mirror-free life in spades. For example, I calculated that by the end of these 365 days I'd have gained *over ninety hours* of time to do . . . whatever. Just by cutting fifteen minutes out of my morning makeup routine. And let's not forget the benefits of feeling increasingly confident about my body and myself as a whole, more in tune with things that made me feel good and kept me healthy. I also cared much less about whether or not I looked like a feminist trophy-wife. And yet, I was still looking forward to seeing what I looked like again! I missed me. But how to celebrate?

I went back and forth between two different options, depending on my mood. When I was feeling calm, confident, and excited (which was pretty often), I wanted to celebrate with a big party, filled with family and friends. I imagined a Body-Positive Bonanza, filled with love-your-body art and activities. I envisioned cool music, delicious beverages, and yummy munchies. Then, when the clock struck midnight, I'd give a little speech and go check myself out in a mirror. Taking things a step further, I wondered if About-Face would want to be involved, as a way to raise awareness about their work. Maybe other Bay Area organizations would want to get involved as well. (What a great way to check off that fourth New Year's resolution goal!)

But sometimes, if I was feeling less secure, I wanted the exact opposite: to take my "first look" completely alone. The big-party option seemed like a great way to commemorate the year in a way that involved all of the people who had supported me throughout it. I knew that my friends and family were excited for me and wanted to be there. (In fact, I was pretty sure Michael's feelings would have been hurt if I'd gone for the solo option.) But involving other people added pressure to the situation. I mean, what if I didn't *like* what I saw in the mirror? What if my first reaction was a cringe—or worse, a meltdown? I prepared myself for the possibility that this could happen. If it happened in front of an audience, I might feel pressured to fake a positive reaction, to write a happy ending to the story. But this wasn't what I wanted for myself. I wanted the moment to be authentic, not for the sake of an audience, but for myself.

One thing was for sure: I wouldn't know which situation I preferred until the moment came. The solution, therefore, was obvious: I needed a plan that gave me the flexibility of a public *or* private first look. In other words, I needed to throw my party somewhere that had a private nook available, just in case. I was also kind of weirded out by the concept of a sudden reveal in the mirror. The idea reminded me too much of reality TV makeover shows. I talked to my friend Laila about this, and she helped me come up with a solution: We could cover the mirror with a collage of images and positive messages that reminded me of who I was on the *inside*. At midnight I'd take the collage down, bit by bit, to see myself gradually while keeping in mind the lessons I'd learned about what really counted.

I felt calmer once this flexible plan was in motion, so I spoke with Jennifer to ask if she wanted About-Face to be involved in my Body-Positive Bonanza idea. Jennifer agreed enthusiastically and promised to help me get in contact with other area organizations, including Volluptuart, an online retailer of body-positive art, HAES activist Marilyn Wann, and The Body Positive, an eating disorder prevention organization.

My next steps were to find the perfect (i.e., really big and un-warped) mirror for my first look and to nail down a venue for the event.

But before I could dive into these remaining tasks, I hit a major roadblock: I managed to catch a horrible cold, which quickly turned into an epic cough. Between sleepless nights and daily coughing fits that left me sweaty, breathless, and mildly incontinent, I barely had enough energy to work on my dissertation research, much less party planning. As I worked my way through endless over-the-counter and folk remedies, I gained a renewed appreciation for health.

I also, oddly enough, gained a renewed appreciation for my sense of smell, which the cold had forced into dormancy. Every time I showered, put on makeup, styled my hair, or spritzed perfume, I felt really sad and numb without the accompanying scents I was used to experiencing. I'd clearly been overenjoying the scents of my various getting-clean-and-ready products in the absence of being able to see their effects. I hoped this scent-sensitivity continued when I went back to using mirrors again (assuming I regained my sense of smell!). Life is richer when you experience it with all of your senses, no?

FEELING SICK AND EXHAUSTED WAS DEPRESSING, SO I DECIDED to boost my spirits by making a list of all of the ways that mirrors were used to help people and improve society.

Thanks to my recent e-mail from Abby, the first item on the list was "libido, and saving the Jewish nation." Next I wrote out the various ways that mirrors have been used for therapeutic treatments, particularly for eating disorder recovery. Called "body exposure" or "mirror confrontation" therapy, eating disorder sufferers stand repeatedly and for prolonged periods of time in front of mirrors, which has been shown to reduce body image disturbances and avoidance behaviors. Often, this therapy involves asking the patient to look into the mirror and describe her body as precisely and as neutrally as possible, while avoiding subjective and negative statements (i.e., by saying

"I have brown hair and freckles" instead of "I am a big fat nobody"). This type of therapy helps eating disorder sufferers reconnect with the reality of their bodies while reducing self-objectification.

I was also fascinated to learn that mirrors are frequently used to help amputees manage phantom limb pain, and to help stroke victims regain use of paralyzed limbs; using mirrors to track limb movement during physical therapy helps the brain reconfigure itself. Although not considered therapy, per se, childhood development experts recommend that infants spend time in front of mirrors, which helps them learn how to focus, track images, and "explore all the wonderful things a face can do."

I also revisited the research I'd read previously about how mirrors impact behavior. Seeing one's reflection prompts self-consciousness and self-awareness. As one psychology text put it, it serves as a reminder of the difference between a person's ideal self and the person's actual self, promoting behavior more in line with the ideal. Thus, the presence of a mirror influences people to be more honest, more helpful, and to express less prejudice—all good things, to be sure. Of course, this is a mixed bag, seen in cases when mirror exposure causes self-objectification, and in the fact that women eat less food when exposed to a mirror. I would try to focus on the good aspects for the time being.

A website in which people were able to pose questions to physicists revealed an inspiring list of scientific technologies that made use of mirrors, from Newtonian telescopes and solar panels to periscopes, searchlights, floodlights, flashlights, spotlights, and single-lens reflex cameras. Car rearview and side mirrors protect our safety, and both dentists and auto mechanics use mirrors to examine hard-to-reach places.

And finally, without mirrors, how would pet parakeets ever keep themselves company?

Coming up with my Mirrors for Good list was both motivating and entertaining. Yet I kept coming back to one of the most basic uses of mirrors I was looking forward to the most: making sure I didn't have anything in my teeth!

N THE FIRST WEEK OF MARCH, I GAVE MY FIRST ABOUT-FACE media literacy workshops of the year at the University of California San Francisco Young Women's Health Conference. I was excited, but nervous. More nervous, in fact, than I'd felt on my first day teaching my own lecture course at UCLA. The conference had been steered by high school girls, and was known to be a high-energy and high-impact event. I would be representing About-Face in two workshops, and it was a big-enough deal that Jennifer decided to accompany me to the conference to help out, in case I needed it. I hoped I wouldn't need help, but was frankly relieved to have her there. I was still sick as heck, and worried that I'd have a coughing fit or lose my voice before finishing!

As I set up the room and my projector, Jennifer brought me a cup of tea. I mentioned that I was worried about keeping my audience of high schoolers engaged and (hopefully) participating. The workshop I was running focused on giving girls tools to understand and resist unhealthy media messages. I'd built my slide deck so that it included a lot of (hopefully) current and hip media examples— like print advertisements, commercials, and even a rap music video—but I feared the ultimate embarrassment: showing an outdated (by teenaged standards) media clip that unknowingly revealed my unhipness. Engaging my audience would be key if I hoped to keep their attention for forty-five minutes. I whispered these concerns to Jennifer as the room began to fill with girls, and she told me to just relax and have fun.

I popped a cherry-flavored throat lozenge into my mouth and got started.

Thankfully, it went well and I enjoyed myself! After reinforcing the three questions that About-Face encourages students to ask when thinking about media (What is the product being sold? How is it being sold? How does the media-maker want you to feel?), I was thrilled to see the girls quickly pick up on the nuances of these questions when faced with media examples. My favorite oft-repeated tropes were advertisements in which the product being sold wasn't even pictured in the advertisement (perfume ads featuring naked and kissing couples are notorious for this), followed closely by hyper-objectifying ads in which the models' sexualized body parts are emphasized and zoomed in on to the extent that their heads end up being cut out of the image entirely. "If there's no face, there's no humanity! Objectification at its worst." I lectured, finding my rhythm. The girls laughed at my jokes, participated enthusiastically during the activities, answered my questions, and waited patiently and politely during an inevitable coughing fit. The forty-five minutes flew by, and by the end I found myself energized, invigorated, and inspired.

After my first presentation, Jennifer gave me a high five and a few tips for improving my talk in the next round. That one went just as smoothly, though my energy barely held out until the end. My cough was quickly outpacing my throat lozenges, and I was relieved when Jennifer offered to drive me home. I was exhausted but content. *This is why I teach,* I thought to myself, feeling satisfied that I was well on my way to fulfilling my goal of engaging more in my community. I made a note to myself to write *You're a good teacher!* as one of the messages I'd see during my first look.

A FEW DAYS LATER, THE GOOD VIBES I'D COLLECTED FROM MY workshop presentations hit a wall. After almost a full month battling my cold/cough, my body finally gave in. I woke up with an excruciating pain in my side; it hurt to breathe in or out too deeply. Coughing or sneezing caused an agony so sharp and severe that I saw spots in my vision. I'd avoided a doctor's visit up until that point, wanting to evade unnecessary antibiotics, but I knew it was time. I managed to get a same-day appointment at the family practice where Hanna worked (thank goodness for family connections!) and prayed for some relief.

I left the office with prescriptions for cough medication, pain medication, and a fourteen-day round of Ciproflaxen. My diagnoses? My first-ever sinus infection, along with a strained muscle in my chest wall.

There was also good news: Other than the cough/cold/sinus infection/strained chest wall muscle, I was given a perfectly clean bill of health! I'd decided to bring along the six-page printout of my complete results from the National Health and Nutrition Examination Survey. My doctor looked over the myriad report findings, which included body measurements of my height, weight, BMI, and body fat percentage, blood pressure and heart rate, oral health, hearing, muscle strength, lung function testing, urine tests, STD tests, a complete blood count, and blood tests for measuring over fifty substances/enzymes/whatever.

Guess what? Other than the measurements of my body size (and an oddly high level of mercury in my blood—damn that sushi habit!), every single test came back normal or excellent. Even my kidney function was decent (just a teeny smidge below normal, but better than it was years ago!). My doctor complimented me on having excellent health. I even tempted fate by asking her about my BMI, waist circumference, and body fat percentage, since these were identified as issues to talk to my doctor about. She responded that I was obviously healthy and that I shouldn't worry about this stuff as long as I continued to eat well, get adequate sleep, and exercise regularly. Huzzah!

HOPED TO FEEL BETTER QUICKLY, THANKS TO MY NEW DRUG cache. Indeed, my pain and cough responded well to the meds, and whatever was going on with my sinuses seemed to be improving. My physical health seemed to be on the rebound, but my emotional health was threatening to collapse. (Mind you, this happened less than ten days before my "first look" party! Not a good time to have a mental breakdown.)

It started with anxiety, and got worse with insomnia. Soon I was downing coffee throughout the day to stay awake through my haze of exhaustion and codeine. After two days of this, the bad dreams began. Even if I managed to fall sleep, I'd wake up in the middle of the night bathed in sweat, fighting to forget the latest nightmare. The worst part? Every dream seemed like a warning that something awful would happen at my First-Look Party. Most of the nightmares are lost to memory, but two were too vivid to forget. I look back at these and am able to laugh at their ridiculousness, but they felt terrifying at the time.

In the first, I was wearing a dress that was at least two sizes too small; I couldn't actually see the dress, but it was so tight that I was literally trapped in it. I felt physically uncomfortable, horrified to have so completely misjudged my physical size, and desperate to escape. Yet I was unable pull the dress over my head because my body was so constrained and my arms were too weak. The dress was, essentially, a straitjacket, and I indeed felt insane. (Ugh, I'm getting yucky shivers just thinking about it!)

My second dream was less horrific but similarly telling: In this one, I was about to look into a mirror and I felt really nervous (weird, huh?). I stared at my feet, urging myself to look up, until I finally found the courage to do so. Staring back at me was . . . A NAKED DUDE. Yeah, I was a dude. Thankfully, I was an incredibly good-looking dude, so I liked what I saw. But it was still completely weird. While admiring my chiseled jawline and Abercrombie abs, I wondered, *Why didn't anyone tell me that I'm a guy?!?!*

They sound funny in the daylight, but I seemed gripped by a fear that I had, or was at risk of, greatly misjudging my body. What did this mean? Was my subconscious trying to warn me of something? And what had happened to all of the confidence and calmness I'd been enjoying? Had I actually made any progress at all? Was I about to have a breakdown?

The only good news was that having these nightmares forced me to acknowledge the very fact that I was fearful, which allowed me to try to process what was happening and why. For example, I realized that part of my anxiety was rooted in the irony of having a "first look" at all. Building up suspense around the first look was in some ways an inappropriate (and false) end to the project. For one thing, looking in the mirror again would actually mark a transition, rather than a climax. Further, emphasizing the moment of looking at myself in the mirror for the first time felt eerily evocative of a cheesy reality TV makeover. (Would I squeal with joy? Should I delicately touch my hands to my face to see if it's *really me* in the mirror? Will my husband say something lame like, "Aww, man, you look soooo good, baby! I'm gonna feel like I'm cheatin' on my old wife with a new lady!" I mean, this *is* the asinine behavior we've all come to expect from the "first look in the mirror" scene, no?) It felt utterly off-putting to conclude this project by emphasizing my appearance, but I couldn't bring mirrors back into my everyday life (which, by the way, I was genuinely looking forward to) if I didn't start with a first look.

Angst and fear abounded, but a few things helped me.

First, I reminded myself that the success of the project wouldn't be determined by my reaction to the first look; the days, weeks, months, and years after would be more telling as to whether I'd changed for the better. Also, unlike a reality TV makeover, my metric for deciding whether I'd changed for the better would be based on *internal* cues, not the extent to which my looks had changed. (Indeed, much of my project had been a calculated physical make*under*, which I was proud of and hoped to continue!)

I also reminded myself that *I would be in control*, and that I wasn't responsible for meeting anybody else's expectations. If I wanted to, I could decide at the last minute to never look in a mirror again. (I was fairly sure that this wouldn't happen, but giving myself the choice felt good!) Or I could kick everybody out of the room and count my pores for an hour or two until only my closest friends and family were left waiting for me. With luck, I'd have a glass or two of champagne in my system, a cherished friend on each arm, and it would simply be silly and joyful. But if I started freaking out, I could make up a plan B on the spot!

Finally, I became determined to replace the memory of my nightmares with a new visualization. I chose to envision the emotional experience of seeing an old friend for the first time in ages.

When we greet our oldest friends after a long separation, we're excited to see them in person because we love them. We might notice physical changes, but we don't pass judgment or change our feelings for that person based on their looks; we're just so glad to finally see them. I tried to wrap myself up in happy memories of hugging cherished friends and relatives at airports, bus stops, and train stations. I hoped that, by really cultivating these memories, I'd prime my brain to have a similar mind-set for the first look.

O N DAY TWELVE OF MY ANTIBIOTIC REGIME I HAD ANOTHER nightmare (involving cupcakes and the inability to stop eating them. Yes, it *was* a nightmare, I swear!). I woke up feeling really anxious and generally lousy. In the midst of bitching at Michael over something petty, it hit me: This did *not* feel like me. Something was up. What—other than an impending First-Look Party—might be going on? (Cue suspenseful music.)

An exhaustive Google search of all the cold/cough/allergy/sinus-infection meds I'd been taking landed me on a place I like to call Planet Duh. It turns out that Ciproflaxen—the antibiotic that had finally banished the last of my symptoms—has some *very interesting* side effects, including "restlessness, insomnia, nightmares, dizziness, tremor, headache, or irritability. . . . Such symptoms can be made worse by coffee."

You read that correctly: insomnia, nightmares, and irritability (oh my!). Add to this the fact that I'd been chugging the joe, and suddenly we had a hypothesis. To test said hypothesis, I cut out the coffee immediately and slept through the night for the first time in ages. I was still pretty anxious during the daytime, but my last dose of Cipro a few days later marked the end of my almost-meltdown. It was a relief to figure out that it was chemically induced rather than rooted somewhere deep in my damaged psyche. And it resolved just in time, a mere two days before my First-Look Party. My positive visualization exercises helped chase away the worst of my lingering fears.

THE DAY BEFORE MY BODY-POSITIVE BONANZA AKA FIRST-LOOK Party went by in such a rush that I barely noticed that it was my last day living mirror-free. I was too busy running around with my family and throwing together last-minute party-planning ideas to really absorb things. I decided that I was okay with that. I mean, by that time really I ought to have been able to run around frantically for a day without worrying about mirrors or what I looked like in them—that was the whole point of this project! I decided to just go with the flow, with plans to overanalyze everything later.

In the mail that day I received two gifts that warmed my heart, and tickled my funny bone: from my maternal grandmother, a beautiful card wishing me luck at my "coming out party," and from Sherry, a magnifying mirror.

THAT EVENING, THE BODY-POSITIVE BONANZA WAS EVERYthing I could have hoped, with the exception of a torrential downpour. The venue, the San Francisco Women's Building, felt perfect for the occasion. My friends and I had decorated the room with mirrors and colorful phrases from my year, including my Top Ten Ways to Be Kjerstin list, plus some of my most memorable "aha" moments. About-Face, Volluptuart, and Marilyn Wann had all set up colorful tables filled with body-positive activities, art, information, and souvenirs. It looked like my friends and family were all having a good time.

I'd had some help with my makeup and hair from Laila and her sister Rana, so I knew I was a step above my everyday look. I was glad; why not dress up a bit for myself? (I stopped short of wearing my wedding gown, though I was tempted!) My friends had set up a table with huge Post-it notes and colorful markers, asking all of the guests to write a positive message for me to read during the first look.

Even with all of this I was still pretty nervous. I wasn't sure what to expect, and I was still scared that I wouldn't like what I saw in the mirror. I worried not only that I'd feel horrible about what I looked like, but also that I'd feel horrible about feeling horrible. For a moment I considered backing out of the public first look and retreating to the coat closet we'd designated as my plan B. I mentioned this to Michael, who reminded me that it was completely my choice. "But," he said, "I promise that you won't be disappointed, and neither will anyone here." Somehow being told that I had the choice (as though I hadn't already had the choice) made me feel more relaxed. I would take my first look in the main room of the party. The lighting in that coat closet looked dreadful, anyway.

Jennifer came by to tell me I had ten minutes. "I'll start gathering people, and we can move your mirror to the center of the room!" My heart started pounding.

Jennifer made an announcement, and everyone started coming in toward the center of the room, where my enormous and completely BeDazzled mirror stood waiting for me. Shaking, I accepted the microphone from Jennifer to say a few words of thanks to everyone who had supported me, especially Michael, who had been beside me for the entire year, and who had also talked me through the final minutes of that evening. I asked everyone to keep in mind that—as exciting as my first look might seem—it marked a transition rather than an end point in my journey.

Somebody shouted out, "It's midnight!" and I shrugged, saying, "I guess it's time to get this over with!" I had asked my mom and Hanna to help me move the positive messages from the mirror to its frame, and the three of us stood in front of the mirror while Michael started chanting a countdown.

At once I began peeling away the Post-it notes, starting at eye level. I felt really freaked out about seeing myself, so I began reading each message out loud. My mom began to follow suit, reading out loud as my eyes started to track the growing uncovered space of the mirror. And then I started to see myself. Pink! Yellow!

My mom continued reading from the messages, and I interrupted her, saying, "Mom, stop! Look! I'm seeing myself!" She laughed, as did everyone else.

I saw color first. The skin of my neck and upper chest was flushed bright pink, and my hair looked pale yellow in comparison. (This always happens when I'm nervous.) I remember thinking that everything looked really lovely. My eyes were sparkly, and my lips were rosy. I had a glow!

The next thing I noticed was the reflection of everybody staring at me, apparently waiting for an official reaction. I couldn't help making a joke: "Well, you guys look great!" I exclaimed, feeling a mix of emotions as I turned back to the mirror, suddenly feeling a bit self-conscious of the fact that I wanted to really take a good long gander! I was so relieved that my first observations were of color instead of my weight. I felt as though I'd passed an important test. I looked at myself, and then again at all of my friends and family circled around me in the background, smiling. I felt beautiful, inside and out.

AFTERWORD/ REFLECTIONS

All life is an experiment. The more experiments you make, the better.

RALPH WALDO EMERSON

As i'd predicted, the end of my year without mirrors marked a point of transition rather than culmination. Here's what happened next.

Once I removed the curtain from my bathroom mirror, I quickly found that I'd become surprisingly prudish. After a year of not seeing my naked body, it felt shocking and almost inappropriate to catch glimpses of it as I stepped out of the shower. Instead of staring I'd turn away, as though it was the only polite thing to do. Luckily, I didn't have this reaction to my fully clothed reflection (indeed, on the morning after my First-Look Party, I spent a few hours trying on most of my closet), so I found the whole thing amusing. Clearly I had a first *naked* look in my near future.

And so, three days after my project ended, I guided myself through a solo version of "mirror confrontation" therapy, by getting buck naked, forcing myself to look into my bathroom mirror for what certainly seemed like a prolonged period of time, during which

I attempted to describe my body as specifically and neutrally as possible, avoiding subjective and negative statements. I was nervous but shouldn't have worried.

Here is what I saw: First of all, I looked pretty much the same as I did when I'd started the project. My hair was shorter, my skin was paler (apparently a common side effect of moving away from Los Angeles), and I noted that the five-ish pounds I'd gained appeared to have settled into my slightly rounder belly. But other than these things it was as though I'd never said good-bye to my reflection at all. Except, of course, my thinking had changed dramatically.

As much as I tried to stay "neutral," I couldn't help *admiring* my clear skin, pink cheeks, and bright eyes. My lips were rosy, my teeth strong and white, and my pale eyelashes (finally growing back!) seemed delicate and lovely. A glance at round hips, a great ass, strong legs, and slightly outturned feet with high arches finalized the image, and I laughed with my reflection as we kissed our flexed biceps. Well done, I thought to myself, well done.

All was not perfect, of course. In that first week I also found myself increasingly fascinated by some of the close-up bodily details that I hadn't even bothered to think about in the past year. Viewed two inches away from my new magnifying mirror, my pores became oddly interesting, as did my eyebrows, and a handful of lone frizzy hairs, which I determinedly tweezed, one by one (though, as did not happen with my pre-wedding eyelash fiasco, I managed to stop before baldness!). I knew full well that imperfect pores, eyebrow stubble, and the occasional frizzy strand of hair would be completely unnoticeable to a common observer, and that obsessing over or "fixing" these things was therefore a waste of my time, but I couldn't help myself. I decided to just go with it for a few days to see what would happen. So I went ahead and inspected my pores to my heart's content, an endeavor amounting to a full hour that night! Then I got bored and stopped. Permanently. I haven't done it since (well, except for the occasional zit).

I decided then that 'curiosity, fascination, and neutral self-observation would be a welcome part of my new vanity and body-image repertoires.

Also, for several weeks after the project ended, I couldn't help but automatically look away from unexpected glimpses of my reflection. This eased by the beginning of May, after five weeks of being able to see myself. And then, for almost two months, I went through what I can only describe as a vanity relapse. I couldn't get enough of the world of makeup, hair, and clothes. I shopped excessively, experimented enthusiastically, and even took to snapping pictures of myself once a week wearing newly configured outfits, proudly posting the images on my blog each Wednesday, which I'd renamed Haute Hump Day. Again, even though these fashion shows were admittedly superficial, I went with it to see what would happen. After all, I was finally *enjoying* my reflection, and after a year without seeing myself I felt I'd earned it.

My indulgent fashion projects lasted from mid-May through the end of June, until, once again, I abruptly stopped. This time, stopping had little to do with boredom, and everything to do with being too busy to bother. Did I stop enjoying fashion and girlie-grooming? No, but I had other things in life that felt more rewarding, and—thanks to my year without mirrors—I knew that the important people in my life weren't going to abandon me for lack of lip gloss.

From that point forward, it was smooth sailing. The calm confidence and happiness I'd experienced in those blissful months after my wedding came flooding back. I went back to my minimalist makeup routine, put away the magnifying mirror for good, and happily shifted my creative energy back to my research, writing, and volunteer work.

The year 2012 marked the first time in my life that I successfully accomplished every one of my New Year's resolutions. I tried new recipes, had more sex, continued volunteering with About-Face, and managed to limp my way across the finish line of a half marathon. My decision to "spend less time living on the surface of my body" continues to shape the daily choices I make for my health and happiness.

I haven't kept up with my yoga practice, and I no longer wear my hair in a ponytail every day, but I do go barefaced on No Makeup Mondays. Nobody seems to have noticed, which I like. I'm slowly (verrrry slowly) growing out my bleach-damaged hair. With luck I'll be back to my natural color by the time my *second* book comes out.

Sherry and I have become closer friends. She's begun e-mailing me links to news articles about body image, and I've challenged myself to learn to cook her signature culinary specialties. We still surprise each other by showing up to events wearing the exact same shirt, usually from the Anthropologie sale rack. This amuses Michael to no end.

The About-Face office has become my second San Francisco home. I'll be donating 5 percent of my book royalties to help ensure that its media literacy programs continue to reach as many girls as possible.

To help other people who are interested in building a healthy body image without a 365-day commitment, I built a webpage filled with a growing list of body-positive activities and experiments.

You can find it at www.kjerstingruys.com/website/Healthy_Body_
Imgage_Activities_and_Experiments.html.

I look at myself in my bathroom mirror pretty much every day
now. I like what I see, more so than I did before I gave up mirrors.
This is nice, but the biggest and most satisfying change to my life
happened when I finally began caring less about my looks than I did
about all the other things that make me who I am. If I feel beautiful,
I am beautiful, and that's all I need to know.

ACKNOWLEDGMENTS

I am grateful to so many people who have contributed to this project and supported me along the way. It would be impossible to thank every one of you without doubling my page count, but I've gathered a list of those who especially deserve recognition.

First, I want to thank my fantastic agent, Mollie Glick, my favorite fast-talking dame, for her enthusiastic support of the book concept in its earliest stages, for her expert guidance through an ambitious proposal submission timeline, and for her spot-on advice throughout the writing and publication process. I am indebted to Beth Duff-Brown for somehow convincing Mollie to take time during her vacation to read my work. Thanks also to the rest of the team at Foundry Literary+Media, especially Katie Hamblin, who was an invaluable advocate for the book, particularly while working on what eventually became a gorgeous and compelling cover.

Thanks also to everyone at Avery. In particular, I am indebted to Marisa Vigilante, my wonderful editor, who truly shared my vision for the book and provided the insightful editing (and moral support!) needed to make it a reality. Also deserving of thanks is publicist Lindsay Gordon, who kept me steady during a few tight spots by helping me stay focused on the big picture.

I am indebted to the friends and colleagues who convinced me that a very weird and fairly personal "life experiment" was worth writing about and sharing with others. In particular, I am forever grateful to my dearest friends, my chosen family, who barely blinked when I shared what I was up to, and then rooted for me the whole way: Sarah Schlabach, Laila Coniglio, Elizabeth Joniak-Grant, Tara McKay, Lindsay Bruno, Mandy Ackermann, and Lisa Kietzer. Thanks to Dave Frederick for being the first to encourage me to blog, and for proposing such a creative and apt title. I am also forever grateful to my mentor, Abigail Saguy, for her invaluable guidance on the writing process, and for graciously supporting my venture into public sociology.

I am extremely lucky to have connected with many mini-mentors and new friends along the way. Thanks to Lisa Wade for providing generous advice about blogging to a technophobic amateur, and for helping me refine my most personal blog post into an essay worthy of Sociological Images. Cara Walker, PR wiz, and Theta Pavis, media specialist for Sociologists for Women in Society, provided timely advice just when I needed it most. I am also grateful for the moral support, structure, and camaraderie I found in the Guerrero Street Writers Group; thanks especially to Lynne Gerber for welcoming me into the club. Autumn Whitefield-Madrano, fellow mirror-faster and feminist beauty blogger, has been a generous and much-appreciated ally throughout our parallel adventures in mirror avoidance, media blitzes, and writing. Thanks also to Stefanie Faucher, my splendid office mate, whose passionate dedication to her own causes continually inspires me to work harder for mine.

The entire About-Face community of activists and volunteers deserves a thousand thanks for their support and unwavering enthusiasm for this project. I wrote much of the manuscript mere yards away from the About-Face epicenter, where I found body-positive inspiration every day. Jennifer Berger, especially, played a central role in this project through her frequent encouragement, experienced writing know-how, generosity in introducing me to other Bay Area body image advocates, and, of course, the cupcakes. The following

About-Face board members and volunteers encouraged me along the way, and pitched in to help make my "first look" a fabulous experience: Lee Ann Bird, Dan Dworkin, Catherine Kelliher, Susan Kimberlin, Yonnie Leung, Elizabeth Nartker, Beth Till, Marcella Raimondo, Stephanie Clowdus, Gracie Janove, Nallaly Jimenez, Suzannah Tipermas Neufeld, Ivette Torres, Stacey Jean Speer, and Tessa Needham. Size-acceptance superhero Marilyn Wann, and Nomi and Mark Dekel of Volluptuart also helped make it the Body Positive Bonanza I'd envisioned.

I am incredibly grateful to my blog readers, whose heartfelt and often hilarious comments helped me stay the course through 365 days without my reflection. Being able to engage with such a diverse and thoughtful group kept me from feeling alone throughout a somewhat isolating adventure. A special thanks goes out to Marilyn Schmidt, my unofficial secular fairy godmother, whose letters and e-mails offered so much wisdom.

Sherry Ackermann, my fabulous mother-in-law, deserves special thanks, not only for raising an amazing human being who happens to be my husband, but also for graciously sharing her story and trusting me to write about it. It is impossible to succinctly describe how much I've learned through our growing friendship and what it has meant to me. I am immensely grateful.

Finally, I want to thank my parents and siblings for their love, bemused enthusiasm, patience, and encouragement throughout my year without mirrors, and again as I tackled the challenges of writing my first book. Most of all, thanks to my amazing husband and partner, Michael. You are my favorite mirror.

RECOMMENDED READING

On Mirrors

Sabine Melchior-Bonnet, *The Mirror: A History*
Jonathan Miller, *On Reflection*
Mark Pendergrast, *Mirror, Mirror: A History of the Human Love Affair with Reflection*

Body Image, Self-Acceptance, and Eating Disorder Prevention

Caitlin Boyle, *Operation Beautiful: Transforming the Way You See Yourself One Post-it Note at a Time*
Kim Brittingham, *Read My Hips: How I Learned to Love My Body, Ditch Dieting, and Live Large*
Brené Brown, *The Gifts of Imperfection: Let Go of Who You Think You're Supposed to Be and Embrace Who You Are*
Cynthia M. Bulik, *The Woman in the Mirror: How to Stop Confusing What You Look Like with Who You Are*
Thomas F. Cash, *The Body Image Workbook: An 8-Step Program for Learning to Like Your Looks*
Ophira Edut, ed., *Body Outlaws: Rewriting the Rules of Beauty and Body Image*
Marya Hornbacher, *Wasted: A Memoir of Anorexia and Bulimia*
Lesley Kinzel, *Two Whole Cakes: How to Stop Dieting and Learn to Love Your Body*

Courtney E. Martin, *Perfect Girls, Starving Daughters: The Frightening New Normalcy of Hating Your Body*

Rosie Molinary, *Beautiful You: A Daily Guide to Radical Self-Acceptance*

Robyn J. A. Silverman, *Good Girls Don't Get Fat: How Weight Obsession Is Messing Up Our Girls and How We Can Help Them Thrive Despite It*

Health at Every Size and Fat Acceptance

Linda Bacon, *Health at Every Size: The Surprising Truth About Your Weight*

Natalie Boero, *Killer Fat: Media, Medicine, and Morals in the American "Obesity Epidemic"*

Paul Campos, *The Obesity Myth: Why America's Obsession with Weight Is Hazardous to Your Health*

Glenn A. Gaesser, *Big Fat Lies: The Truth About Your Weight and Your Health*

Kate Harding and Marianne Kirby, *Lessons from the Fat-o-Sphere: Quit Dieting and Declare a Truce with Your Body*

Golda Poretsky, *Stop Dieting Now!: 25 Reasons to Stop, 25 Reasons to Heal*

Abigail Saguy, *What's Wrong with Fat?*

Evelyn Tribole and Elyse Resch, *Intuitive Eating: A Revolutionary Program That Works*

Examples of Other People's Inspiring Yearlong Life Experiments

Colin Beavan, *No Impact Man: The Adventures of a Guilty Liberal Who Attempts to Save the Planet and the Discoveries He Makes About Himself and Our Way of Life in the Process*

Sara Bongiorni, *A Year Without "Made in China": One Family's True Life Adventure in the Global Economy*

Vanessa Farquharson, *Sleeping Naked Is Green: How an Eco-Cynic Unplugged Her Fridge, Sold Her Car, and Found Love in 366 Days*

Phoebe Baker Hyde, *The Beauty Experiment: How I Skipped Lipstick, Ditched Fashion, Faced the World Without Concealer, and Learned to Love the Real Me*

A. J. Jacobs, *Drop Dead Healthy: One Man's Humble Quest for Bodily Perfection*

A. J. Jacobs, *My Life as an Experiment: One Man's Humble Quest to Improve Himself Living as a Woman, Becoming George Washington, Telling No Lies, and Other Radical Tests*

A. J. Jacobs, *The Year of Living Biblically: One Man's Humble Quest to Follow the Bible as Literally as Possible*

Judith Levine, *Not Buying It: My Year Without Shopping*

Julie Powell, *Julie and Julia: My Year of Cooking Dangerously*

Gretchen Rubin, *The Happiness Project: Or, Why I Spent a Year Trying to Sing in the Morning, Clean My Closets, Fight Right, Read Aristotle, and Generally Have More Fun*

Body Politics and Beauty Science

Susan Bordo, *Unbearable Weight: Feminism, Western Culture, and the Body*

Nancy Etcoff, *Survival of the Prettiest: The Science of Beauty*

Lynne Gerber, *Seeking the Straight and Narrow: Weight Loss and Sexual Orientation in Evangelical America*

Daniel S. Hamermesh, *Beauty Pays: Why Attractive People Are More Successful*

Anna Kirkland, *Fat Rights: Dilemmas of Difference and Personhood*

Deborah L. Rhode, *The Beauty Bias: The Injustice of Appearance in Life and Law*

Esther Rothblum and Sondra Solovay, eds., *The Fat Studies Reader*

Nicole Sault, ed., *Many Mirrors: Body Image and Social Relations*

Sondra Solovay, *Tipping the Scales of Justice: Fighting Weight-Based Discrimination*

Marilyn Wann, *Fat!So? Because You Don't Have to Apologize for Your Size*

Naomi Wolf, *The Beauty Myth: How Images of Beauty Are Used Against Women*